Northwestern University
STUDIES IN *Phenomenology &*
Existential Philosophy

Nature, History, and Existentialism

KARL LÖWITH is Professor of Philosophy at the
University of Heidelberg. An internationally
known philosopher, perhaps his best known work
is *Meaning in History*. He was born in 1897
and studied philosophy and biology in Munich,
Freiburg, and Marburg. In 1928 he joined his
former teacher, Martin Heidegger, on the faculty
of the University of Marburg. From 1934 to 1936
he was a Rockefeller Fellow in Rome, going on
to become Professor of Philosophy at Tohoku
University, Sendai, Japan. After spending six
years in Japan, Löwith came to the United States
and was appointed Professor of Philosophy at
Hartford Theological Seminary. From 1949 to
1952 he was Professor of Philosophy at the New
School for Social Research, New York City.

ARNOLD LEVISON is currently Assistant Professor
of Philosophy at the University of Illinois,
Chicago Circle. Assisting with the translations
were Jamey Daley, Assistant Professor of Philosophy at Knox College, and Sandra Bartky,
Assistant Professor of Philosophy at the University of Illinois, Chicago Circle.

Karl Löwith

Edited with a Critical Introduction by

Nature, History, and Existentialism

and Other Essays in the Philosophy of History

ARNOLD LEVISON

NORTHWESTERN UNIVERSITY PRESS

EVANSTON   1 9 6 6

Acknowledgments

THE EDITOR would like to express his thanks to the Northwestern University Faculty Committee on Research for providing him with a grant for the summer of 1964, during the tenure of which the introduction to this volume was written. Thanks are also due to the translators, Dr. Sandra Bartky and Mr. James Daley, who gave generously of their time and energy.

Acknowledgment is due to the editors of the following periodicals for their generous permission to reprint essays that first appeared in the pages of their journals: To the editors of *Social Research* for permission to reprint "Nature, History, and Existentialism," Vol. 19, No. 1, 1952; "Heidegger: Problem and Background of Existentialism," Vol. 15, No. 3, 1948; "Skepticism and Faith," Vol. 18, No. 1, 1951; "Man's Self-Alienation in the Early Writings of Marx," Vol. 21, No. 2, 1954. To the editors of *Theology Today* for permission to reprint, "Can There Be a Christian Gentleman?" Vol. 5, No. 1, April, 1948. To the editor of *Philosophy and Phenomenological Research* for permission to reprint "M. Heidegger and F. Rosenzweig or Temporality and Eternity," Vol. 3, No. 1, September, 1942. To Professor Reinhold Niebuhr for permission to reprint "The Historical Background of European Nihilism," which originally appeared in *Christianity and Society*, Summer, 1943. Finally, thanks are due to Mr. Henry Regnery, President, Henry Regnery Publishers, for his kind permission to reprint "Man between Infinites," which originally appeared in *Measure*, Vol. 1, No. 3, 1950.

Note on Text

THE SELECTION, order of appearance, and titles of the essays in the present volume were determined by the author. Some inconsistencies in spelling, punctuation, and footnoting may be noticed. These are due to the fact that the present edition follows the conventions employed in the original publications. Chapter 6 repeats some of the content and wording of Chapter 2. Since these repetitions could not be eliminated without sacrificing the whole of Chapter 6, and since Chapter 6 contains much that is new and important for understanding the author's thought, it was decided to permit these repetitions to stand. The translated essays were reviewed in manuscript by the author, who made many suggestions for improvement. However, the editor must assume the final responsibility for any errors or imperfections that remain.

The translated essays form Chapters 8, 9, and 10 of the present volume, and were originally published in German under the titles, respectively, of "Vom Sinn der Geschichte," "Das Verhängnis des Fortschritts," and "Hegels Aufhebung der christlichen Religion." The remaining papers were first published in English by the author.

Contents

Nature and Existence

KARL LÖWITH, the author of the essays included in the present volume, is known to most English readers very slightly if at all, and even those who are familiar with his name regard him primarily as a theologian and historian of ideas. This reputation is based largely upon his work, *Meaning in History* (1949), which for a long time was the only one of his books available in English.[1] Recently, however, an English translation of his *Von Hegel zu Nietzsche* (1941), a book well known in Europe, has appeared under the title: *From Hegel to Nietzsche: The Revolution in Nineteenth-Century Thought* (1964). The publication of the present volume by the Northwestern University Press, following shortly after that of the above work, should make possible a more adequate appraisal of Löwith's contributions than has hitherto been the case among English readers, and it should also enable us to see *Meaning in History* in its proper perspective. For together, these works reveal that Karl Löwith is not primarily a historian of ideas but a gifted philosopher who happens to have taken history and the historical interplay of ideas as a subject for philosophical analysis, critique, and interpretation. For Löwith, history is not merely the objective record of past events involving human actions, but also and more importantly, a kind of arena or testing ground in which the independently derived conclusions of theology, philosophy, and natural science confront one another as matters for decision and belief, thereby forcing upon us the

1. A selected bibliography of Löwith's works is given at the end of the present volume.

necessity of resolving the conflicts they engender. Löwith's writings are therefore an attempt to grapple with history directly and decisively, but at the same time philosophically, i.e., in terms of the fundamental ideas which make themselves felt as determinative influences shaping our historical destiny. That Löwith writes within a theological and specifically Christian perspective in no way vitiates the philosophical character of his critique, although it may determine the direction of his interests and the kinds of questions he thinks are worth raising and answering.

Although the papers included in the present volume have previously appeared in American or German periodicals, they have not been previously published together in book form. In addition, three of the papers, including one of monograph length, have been translated from the German for the first time expressly for inclusion in this book. While the individual essays touch on diverse themes, as a glance at the Table of Contents will show, they contain an underlying theme in common which gives the volume a high degree of unity, namely the critique of "historical existence," as Löwith calls it. That is to say, these essays provide a critical study of some of the main, current ways of conceptualizing human existence in its relationship to history and nature, going back as far as Pascal's reaction to the conceptual innovations which took place in the seventeenth century in connection with the birth of modern science. Nature is considered by the author both from the standpoint of the experiencing subject and from the standpoint of what has been disclosed about it through the investigations of modern natural science. He considers not only such standard topics as nihilism, the concept of progress, the historical alienation of the individual from nature, and so on, but also such diverse questions as the significance of Hegel's attempt to exhibit philosophy as the fulfillment in history of the teachings of Christianity, and whether it is possible for a Christian believer consistently to follow a conventional bourgeois ethic. Regarded as a group, these essays may be said to constitute a study in the philosophical implications of modern natural science and recent history for the subjective appraisal of our own existence in relation to nature, history, and the possibility of there being a specifically religious and revealed truth.

In this introduction, I shall not attempt to comment separately on the several essays included in the volume. Nor shall I attempt to comment on the theological aspects of Löwith's thought. Instead, I shall attempt to seize upon a theme that underlies many of the essays and directly involves the "critique of historical existence" considered as a purely philosophical task. In this way, I shall try to extend the range of Löwith's own discussions by independently examining some of the issues he raises, and thereby show the reader what there is in these essays of specifically philosophical significance.

[I] NATURALISM AND EXISTENTIALISM

In the first place, despite the difficulty of stating precisely what the issues are, we must be prepared to admit that our conduct of life *is* inescapably influenced by our view of what is the case in the world around us and by our view of what kind of relation we can have to the world, in other words, by our understanding of reality. Many novels of a philosophical nature, for example, are concerned with this kind of theme. One has only to think of such works as Dostoyevsky's *Brothers Karamazov,* Samuel Butler's *The Way of All Flesh,* or Thomas Hardy's *Jude the Obscure.* Specifically philosophical treatises may also be cited in this connection, such as Hume's *Dialogues Concerning Natural Religion* or Mill's essay on *Liberty.* And as Peter Winch has recently pointed out in his monograph, *The Idea of a Social Science,*[2] a philosophical discussion of what an understanding of reality consists in "merges into the discussion of the difference the possession of such an understanding may be expected to make to the life of a man." In so far as the disclosures of modern natural science affect our understanding of reality, therefore, they affect our conduct of life; and a philosophical investigation of the relationship between the disclosures of science and the human understanding of reality is therefore necessary. The fact that no such investigation can ever be complete or decisive, or even that the issues cannot be precisely defined, does not entail that we should never concern ourselves with it.

Among current ways of coping philosophically with this question, we may distinguish two that are dominant in contemporary discussions: naturalism and existentialism. The term "naturalism" denotes that perspective on the world which is connected historically with the emergence of modern natural science and involves

2. Peter Winch, *The Idea of a Social Science: and Its Relation to Philosophy* (London: Routledge & Kegan Paul, 1958), p. 22.

a philosophy of nature in which human self-consciousness and knowledge are regarded as occurrences on a par with other natural occurrences such as physical motion and organic life. "Existentialism," on the other hand, is usually thought of as denoting a perspective whose historical roots are in religion and rationalistic philosophy exclusively and whose theory of man presupposes a sharp break between natural occurrences and human existence. By "nature," in this context, I refer to the relatively permanent processes and structures on which our existence depends, at least externally, in the sense that by its means are provided those physical and biological conditions which are necessary causes for our birth, for sustaining our lives, and finally for our death. "Nature" in this sense is not the existentialist conception of "nature" as something we encounter only in our own experience, which is therefore created or invented by man, but is rather the necessary condition of any experience. It is in this latter sense also that Dr. Löwith, for the most part, uses the term "nature." On the other hand, by the term "human existence" I do not refer necessarily to the existentialist doctrine of "subjectivity" as a dimension of reality distinct from the existence of natural entities, or what is sometimes called simply "existence." For the purposes of this introduction, I wish merely to take "conscious awareness" as a fact, without prejudging the question whether it can be adequately explained in terms of organic-functional characteristics or whether its adequate explanation involves an ontological dualism.

What I want to argue in this introduction is that existentialism and naturalism, despite their obvious differences, have much more in common than the usual accounts of these two ways of viewing the world suggest. I shall argue that neither naturalism nor existentialism provides a satisfactory way of understanding reality and that they are rather symptomatic expressions of our modern inability to conceptualize satisfactorily the relation between man and nature. In order to show this, I shall begin with a discussion of the existentialist attitude toward nature and natural science and proceed from there to discuss some of the main tenets of naturalism, especially the naturalistic conception of nature and of scientific method. I shall then investigate the conception of the relation between nature and human existence in both naturalism and existentialism and conclude by discussing some of the historical connections and interrelations of these contrasting ways of understanding reality.

[II] THE EXISTENTIALIST'S ATTITUDE TOWARD NATURE AND SCIENCE

Regarding the existentialist's attitude toward nature and natural science, Dr. Löwith points out the following:

In Sartre's *Etre et le néant,* nature is an opaque *en-soi* over against the *pour-soi* of human existence. It is accessible only in the natural appetites of the human body. In Heidegger's *Being and Time,* nature is comprised under the lowest category of the merely "extant" [*Vorhandensein*] in contrast to human existence [*Dasein*] which alone has a world and can have meaning. Kierkegaard is exclusively concerned with the inwardness of selfhood. He scorned the discoveries of telescope and microscope. A thoughtful person, he says, who wants to understand what it means to exist as a self . . . cannot be interested in natural science. . . . To busy oneself with billions of years of cosmic history . . . is, according to him, but an escape from authentic existence.[3]

This attitude toward natural science and nature still characterizes existentialist views. For example, John Wild has recently written that the

. . . scientific, calculative mode of understanding, thoroughly grounded and prepared for by the whole course of Western metaphysics, has now become dominant in our time, and is making exclusive claims for itself as the only sound and verifiable way of looking at all beings, including man. These absolute claims, however, are unjustified, for objective science has limits . . . it is incapable of giving us an adequate grasp of our existence in the world. It is blind to what is essentially human and, if left to itself, will destroy us.[4]

Wild's comment is an expression of the concern that many thinkers feel about "scientific" tendencies in contemporary thought. "Scientism" has been defined as "the slavish imitation of the method and language of science" or "the imitation of what certain people mistake for the method and language of science."[5] Wild's claim that there are certain inherent conditions limiting the scope of applicability of scientific method (to which, however, proponents of the universal applicability of scientific method are blind), would indicate that for him "scientism" would be the attempt to extend the scope of scientific method beyond the realm of its

3. See below, p. 103.
4. "Symposium: Martin Heidegger, The Philosophy of Martin Heidegger," *The Journal of Philosophy,* LX, no. 22 (Oct. 24, 1963), 664–77.
5. Karl Popper, *The Poverty of Historicism* (London: Routledge & Kegan Paul, 1961), p. 105.

legitimate application, e.g., from the explanation of natural relations to the explanation of human existence in the world.

One might summarize the philosophical points expressed in the passages quoted above as follows. Nature and natural entities, considered by themselves, are devoid of meaning or interest. A universe without human or other similarly endowed conscious beings would be a mere blindly functioning automaton with respect to which any predications of value would be nonsensical. That is to say, nature, considered as it is in itself and without any relation to human life, would not be valuable or valueless so much as it would be totally outside the category of value-attribution. Human existence, on the other hand, has value and meaning, and nature or natural entities gain these attributes only in so far as they can enter into relation with human existence.

Consequently, a person who is concerned with what it means to exist as a self cannot be authentically concerned with nature for its own sake and any such exhibition of concern is a mere escape from the realities of human existence, or from the burdens of being an individual with an identifiable personality who is responsible to his existence and faces death. However, concern with nature for its own sake, as a matter of historical fact, has tended to dominate Western thought and has led to the development of the "scientific, calculative mode of understanding," which has now been extended to the analysis of human existence itself— but of human existence considered only as a natural object among other natural objects. But if nature and human existence are distinct ontological dimensions of reality, then the objective methods of natural science, which were invented for the purpose of investigating nature, are logically incapable of giving us an "adequate grasp of our existence in the world." The paradox of modern thinking, then, according to this existentialist view, is that scientific modes of thinking, which developed in the first place as an "escape" from authentic human existence or self-concern, are now being held to be the only sound ways of understanding human life itself. And thus a thoroughly destructive circle is being brought to completion.

[III] PHILOSOPHICAL IMPLICATIONS OF NATURAL SCIENCE

It is not easy to find any philosopher who is an adherent of what we might call the "scientific outlook" who is willing to discuss the kind of criticism of the scientific mode of understanding as such which is expressed by Wild and the existentialists. Perhaps the closest we can come to a contemporary philosopher of science who has taken serious notice of such criticisms is Ernest Nagel in his book, *Logic Without Metaphysics*.[6] In that work, Nagel attempts to outline a viable philosophy of nature and human life based exclusively on an application of what Wild calls the "scientific, calculative mode of understanding." I shall now attempt to summarize the main tenets of this view and to draw out its consequences for our conception of human existence and its relation, or lack of relation, to nature.

Naturalism, as Nagel conceives it, is an attempt to express what we might call "the world view of modern natural science."

... it is the inclusive intellectual image of nature and man which naturalism supplies that sets it off from other comprehensive philosophies. . . . Naturalism embraces a generalized account of the cosmic scheme and of man's place in it, as well as a logic of inquiry [i.e., a philosophy of science].[7]

A question arises as to the type of relation Nagel is presupposing here between naturalism, considered as a comprehensive philosophy of man and nature, and the conceptions, procedures, and results of modern natural science. A rather extreme view would hold that naturalism is in some way logically implied, or proved, by the established results of science. However, in claiming that naturalism best expresses the world view of modern natural science, Nagel does not argue that the established results of science prove the truth of naturalism, or that naturalism is directly supported by the evidence which supports the best tested scientific theories. What he claims is only that naturalism is a "distillation" from knowledge "acquired in the usual way in daily encounters with the world or in specialized scientific inquiry." [8] That is to say, naturalism is not itself a scientific theory and does not enjoy the same kind of evidential status as a scientific theory. Rather, naturalism is an attempt to formulate a comprehensive set of principles that at most could *imply* the conceptions, methods, and results of science (among other possible consequences); and that would at least be *consistent* with established scientific results. But the philosophical principles of naturalism could not themselves *be implied in turn* by those conceptions and results. That is to say, conceivably some *other* world view besides naturalism could

6. Ernest Nagel, *Logic Without Metaphysics* (Glencoe, Ill.: The Free Press, 1956).

7. *Ibid.*, p. 6.

8. *Ibid.*

enjoy the *same* logical relation to the conceptions, procedures, and results of natural science that naturalism enjoys, namely that of *implying but not being implied in turn* by those conceptions and results. Quite often, if not always, there can be more than one explanation of the same set of facts, even at the level of strict scientific experimentation, and we should expect the same situation to prevail at the level of generality which is involved when we discuss a comprehensive world view such as that of naturalism. And in fact, no world view, whether it be naturalism or existentialism or any other, could lay *exclusive* claim to being *the* philosophy of modern natural science unless it were implied by premises that are found in the context of a scientific theory considered merely as such. But it is doubtful that any physical theory, for example (such as the kinetic theory of matter), is capable of having any philosophical implications that might logically imply a philosophical world view, if for no other reason than that the relation of a physical theory to concrete nature is too complex and too ambiguous to admit of only a single plausible or reasonable interpretation. But what holds for any physical theory must also hold for any biological or psychological theory that is susceptible of laboratory verification.

Therefore, when we speak of the "philosophical implications of modern natural science," and discuss what world view is most reasonable on the basis of investigations and disclosures of science, we cannot reasonably intend the word "implication" to be taken in its strict logical sense. We may, however, speak of the "philosophical implications of science" in a looser, problematic sense. At the same time, we cannot reasonably mean by "science," in such contexts, specific laboratory theories, such as the kinetic theory of matter. What we must mean is the whole scientific enterprise considered as a historically conditioned process of inquiry, which has been efficacious in shaping our conceptions of the world and of human existence in the world, however vague these conceptions may be prior to the attempt by philosophers to give them a more precise expression. Naturalism, therefore, expresses the philosophy of modern natural science only in the sense that it is the statement of comprehensive principles most likely to be accepted by one who believes in the adequacy of scientific methods of thought to interpret every item of our experience and not in the sense that it is uniquely proved or established by scientific results. It is for this reason that there may be wide divergencies of opinion even within the group of those thinkers who are attempting to give a satisfactory expression of what would be called a "naturalistic" point of view.

[IV] THE PRINCIPLES OF NATURALISM

Three theses are central to naturalism as Nagel conceives it. The first of these three

. . . is the existential and causal primacy of organized matter in the executive order of nature. This is the assumption that the occurrence of events, qualities, and processes, and the characteristic behaviors of various individuals, are contingent on the organization of spatio-temporally located bodies, whose internal structures and external relations determine and limit the appearance and disappearance of everything that happens.[9]

This first thesis might be thought to be an expression of materialism rather than of naturalism. However, while it expresses a kind of materialism, it is not the *reductive* kind of materialism. Reductive materialism is the view that predicates descriptive of non-material entities can be systematically replaced, without loss of truth value, by complex physical descriptions. For example, my claim to be "thinking" now, or to be in possession of a set of "ideas," could be translated, at least in principle, according to reductive materialism into a set of statements describing measurable physical occurrences, e.g., certain brain events, which would be equivalent to my original "psychological" statement. The kind of "equivalence" which would hold between the physical and the "mental" description would not be an equivalence in *meaning* (synonymy) but only an equivalence in the sense in which a phenomenological description of colors, for example, is "equivalent" to a physical description in terms of frequencies of light waves. But the "materialism" which Nagel offers as the first thesis of a naturalistic world view is not this type of reductive materialism. Rather, it is a *dualistic* view with which it would be consistent to conceive of non-material things existing, that is, things that are not "material bodies" or "organizations of material bodies." He gives as examples of such non-material entities "modes of action, relations of meaning, dreams, joys, plans, and aspirations." [10] However, according to Nagel, such non-material entities ought to be construed as nothing more than "*forms* of behavior or *functions*

9. *Ibid.*, p. 7.
10. *Ibid.*

of material systems" and although they are "indefeasibly parts of nature," they are not themselves construable as "causal agents in their own realization or in the realization of anything else." While this is not reductionism, it effectively removes non-material entities from playing any fundamental role in determining natural processes or the real constitution of events. Thus we might say that, according to this version of naturalism, although mental events "really exist" and are not reducible to brain states or processes, they are merely remote effects of a complex chain of physical causes without any causal power of their own to affect the course of nature.

It may be observed that the items of experience which Nagel lists as non-material entities constitute what existentialists regard as the "essentially human" or the "world of lived experience." Thus we should have to conclude that according to the view of naturalism, the world of the "essentially human" plays no fundamental role in shaping the course of nature or history and that man in relation to wider nature has a status analogous to that of a political exile who can live in a certain country (nature) but can take no part in the activities whereby the country is effectively regulated (causal agencies). The remarkable coincidence of this view with some existentialist expressions of "the human predicament" is worthy of note.

The other basic principles to which we would have to give expression in formulating a naturalistic outlook, according to Nagel, are that

... the manifest plurality and variety of things, of their qualities and their functions, are an irreducible feature of the cosmos, not a deceptive appearance cloaking some more homogeneous, "ultimate reality" ... and ... the sequential orders in which events occur or the manifold relations of dependence in which things exist are *contingent* connections, not the embodiments of a fixed and unified pattern of logically necessary links. ... In brief ... irreducible variety and logical contingency are fundamental traits of the world we actually inhabit.[11]

We have here three principles: that of the *causal primacy of organized matter in the order of nature,* that of *pluralism,* and that of the *contingency of all existence.*

What is meant by the principle of the contingency of all existence is that necessary truths, such as those of logic or mathematics, do not describe or express any traits of existing things or of the structure of existing things. Thus, according to this principle, no existent thing is necessarily what it is except in

11. *Ibid.,* p. 9.

relation to antecedent conditions that taken by themselves might have been otherwise. From this point of view, it would make no sense to speak of there being any *reasons*, as opposed to *causes*, for things being what they are; and the "order of nature" that we discover in our experience could not be the eternal and immutable order of Greek Rationalism, but could only be itself the product of contingent connections between events. The "order of nature," in other words, may involve "exceptionless regularity" but cannot involve "necessity."

As we shall see, these three principles, fundamental to a naturalistic world view, have a remarkable similarity to the fundamental principles of existentialism.

[V] EXISTENTIALISM AND SCIENCE

No one, I think, would object to the claim that the principles of the contingency and plurality of all existence are shared by existentialism. As Dr. Löwith points out, one of the basic experiences of existentialism is that of the "contingency of human existence within the whole of the natural world." And existentialism, being itself based partly on a critique of idealism and monistic tendencies of thought, is indisputably committed to what Nagel calls "the manifest plurality and variety of things" as an "irreducible feature of the cosmos."

The remaining principle, that "organized matter" or "body" is causally primary in the "executive order of nature," would also have to be admitted by existentialists, so long as the principle is confined to the characterization of the events and processes of nature and so long as "nature" is not identified with the whole of reality. That is to say, existentialism appears to share with the outlook of naturalism its conception of nature and nature's causal agencies, although existentialists differ on the important question of whether human existence is a part of nature, that is, whether human actions, thoughts, and feelings are properly categorized as effects of natural causes. These points may profitably be considered in more detail.

The fundamental tenet of the contingency of existence is expressed in existentialist terms by the notion that man is "cast" into the world, that nothing can relieve him of the "burden" of the "sheer factuality" of his being. Perhaps the only difference between naturalism and existentialism as regards this tenet is that while the adherent of the outlook of naturalism is content to describe what he regards as the fact that man's life is contingent, the existentialist implicitly contrasts this conception of human existence as a contingency with the traditional conception of man as having a "place" and a "purpose" in a scheme of things. He thus draws out in full his sense of the pathos of human existence in the modern world by contrasting it historically with man's former conceptions of his existence. For example, Kierkegaard, in a well-known passage, gives vent to the feelings that the contingency or "factuality" of human existence aroused in him.

My life has been brought to an *impasse*. I loathe existence, it is without savor, lacking salt and sense. . . . One sticks one's finger into the soil to tell by the smell in what land one is: I stick my finger into existence—it smells of nothing. Where am I? Who am I? How came I here? What is this thing called the world . . . ? Who is it that has lured me into the thing and now leaves me there . . . ? Why was I not consulted . . . ? How did I obtain an interest in this big enterprise they call reality . . . ? And if I am compelled to take part in it, where is the director? I should like to make a remark to him.[12]

Clearly, the anthropomorphism expressed in this passage is not intended to be taken literally, but ironically. Kierkegaard wishes to bring out what he regards as the absurdity of the human condition in the world by characterizing the world with predicates that apply meaningfully only to interrelations with human beings. The "world," for Kierkegaard, is nature *and* history. The contingency of the world makes it possible to ask why the world is not a place to which human predicates *could* apply without absurdity.

This passage from Kierkegaard can be compared with Nagel's comments on the same theme. According to naturalism, Nagel says, "the emergence and the continuance of human society [is] dependent on physical and physiological conditions that have not always obtained and that will not permanently endure." [13] Furthermore, naturalism offers no "cosmic consolation for the unmerited defeats and undeserved sufferings which all men experience in one form or another," since, according to this doctrine, "human destiny" is "an episode between two oblivions." [14] By pointing to the finiteness of human existence and the absoluteness of death for the individual and by speaking of human life as an "episode between two oblivions," Nagel presupposes that conception of

12. Soren Kierkegaard, *Repetition* (Princeton: Princeton University Press, 1941), p. 114.
13. Nagel, *op. cit.*, p. 9.
14. *Ibid.*, p. 17.

nature as an *"en-soi,"* devoid of meaning or interest, that the existentialist also presupposes.

However, Nagel refuses to draw the typical existentialist conclusions from this characterization of human existence. He insists that, despite its transitory nature, "human good is nonetheless a good." And though he admits that there are "irremediable evils" in human life, he claims that "it is impossible to decide responsibly, *antecedent* to inquiry, *which* . . . human ills can be mitigated . . . by extending the operations of scientific reason into human affairs. . . ." [15] In other words, human reason, he believes, while not an "omnipotent instrument for the achievement of human goods" is nonetheless the "only instrument we do possess" and it *is* potent against "remediable evils." Thus naturalism, according to Nagel, while "sensitive to the actual limitations of rational effort," does not "warrant a romantic philosophy of general despair." [16] This last phrase is presumably an allusion to existentialism.

This examination shows, I believe, that with respect to the fundamental principle of the contingency of human existence, the only difference between naturalism, as Nagel represents it, and existentialism, is that the former recommends an attitude of optimism qualified by intelligent resignation about the evils that we can do nothing to remedy, while the latter is in part an expression of protest. Kierkegaard's attitude of protest, for example, seems to be a result of a wish on his part that the world should have been a different sort of place than science reveals it to be; specifically, that man should have had some definite place in a scheme of things, or that his existence should have served some kind of detectable purpose. The pathos in his expression arises from his clear perception that the world is just not that sort of place. But his conception of nature seems to be the same as that which we gain through the investigations of modern natural science, and which is presupposed by naturalism.

Let us go on to examine the third basic principle of naturalism, that of the causal primacy of organized matter in the order of nature. (The second fundamental principle, that of the plurality of existing things, need not detain us.) It appears that the fundamental existentialist distinction, already alluded to, between two kinds of being that are different in principle, expresses the same apprehension of natural entities that is characteristic of

15. *Ibid.*, pp. 17–18.
16. *Ibid.*, p. 18.

naturalism. This is the distinction between human *Dasein*, which exists "because it is spontaneously related to the world and to itself," and, on the other hand, beings which are not self-related, i.e., natural entities properly speaking. The point of disagreement between naturalism and existentialism turns solely on the question of how we are to conceive of specifically *human* existence; that is, whether we are to conceive of human existence as a natural product, distinctive from and yet emergent from natural processes (naturalism), or as a mode of existence which, in its capacity for being self-related, is different in principle from the existence of natural entities, however it may have originated (existentialism). The question, in other words, is what significance ought to be attached to the fact that only man has a sense of selfhood to any developed degree, or, in existentialist terms, that only man is capable of "questioning Being."

What existentialists mean by "existence" is characterized by Löwith as follows:

Existence is . . . not a fixed quality, like being tall or short. It is a constant possibility. We *can* exist in this or that manner, authentically or unauthentically. . . . However we choose to be, these possibilities remain *each one's* own possibilities. Man's *Dasein,* which chooses and pursues one of his possibilities, is always *my* personal or *your* personal existence, amidst and in spite of all sociality. In all his taking care of something and caring for others, man is ultimately concerned with his own being and possibilities, which rest, however, on the sheer fact of his being-there.[17]

In other words, for the existentialist, man is like other natural beings to the extent that he is not responsible *for* his being-there, but unlike other natural beings to the extent that he is responsible *to* his existence, in the sense that he alone among natural beings can question his existence and can choose from a number of possibilities the manner of his existence, or even not to exist. This means, in a less exotic language, that material factors or contingent causes are the source of human life, but that once a human life is launched, its mode of existence is fundamentally different from that of natural entities in general, concerning which it makes no sense to say that they might "choose" their manner of existence or might "withdraw" from existence.

To compare this view of human existence with that of naturalism, it might be thought that the latter would take a very different view, perhaps going so far as to classify man's existence as another kind of *Vorhandensein,* or as a being that is merely

17. See below, p. 35.

"extant." This is by no means the case, however. Thus the existentialist, in charging that scientific method is inherently incapable of grasping our human existence in the world because it treats man as a natural object among other natural objects, fails to note a possible distinction between types of natural objects. For Nagel, many human traits, though natural products, appear to be distinctive of man, in that many terms have an "identifiable content only in reference to the human psyche." [18] Any social concept, such as "profit and loss," "hara-kiri," or "ambition," would be an example of such a term. Nagel in fact criticizes the tendency of many philosophers who wish to express a naturalistic outlook to make a "fetish of continuity" between the "typically human on the one hand, and the physical and biological on the other." [19] In other words, a simple-minded belief in continuity is not an essential feature of a naturalistic outlook. As against continuity. Nagel prefers to stress "the emergence of novel forms in physical and biological evolution"—and in this way to show how it is possible for human traits to be natural products and yet not be identical with the traits from which they emerge. Nagel says that a sophisticated scientific outlook would seek to understand "what man is, not in terms of a discovered or postulated continuity between what is distinctive of him and what is pervasive in all things," but rather in terms of his most distinctive traits, without having to deny, on the other hand, that those traits are dependent on non-human causal agencies for their origin.[20] But the distinctiveness of human traits in the natural world does not, according to Nagel, mean that we must "regard man and his works" as "intrusions into nature," any more than we have to construe as "intrusions the presence of heavenly bodies or of terrestrial protozoa."

The stars are no more foreign to the cosmos than are men, even if the conditions for the existence of both stars and men are realized only occasionally or only in a few regions. Indeed, the conception of human life as a war with nature, as a struggle with an implacable foe that has doomed man to extinction, is but an inverted theology. . . . It is a conception that is . . . anthropomorphic in the importance it imputes to man in the scheme of things.[21]

This way of conceiving human existence, as a natural product but unique among natural entities in possessing a highly developed

18. Nagel, *op cit.*, p. 9.
19. *Ibid.*, p. 10.
20. *Ibid.*, pp 10–11.
21. *Ibid.*, p. 9.

psychic dimension, yet for all that enjoying no special or privileged status in or outside of nature, is curiously similar to the existentialist conception of human existence. The existentialist, it is true, gives a very different account of the "uniqueness" and "isolation" of human existence in the natural world, even going so far as to suggest that man is, after all, an "intrusion into nature." But the major point of conflict between naturalism and existentialism seems to turn less on the description of the facts of human existence and more on what significance or importance ought to be attached to those facts. Does the fact that man alone among natural beings can question his existence as a matter of principle mean that subjective human existence amounts to a unique ontological dimension, a specifically human reality, and therefore cannot unambiguously be described as "natural"? Does Nagel, in admitting that there are "distinctive human traits" not in any sense shared by other natural entities, implicitly commit himself to a doctrine of "human reality" as a unique ontological dimension? If so, which position gives the fuller and more adequate description of "human reality" and its relation to wider nature? The answer seems already to have been given. Existentialists describe modern human existence by implicitly contrasting it with traditional conceptions of man as having a definite place in a scheme of things, whereas naturalistic thinkers such as Nagel describe it without reference to any historical situation, confining themselves, so to speak, to descriptions of its logical structure.

It is true that Heidegger has claimed that nature cannot elucidate the ontological character of our world and of our being in it because nature is only a kind of being within our world. However, the Heideggerean notion of *Geworfenheit,* of "being thrown into" existence, i.e., the notion that *Dasein* does not *decide* whether it wants to come into existence and thus that it is unintelligible *why* we have to be—this notion already presupposes the ontological priority of nature over history in a more fundamental sense of "nature," and thus presupposes that "nature" in this fundamental sense exists independently of our historical world. It is true that this priority of nature does not of itself elucidate the "ontological character of our world," but that character evidently could not have been grasped in the first place, apart from the concept of a prior and independent nature, which is responsible for our historical existence. Thus, the fact that from our perspective we encounter nature only in history does not entail that nature is itself only a manifestation of human history. Similarly, the existentialist conception of *Geworfenheit* seems to presuppose the same principle of the causal primacy of organized bodies in the order of nature that is presupposed by naturalism. It is this presupposition which makes intelligible the existentialist notion of the alienation of human historical existence from nature.

[VI] HISTORICAL CONSIDERATIONS

Löwith criticizes existentialists for being ignorant of or indifferent to the historical origins of their fundamental tenets in the same conceptions that underlie the investigations of modern natural science.

To understand existentialism historically as well as systematically, we have to refer to the new concept of an infinite universe which seems at first to be the farthest removed from any immediate existential concern of a self with itself. It is my thesis here that we "exist" (in the sense of existentialism) because we are lost in the universe of modern natural science.[22]

In this connection, Löwith observes that:

If we reflect upon the history of Western thinking, a distinct turning point can be seen when the pre-modern concept of an essential human existence within an orderly *cosmos* changes into a chance-existence. The change occurred at the beginning of the seventeenth century, as a consequence of the astronomical discoveries of the sixteenth century.[23]

These astronomical discoveries led to the "negative experience that man has no definite place and nature within the natural universe."

This metaphysical displacement is, however, not a novelty of the twentieth century, but rather *the* modern destiny. "Since Copernicus," Nietzsche said, "man is falling from a center toward an *x*." This universal destiny is aggravated by man's social solitariness amid a modern mass-society.[24]

Prior to the seventeenth century, men who thought about it at all believed that the universe was an "encompassable world order," this *order* being reflected in human reason and thus recognizable *a priori* as a part of one's personal or subjective experience of the world. Seventeenth-century physical investigations of the cosmos, however, had a shattering effect on this comfortable conviction. An apparently insignificant factor, that of the sheer extent or size of the physical universe, seems to have played a major role in causing this conceptual upheaval. For as the universe increased

22. See below, p. 102.
23. See below, p. 24.
24. See below, p. 104.

in size in man's conception of it, it seemed to decrease proportion-
ally in the degree of rational order that could plausibly be attributed
to it. In other words, as man's conception of the physical universe
shifted from one of finite to one of infinite extent, his sense of
being positively and intimately related to any possible order of the
universe correspondingly diminished. Since the size of the universe
no longer fit his preconceptions and since an infinite universe
could no longer be represented to him as an "encompassable world
order," doubt was engendered that the universe embodied a principle of order similar to that which man recognized in his reason.
It was then theorized that the universe originated in an explosion
and that the present order of nature is the chance result of
statistical probabilities. But as Löwith observes:

No social order of whatever kind, not even order plus freedom, can possibly make up for that lack of fundamental order in the universe. Hence,
we have indeed "to be," or exist, in all those descriptive terms of sheer
factuality, contingency, and absurdity which existentialism has brought to
light.... *It is the character of our world and world concept which makes
us exist existentially.*[25]

Of course, the shift in the conception of the size of the universe
was not merely from a smaller to a larger one, but from a finite
to an infinite one; and it is this notion of an infinite universe that
is the source, according to Löwith, of the modern sense of man's
homelessness in nature.

To say, as Nagel does, that man is at home in nature as much
as anything is at home in nature [26] misses the fundamental pathos
of the condition of modern man, which is not merely natural, but
also historical in character. It is only historically, that is to say,
that the concept of man's "homelessness" in nature can be understood. It is significant that the shift from a finite to an infinite
universe should have taken place at the same time, historically
speaking, that the fundamental tenet of the contingency of all
existence was gaining the ascendancy; and that the immediately
preceding world-concept should have been one in which man had
a necessary place in a total world-process, including history as well
as nature. Man has thus lost his place historically in a scheme of
things and nothing in modern intellectual developments has
convincingly restored him to such a place. The "plight" of modern

25. See below, p. 105.
26. Nagel, *op. cit.*, p. 9.

man, then, according to Löwith, is that while nothing remains of man's relation to the universe but "radical, universal contingency of existence, or existence 'without support,'" such a thought is, in Kant's phrase, "intolerable to human reason," while its opposite, "inner necessity," is undemonstrable for it. "The difference between Kant and contemporary existentialists," Löwith ironically remarks, "is that the latter apparently have managed to find radical contingency tolerable and even liberating, and the demonstrability of an inherent necessity of existence to be unnecessary." [27]

The aim of Löwith's analysis seems to be to persuade us that while existentialism is the only authentic philosophical expression of man's current historical situation, it cannot be regarded as a satisfactory stopping place. Existentialism, in other words, and *a forteriori* naturalism, is a philosophy that must be overcome; but it has to be understood properly before it *can* be significantly overcome. However, if there is a historical or theoretical alternative to modern existentialism, Löwith does not believe that it will be easily achieved, if indeed it can be achieved at all. For if there were such an alternative, he argues, it would have to be

... the choice of understanding the world and man's place in it either as an immutable natural order—that is, with the eyes of Greek contemplation —or as divine creation—that is, with the eyes of ... faith. Either choice would indeed be persuasive, since one cannot wish to remain forever nailed on the cross of contingency, absurdity and total displacement. But choosing between one or the other ... would still be an existential attitude and decision, and therefore contradictory to the nature of the chosen world view. For neither of them is a mere project of human choice and decision. The one is revealed and intelligible only to faith; the other ... is revealed ... in and by nature itself to the nature of man. We cannot choose not to be modern, if it is true that modernity has, since Descartes, rested on the choice of a standpoint and viewpoint. *We would have to overcome in principle the modern attitude as such toward the whole of Being if we are to overcome existentialism.*[28]

In other words, the fact that in order to overcome existentialism one has to make a choice of world view embodying a different conception of nature and existence is precisely the predicament on which existentialism as a philosophical expression of man's current historical situation is based, namely the predicament of being free to make such a choice. For the ancient Greek, or the medieval believer, no such choice could be contemplated, since it

27. See below, p. 26.
28. See below, p. 49.

was already a part of his world view that human existence was a necessary element in a natural or divine order that was rational in character. Thus in order to overcome existentialism, according to Löwith, we should literally have to cease to be "modern," we should have to overcome the modern attitude as such to the whole of nature.

[VII] Criticism of Löwith's Argument

The fundamental question raised by Löwith's argument is whether the ambiguity of human existence as both natural object and reflective subject can be resolved by some conceptual effort or realignment of concepts which would have the effect of "putting man back into nature." Löwith argues that since the problem is not merely conceptual or abstract, but involves as well the concrete historical situation of modern man, such an attempt on the abstract level only would be futile, because it would necessarily have to pass over the fundamental problem. A philosophical analysis can bring out the meanings and interrelations among the facts, but it cannot change or alter them. Yet the latter is precisely what would have to be done by those who hope to resolve this problem by redefining what we mean by "nature." Many recent thinkers, for example, have attempted to interpret the fundamental reality allegedly disclosed by the investigations of modern natural science, especially by modern relativity and quantum theories, in a manner less adverse for the prospects of human existence than was possible on the nineteenth-century version of physical science.[29]

The nineteenth-century conception of the physical world and man's place in it is well expressed in the novel, *Jude the Obscure,* by Thomas Hardy.

... the First Cause worked automatically like a somnambulist, and not reflectively like a sage; ... at the framing of the terrestrial conditions there seemed never to have been contemplated such a development of emotional perceptiveness among the creatures subject to those conditions as that reached by thinking and educated humanity.[30]

29. See, for example, A. N. Whitehead's "Nature and Life" in *Modes of Thought* (New York: Macmillan, 1938), pp. 173–238; and C. F. von Weizsäcker's *History of Nature* (Chicago: University of Chicago Press, 1949), Chap. 1 and *passim.*

30. Thomas Hardy, *Jude the Obscure* (New York: The Modern Library), p. 407.

It might be objected that Hardy is influenced mainly by what in the nineteenth century was thought to be revealed about the universe by science, namely, that the world is a physical mechanism operating solely in accordance with mechanical laws. The expressions of the meaninglessness and alienation of human existence which he gives, and which are echoed by Löwith, would not carry over into twentieth-century revisions of the physical picture of the world, according to which the world is no longer considered to be infinitely extended in space and time. Whitehead, for example, attempts to interpret our conception of the basic physical particles as involving emotional qualities not different in principle from those of human organisms; and Weizsäcker attempts to show, in opposition to Hardy, that human reflective experience of a self developing in time is not an aberration or a "mere appearance" but is, on the contrary, "fundamental to the new physical-cosmological world picture, considered quite apart from man's experience—that, indeed, there is a history of nature from both points of view" [that is, objective and subjective viewpoints], and thus "quite certainly an historic nature in fact." [31]

Thus, Hardy's notion that the universe works "automatically like a somnambulist" rather than "reflectively like a sage" clearly suggests a mechanistic as opposed to a teleological model of natural reality, and would be rejected by both Whitehead and Weizsäcker as an unjustified inference from the investigations of science. Whitehead, for example, would reject this interpretation on the grounds that teleology is an observable component in nature, and both Whitehead and Weizsäcker would reject it on the grounds that nature itself has an "inner" or "subjective" aspect, as well as an "outer" or objective" aspect, just as men do. Further the fact that Hardy finds the "development of emotional perceptiveness" a contingency that does not prepare the creatures in whom it occurs for a life under "terrestrial conditions," suggests that he views "emotional perceptiveness" as the exception rather than the rule of natural existence, a view which surely reflects the nineteenth-century picture of nature as a vast machine.

However, while Whitehead presents an alternative analysis of the nature revealed by natural science, in which emotional perceptiveness is the bond uniting all natural entities, this analysis does not affect the question which is raised by Löwith. This problem concerns the alienation of emotionally perceptive persons from

31. The quoted phrases immediately preceding are from J. J. Compton, "Understanding Science," *Dialectica*, XVI, 16, no. 2, 173.

the nature disclosed by the investigations of natural science. The question behind this alienation is not so much what is the most general character of natural entities, as Whitehead seems to think, or even—to use Heidegger's famous phrase—why there is anything at all rather than nothing. The question is rather, why are there creatures endowed with the capacity for reflection and emotional perceptiveness of a high order in a universe to which these characteristics have no positive relation? If, as Whitehead seems to suggest, so-called physical objects can have "feelings," these feelings are still not of a sufficiently high order to produce experiences such as alienation, suffering, and heartbreak, and it is this capacity for apparently useless suffering that has to be explained. Even if, as Whitehead argues, "feelings" are the concrete bonds interrelating natural entities, and even if the patterns formulated in scientific laws ultimately refer to these "felt" interconnections, it would still not be appropriate to predicate human capacities of emotional perceptiveness to these entities. Presumably, for example, roses do not suffer by being picked, nor do stones develop a sense of alienation through being dropped. Whether, therefore, man is "in" or "out" of nature in the sense of Whitehead and Weizsäcker is irrelevant to the question expressed by Hardy and investigated by Löwith.

The answer given to the question, why are there creatures endowed with the capacity for reflection and emotional perceptiveness in the universe of modern natural science, is no more satisfactory in terms of quantum and relativity physics than it is in terms of nineteenth-century mechanistic conceptions. The answer is, in both cases, fundamentally the same, namely that there is no *reason* which can explain the existence of such capacities, and such capacities, and such mechanistic or quantum-theoretic causes as we might uncover would be of no more subjective interest than the scientific explanation of the causes of the rainbow. Even teleological causes, such as might be required in a science like biology in order to explain evolution, would still be only contingent, that is to say, non-rational or non-intelligible causes. The whole point of Löwith's argument is that if the sense of alienation follows from the discovery that events do not occur for a reason, including the event which is one's own life, and if this discovery reveals the genuine condition of reflective human existence in the universe of modern natural science, then no amount of conceptual realignment or discovering correlates of consciousness in external nature can alter or diminish this sense of alienation. For the question is not whether, on the basis of the laws of the behavior of the micro-entities of modern physics, it is possible for certain complex organizations to arise with all the traits, including consciousness, that we usually associate with human beings. The question is rather, as Kant saw it: [32] how can we make our own existence intelligible to ourselves short of discovering a *necessary* ground of the being of consciousness? Thus, the notion of the alienation of man from nature, as a historical fact, comes to take on this significance: what is most important to ourselves as reflective subjects evidently has no particular bearing on, or relation to, the fundamental natural conditions which ultimately both sustain and destroy our existence. Thus, the fact that there may be naturalistic or scientific explanations of the origin of consciousness, as giving not indeed the only *possible* explanation of consciousness, but one that is *sufficient* to account for all the facts of consciousness in terms of antecedent natural conditions, is not a *solution* to the problem of alienation, but a restatement of the problem itself, or an explanation of how the problem *arises* in the context of history. Modern man is both a part of nature and at the same time alienated from it. He is, as it were, according to his own conceptions, nature's stepchild.

Nevertheless, Löwith's argument may be objected to on the grounds that it is excessively historicist in character. For after all, both existentialism and naturalism, if the arguments of this introduction have been sound, stem from the basic principles of the contingency of all existence and of the causal primacy of organized bodies in the order of nature. The existentialist's sense of the alienation of man's existence arises from these principles together with the arguments showing the uniqueness and isolation of human life in the natural world, as revealed by modern science. This sense of pathos is heightened by contrasting the resultant modern conception of the human condition with the traditional conception of man as having a status in a universal rational order. But if we wish to "overcome" a philosophical world view such as extentialism or naturalism, the problem is not one of *choosing* another world view, but of showing that the fundamental principles on which the philosophy in question is based are false and that another set of principles is true or at least more likely to be true. For example, it can certainly be questioned to what extent the principle of the contingency of all existence is true, or even logically tenable. And the arguments that might refute this principle, and consequently existentialism and other world views based on it, would not necessarily be historicist in character but could as well be

32. See above, p. xxxii.

logical and abstract. Löwith himself recognizes this when he speaks of the need to subject the modern world to a radical criticism.

Investigations like those carried out by Löwith are important for the light they shed on the historical origins and consequences of our favorite assumptions and for what they do to show us that these assumptions have not always been held by thinking men. Thus, if Löwith's argument is correct, at least in its main principle, and if it is true that the existentialist conception of existence cannot be understood apart from an understanding of the modern scientific conception of nature, then the existentialist tendency to characterize distinctive human existence as a "pour-soi," a complete and unambiguous transcendence, cannot be accepted. For human existence on any theory cannot adequately be comprehended except in its relation to the physical universe and to the natural processes that ultimately condition it, even if only externally. Nature, therefore, is not a mere insignificant background to modern man's "forlorn historical existence." Rather, it is the character of physical nature that *makes* man's existence "forlorn," when that existence is contrasted with the traditional conceptions. Kierkegaard is surely going to extremes, therefore, when he dismisses the methods and results of natural science as irrelevant for questions of personal existence and self-knowledge. For as we have seen, the nature of our understanding of reality affects our conduct of life. Indeed, if Löwith's argument is correct, the historical origins of Kierkegaard's own most basic convictions belie this dismissal.

Löwith points out that the existentialist's emphasis on human existence and on the world as a historical one has a concomitant in the lack of sense for that which is natural. The existentialist's attitude toward nature, as Löwith characterizes it here, is the exact inverse of the attitude of the naturalistic outlook to history. While the latter hardly acknowledges the possibility that specific historical conditions might play a role in shaping our conception of nature (as opposed to sense perceptions), existentialism recognizes the importance of the historical factor, but tends to exaggerate the difference between human and other natural existents, and to relegate nature to an insignificant background of the unfolding drama of human historical existence. Both outlooks, therefore, the naturalistic and the existentialist, are really two sides of the same coin, and both are equally symptomatic expressions of our modern inability to conceptualize the relation between nature, history, and human existence in a way that does justice both to the continuity and discontinuity between man and nature and to the respective roles of history and nature in determining our conceptions of things.

[VIII] Conclusion

Löwith argues that the existentialists

... denaturation of human life to historical existence did not ... arise with modern historicism and existentialism, but with modern natural science. It is against the background of nature as conceived by modern natural science that existentialism itself comes into existence, for its basic experience is not the historicity, but the contingency of human existence within the whole of the natural world.[33]

Löwith's emphasis on the factor of "contingency" is justified by the preceding analysis. Furthermore, it is on this matter of the contingency of existence that existentialism and naturalism are most closely alike. If existentialism involves the neglect of nature, one might say equally that the naturalistic emphasis on the world as a physical one and on human existence merely as a phase in the panorama of meaningless nature has a concomitant in the lack of sense for that which is historical and personal. Curiously, it is precisely the non-human character of the concept of nature, borrowed from natural science, that concerns the existentialist and makes him conscious of the human "plight." Thus, the existentialist cannot afford to anthropomorphize nature any more than the naturalistic philosopher, for he could not then still maintain his essential thesis, namely that man has no "place" in nature.

Modern thought seems to have revolved between the two extremes of seeing human existence either as a pure transcendence, or as a mere occurrence of physical nature on a par with other physical and organic events. Nagel makes an attempt to find a middle path between these extremes, but fails to make any more intelligible for us the nature of the relation that holds between subjective human existence and the rest of nature than does existentialism. Nor does there seem to be any verifiable claim in Nagel's "naturalism" that could contradict the conclusions of existentialism, or vice versa. Even the view that material factors ultimately control human actions applies, according to Nagel, only to the external conditions of those actions and not to their appearance to the subject, i.e., to his inner life. And while the capacity for reflective thought seems to make the important difference between man's existence and mere physical or animal existence, this capacity may not be an essential or specific difference, but only a difference in degree. So much, at least, we can credit to the arguments of Whitehead. Consciousness to some extent is shared by the animals most closely related to man biologically, and such

33. See below, p. 24.

animals appear to be capable in a rudimentary way of every kind of behavior of which human beings are capable, except perhaps those forms of behavior which are uniquely dependent on the development of speech. Thus the capacity for reflection can be conceived of as necessarily standing outside of "nature" only by a conceit. But even if this is so, "nature," in the broadest sense, seems to take on the same kind of indeterminacy that human existence does in existentialist conceptions, and "nature" in this sense is no longer a suitable name for the purely physical or non-reflective, or the merely blind. As opposed to such a conception, we have the alternative of understanding man's "placelessness" in nature not as an aberration of the natural order, but precisely as a natural concomitant of the development of man's reflective capacity to question his existence. Man's "placelessness," viewed in this way, might be said to be the key to understanding his natural condition, namely to exist between the tension of these opposites, between the extremes of being a blind physical mechanism, on the one hand, and a pure consciousness or self-awareness on the other.

ARNOLD LEVISON

Evanston, Illinois
June, 1965

Nature, History, and Existentialism

1 / The Historical Background
of European Nihilism

THE DISSOLUTION OF OLD-EUROPE

THE DISSOLUTION of the religious and moral unity of the Christian Occident began with the German Reformation. Its political tradition was shattered by the French Revolution, which was to be continued by the Russian Revolution, for Bolshevism originated in western Europe, with the Jacobins. The events of 1789, 1848, and 1917 belong to the same movement. Together, the French and the Russian revolutions made a clean sweep of the past. Both mark an epochal incision in European history. Carlyle called the French Revolution the third act of the world's history; for him the whole history of Christianity was but one single epoch in relation to this revolution, the second act after the first of antiquity. He held the opinion that the European race had burst out into anarchy and several "grossly excited" centuries were ahead before the old house would be completely gutted by fire and something new could take its place. In their counterrevolutionary writings, Bonald and De Maistre in France, Burke in England, and Gentz in Germany emphasized no less, each in his own fashion, that Europe faced a crisis. Napoleon's desire was to bridge the chasm opened by the revolution; his great project failed and the revolution of July 1830 made it obvious that the restoration which meanwhile had taken place was but an interlude. Accordingly, one may say that since 1789 Europe has been living in a still unfinished era of revolutions.

In 1830 Niebuhr, the German historian, believed he saw a rising tide of subversion such as the world had seen during the third century: annihilation of wealth, liberty, civilization, and science. Goethe concurred when he prophesied an impending barbarism, even declaring: "We are already right in it." In a conversation in 1829 on Europe's plight, he said that the nineteenth century

[3]

was not simply the continuation of the preceding century, but the beginning of a new period. He saw the time coming when God would no longer be glad of this world and "will have to smash up the whole for a renewed creation." He deemed the foundations of bourgeois society and its forms of intercourse destroyed and looked upon Saint-Simon's writings as the clever outline of a thorough overthrow of the existing order. He saw in the modern French novels a "literature of despair," pressing upon the reader the opposite of all that man ought to be told for his own good. "To excel the ugly, the hideous, the cruel, the contemptible along with the whole kinship of the depraved, that is their satanic business." Everything is now "ultra," perpetually "transcendent" in thought as in action:

> No one knows himself any longer, no one understands the element in which he moves and works, or the subject which he is treating. Pure simplicity is out of the question; of simpletons we have enough. Young people are excited much too early and then carried away in the whirl of the times. Wealth and rapidity are what the world admires and what everyone strives to attain. Railways, quick mails, steamships, and every possible kind of rapid communications are what the educated world has in view so that it over-educates itself and thereby continues in a state of mediocrity. It is, moreover, the result of universality that a mediocre culture becomes common. . . . This is a century for men with heads on their shoulders, for practical men of quick perceptions who, because they possess a certain adroitness, feel their superiority above the multitude, even though they themselves may not be gifted in the highest degree. . . . We and perhaps a few others will be the last of an epoch which will not soon return.
>
> (Letter to Zelter, 1825)

Burckhardt makes up his mind in 1846. He departs from the political radicalism of his early friends and henceforth restricts himself to the culture of "Old-Europe." According to Burckhardt, some sort of Roman Caesarism with great national wars looming on the horizon was in store for Europe. The state will again become all-powerful on the basis of democratic leveling and thus bid the masses "to shut up." Questions of pure legality have never arisen where movements of whole nations are concerned, but this time it would seem "as though there were no law and no question left at all." This despotism would not be exercised by tenderhearted dynasties, but by military authorities which are able to govern with absolute brutality, scornful of law, material wealth, sovereignty of the people, or even science. Possibly such despotisms will succeed to a great degree and subdue the European world even in an absolutistic sense. The two claws of the pincers, between which so-called culture will find itself crushed and which have operated since 1840, are the working classes from below and the military hierarchy from above. The result may again be a Roman Empire, after the intervening appearance of several minor successor states.

"Terrible simplificateurs" will come over Old-Europe, and the pattern of all life, even more than now, will be the expediency of thorough-going militarism. Quite unpredictable, however, will be the fate of the working classes: "a fixed and controlled amount of misery, glorified by military advancement and uniforms, begun and finished with a roll of drums, is the logical thing to come." There can be no question of stopping on this road—and perhaps it will be in Germany that the sovereignty of a militarized state will first mature. "Alas! How much that was dear to the educated man will have to be thrown overboard as spiritual luxury! And how strangely different from what we are will the new generation be. . . . 'Prepare for death,' that's the wisest thing for all of us to do, in all of Central Europe. Everything will change."

The same thought is found in the writings of Bruno Bauer, a radical disciple of Hegel. He believed that imperialistic dictatorships would dominate Europe and they would decide the question: "Russia or Europe."

The illusion of the revolution of 1848, that the time had arrived when the members of the historical family of nations, fortified by the new principle of equal rights and self-determination, will constitute themselves independently and cooperate peacefully, this illusion has the same fate as all illusions dating the era of a new freedom from the downfall of existing barriers to personal activity. This illusion cannot but dissolve through the force of a sterner authority. It shares the fate of that other illusion which sees in individualism the result of the last sixty revolutionary years, the solution of all problems, while it is proved daily that it is only a makeshift condition, shaping one side only and riveted by an iron law to its opposite: imperialism and dictatorship.

For the overthrow of the old order of associations and classes deprived the individual of his personal significance as a member of certain corporations, subduing him thus to an extended system of centralization and to the omnipotence of the whole. "Labor is freed but unchained it will aim at a sterner centralization, dragging in with arms of steel all the single human beings that felt well and secure in their former seclusion and forcing them to submit or to die." Bauer thought that laws would again be passed which, as in the old "military-theological world" before the French Revolution, would keep men under discipline and determine their feeling, thinking, and wishing according to fixed standards. Still lacking, however, would be the science of historical laws, which could seize upon the mind and the soul of the masses as the old moral order had done. In this respect, the social sciences have not yet caught up with the natural sciences. Between present anarchy and the future shape of government and society, Bauer's contemporaries are unsteady individuals who ask timidly "What now?" and think their dissatisfaction with the present contains the strength of the future.

The question for Bauer is

whether the Germanic world will survive the decline of the old civilization— for nothing is more certain than this decline—or whether the Russian nation alone will determine the new, whether the incipient era will be called Russian, or whether conjointly with Russianism, Germanism too will confer its name upon it. . . . The German and the Russian questions are the only two vital questions of modern Europe. The latter question, however, had already been posed so precisely by Catherine that the reply to it will precede the answer to the other, for it is supported by such a great organization that the power in control of it can set the time to bring matters to a crisis and cut the Gordian knot.

One decade later in France, Proudhon sketched the disintegration of Old-Europe:

Today civilization is truly in a critical stage which has only one historical analogy, the crisis caused by the rise of Christianity. All traditions are used up, all faith is worn out. On the other hand, the new program is neither ready nor has it entered yet the consciousness of the masses. Hence, what I call disintgration. It is the most terrible moment in the life of society. Everything combines in order to sadden people of good will: the prostitution of conscience, the triumph of mediocrity, the confusion of true and false, the betrayal of principles; baseness of passions, negligence of morals, suppression of truth, a prize for lying. I do not delude myself. I do not expect tomorrow the return of liberty, regard for right, public decency, freedom of speech, integrity of the newspapers, morality of the government, good sense of the citizens, and public-mindedness of the plebians—all to be reborn in our country by means of a magician's rod. No, no, I cannot see the end of the decadence: it will not diminish within one or two generations; that is our lot. . . . I shall see the evil only, and shall die in utter darkness, marked by the past with the seal of rejection. . . . Havoc will result and the depression following the blood bath will be terrible. We shan't see the dawn of the new era, we shall struggle by night and it is necessary to prepare for endurance by doing our duty with a minimum of sadness. Let us stand by each other, call out to each other in the dark, and do justice as often as opportunity presents itself.

Again, a decade later, after the Franco-Prussian war, E. Renan's *La Reforme intellectuelle et morale* appeared, while in Germany, Nietzsche was writing his Meditations, likewise a diagnosis of the time and an attempt to find a way out. In the third of the *Unzeitgemässe Betrachtungen* (1874), Europe's plight is described in a tone like Burckhardt's.

From Proudhon, Renan, and Nietzsche the road leads to Georges Sorel, whose books have helped to shape the Fascist movement. Since the middle of the nineteenth century, European historians no longer follow the pattern of progress, but that of decay.

NIHILISM IN EUROPEAN LITERATURE

IN THE MIDST of frantic progress, of domination and exploitation of the world by means of the new technical inventions, a feeling of aimlessness and a spiritual pessimism cast its shadow upon Europe's finer spirits. During the middle of the century, European literature produced a type of nihilism formerly unknown. Immermann's novel *Die Epigonen* (1830), Gutzkow's *Die Nihilisten* (1853), and Turgenev's *Fathers and Sons* (1860) provoked very lively discussions. This nihilism found its most sophisticated expression in Flaubert and Baudelaire.

Having shown up in the *Temptation of St. Anthony* all sorts of current beliefs and superstitions, Flaubert set about to disentangle and analyze the chaos of scientific culture. He made a list of human follies, intended as an ironical glorification of all that had passed as truth. The result of these absurd studies was the novel *Bouvard et Pecuhet:* two Philistines, sincerely striving for their higher education, good natured and men of sense who had been office clerks. They ramble, in their happily acquired country seat, through the entire maze of piled-up knowledge from horticulture, chemistry, and medicine to history, archeology, politics, pedagogy, and philosophy only to return to their copying by making extracts from the books they had perused in vain. The whole work leads to the conclusion that our entire education is inane. Doctrines of age-long standing are expounded and developed in a few lines, then they are disposed of by other doctrines which are arraigned against them, and then with equal precision and passion destroyed in their turn. Page after page, line after line, some new kind of knowledge turns up, but at once another appears to knock the first one down and then it, too, topples over, hit by a third. At the end of the unfinished sketch, Pecuchet draws a gloomy picture, and

Bouvard a rosy one, of the future of European mankind. According to the one, the end of the debased human race, sunk into general depravity, approaches. There are three alternative possibilities: 1) radicalism severs every tie with the past, entailing inhumane despotism; 2) if theistic absolutism should be victorious, liberalism, with which mankind has been imbued since the French Revolution, will perish and a revolutionary change will take place; 3) if the convulsions of 1789 continue, their waves will carry us away and there will no longer be ideals or religion or morality; America will conquer the world. According to the second picture, Europe will be rejuvenated with the aid of Asia, and there will develop undreamt of techniques of communications, U-boats, and balloons; new sciences will be born enabling man to place the powers of the universe at the service of civilization and, when the earth is exhausted, to emigrate to other stars. Together with human wants, evil will cease, and philosophy will become religion.

Baudelaire's intention to compose "The end of the world" dates from the same period. Some fragments of it, entitled *Fusées*, appeared three years after the revolution of February, 1848. Like almost all young intellectuals, Baudelaire had a hand in this revolt against the bourgeois order, eager as he was for revenge and destruction and full of literary excitement. Later, he regretted this ardor of 1848, not from reactionary motives, but because he wished to separate himself even more completely from the exciting social order and to live in solitude and independence. The lowering of culture to a general level of mediocrity foreseen by Goethe, is to Baudelaire a downright Luciferian fall into nothingness, from which only "artificial paradises" can deliver us:

The world is drawing to a close. Only for one reason can it last longer: just because it happens to exist. But how weak a reason is this compared with all that forebodes the contrary, particularly with the question: What is left to the world of man in the future? Supposing it should continue materially, would that be an existence worthy of its name and of the historical dictionary? I do not say the world would fall back into a spectral condition and the odd disorder of South America republics; nor do I say that we should return to primitive savagery and, with a rifle in our arms, hunt for food through the grass-covered ruins of our civilization. No, such adventures would still call for a certain vital energy, an echo from primordial times. We shall furnish a new example of the inexorability of the spiritual and moral laws and shall be their new victims: we *shall perish by the very thing by which we fancy that we live.* Technocracy will americanize us; progress will starve our spirituality so far that nothing of the blood thirsty, frivolous or unnatural dreams of the utopists will be comparable to these positive facts. I invite any thinking person to show me what is left of life. Religion! It is useless to talk about it, or to look for its remnants; it is a scandal that one takes the trouble even of denying God. Private property! It was—strictly speaking—abolished with the suppression of the right of primogeniture; yet the time will come when mankind like a revengeful cannibal will snatch the last piece from those who rightfully deemed themselves the heirs of revolutions. And even this will not be the worst. . . . Universal ruin will manifest itself not solely or particularly in political institutions or general progress or whatever else might be a proper name for it; it will be seen, above all, in the baseness of hearts. Shall I add that that little left-over of sociability will hardly resist the sweeping brutality, and that the rulers, in order to hold their own and to produce a sham order, will ruthlessly resort to measures which will make us, who already are callous, shudder?

The same picture of the future as that drawn by Flaubert and Baudelaire appears in the Russian criticism of Europe. In 1880, Dostoyevsky, in his *Diary of a Writer*, argues against the Russian enthusiasts for Western culture that, in view of the failure of Europe to solve its own problems and of its imminent terrible collapse, it is ridiculous to demand that the Russians import European institutions in order to catch up with the progress of the West. "The European anthill built up without a church and without Christianity—for everywhere in Europe the church has lost her ideal and has turned into a state—this anthill on a rotten foundation, lacking every universal and absolute, is completely undermined." What good will it do to take over from Europe institutions which will break down there tomorrow—institutions in which the most intelligent Europeans themselves no longer believe, while they are being slavishly copied by Russians as though the comedy of the bourgeois order were the normal form of human society?

Tolstoi, in 1910, the last year of his life, wrote the following piece of radical criticism of the European civilization which was corrupting not only Europe, but also India, Africa, China, and Japan:

The medieval theology, or the Roman corruption of morals, poisoned only their own people, a small part of mankind; today, electricity, railways and telegraphs spoil the whole world. Everyone makes these things his own. He simply cannot help making them his own. Everyone suffers in the same way, is forced to the same extent to change his way of life. All are under the necessity of betraying what is most important for their lives, the understanding of life itself, religion. Machines—to produce what? The telegraph—to despatch what? Books, papers—to spread what kind of news? Railways—to go to whom and to what place? Millions of people herded together and subject to a supreme power—to accomplish what? Hospitals, physicians, dispensaries in order to prolong life—for what? How easily do individuals as well as whole nations take their own so-called civilization as the true civilization: finishing one's studies, keeping one's nails clean, using the tailor's and the barber's services, travelling abroad and the most civilized man is complete. And with regard to nations: as many railways as possible, academies, industrial works, battleships, forts, newspapers, books, parties, parliaments. Thus the most civilized nation is complete. Enough individuals, therefore, as well as nations can be interested in civilization but not in true enlightenment. The former is easy and meets with approval; the latter requires rigorous efforts and therefore, from the great majority, always meets with nothing but contempt and hatred, for it exposes the lie of civilization.

Further documents of this kind extending up to the present day could easily be added. Nihilism as the disavowal of existing civilization was the only real belief of all truly educated people at the beginning of the twentieth century. Nihilism is not a result of the Great War but, on the contrary, its cause. Most fully aware of all this was the literary circle around the poet Stefan George. In the preface to the third annual issue of the *Yearbook for the Spiritual Movement* (1912), edited by Gundolf and Wolters, we read:

Even the dim eye does not fail to observe the general cheerlessness spreading despite all improvements, alleviations and amusements, provoking the comparison with the late Roman Empire. From the Emperor to the humblest worker everyone feels that it cannot go on in this way. Everyone is willing to admit that, at least for departments not affecting him directly. What sustains is merely the individual's concern for office, goods and chattels. Nobody believes any longer in the foundations of the present state of the world. These pessimistic presentiments and divinations represent the truest feelings of the time and all hopes to build something on nothing have, therefore, the look of despair.

Turning Points in European Philosophy

HEGEL MARKS the end of the history of the old European spirit. Being on the historical road of "progress in the consciousness of freedom," the spirit finally attains in Hegel its perfect knowing and being, thus consummating its history in a double sense. In Hegel's system, the history of the spirit comes to its fulfillment [*Voll-endung*], i.e., to its greatest fullness as well as to its final end. The principle of "final" construction underlies not only the closing chapter of phenomenology, the system of the encyclopedia, and the "conclusion" of logic, but also all special kinds of knowledge. Both the history of the world and most clearly that of the arts end in a state of perfection. According to Hegel's division of the history of philosophy, his own system stands at the end of the third epoch. The first extends from Thales to Proclus and comprises the beginning and the decline of the ancient world. In its culmination in Proclus, the ancient reconciliation between the temporal and celestial world comes to pass. The second epoch extends from the beginning of the Christian era to the Reformation. In it, though on a higher level, the same reconciliation of the finite and the infinite comes to pass again in order to be consummated in the third epoch, in the philosophy from Descartes to Hegel, by the latter. Like Proclus, Hegel has united the world of the Christian Logos with the absolute totality of the concretely organized idea and thus he is the conclusion of all three epochs. With Proclus, the spirit of the world is to be found at a great turning point before the absolute break, i.e., the onset of Christianity into the pagan world. In a letter to Creuzer, Hegel likewise mentions this "tremendous step" due particularly to Proclus as representing the true turning point of the transition from ancient philosophy to Christianity. Now it is again time to take "a similar step."

But what is the consequence of Hegel's consummation of the Christian philosophy? Obviously, that it must be the last step before a new turn, a break with Christianity! Then, indeed, Hegel's consummation is the same as that of Proclus: a "reconciliation of decay." The highest development is simultaneous with the beginning of a decline at a time when "everything is about to dissolve and to strive for something new." To this new era Hegel gave only an indirect expression. He thinks in terms of the remembrance of the past, in the "grey old age of the spirit," and at the same time in the anticipation of a potentially new territory of the spirit, though explicitly leaving aside the knowledge of it. There are a few bare references to America, which since the beginning of the century is held to be the future country of liberty. He envisages the possibility of the spirit of the world emigrating from Europe.

America is thus the country of the future in which in times to come . . . the momentousness of the history of the world shall reveal itself; it is the longed-for country of all those who are tired of the historical arsenal of old Europe. Napoleon is said to have exclaimed: *cette vieille Europe m'ennuie.* . . . However, what has been happening there (in America) is only an echo of the old world and the expression of an alien life; moreover, as a country of the future, it does not concern us here at all.

Similarly, Hegel concludes a reference to the future importance of the Slavic world, understood by him as an intermediate organism in the struggle of Christian Europe with Asia, with the sentence that he does not deal with this complex of data because it has not yet materialized as an independent element in the succession of the forms of the Logos. "Whether this will happen later on, does not interest us here."

Most radical-minded among all Hegelians with regard to Hegel's consummation of history were Marx and Kierkegaard. Both found themselves confronted with the question, how to go further. They answered that a new start can be made not by continuing the course followed to its very end by Hegel, but only by a distinct break with him. Marx achieved this break in the name of social action and Kierkegaard in that of ethical passion. Both saw that Hegel's mediation between reason and reality was without validity. Consequently, they set a "decision" over against his "mediation"—Marx for a new, earthly world and Kierkegaard for the old Christian God. To the *Communist Manifesto* (1847) corresponds Kierkegaard's *The Present Age* (1846). Marx's criticism of the bourgeois-capitalistic world and Kierkegaard's criticism of the bourgeois-Christian world are related to each other as the obverse of a coin is to its reverse.

That Marx demands a political decision concerning the masses and Kierkegaard a religious decision of the individual in his singleness, that Marx philosophizes without God and Kierkegaard before God—these obvious contrasts have a common ground in their falling out with the world and with God. Due to a common opposition to Hegel's "reasonable world," they sever what had been united by him. Marx decided in favor of a humanitarian world, Kierkegaard in favor of a worldless Christianity. They conceive "what exists" as a world defined in terms of goods and money or as an existence permeated by irony and boredom. Hegel's "spirit-realm" turns into a world of labor and despair; his "idea in and for itself" with Marx turns into a "German Ideology," and the "self-delight" of the absolute spirit becomes a "sickness unto death" with Kierkegaard. Hegel's consummation of history signifies for both a "pre-history" before an extensive revolution or an intensive reformation.

Simultaneously with Marx and Kierkegaard, the other radical pupils of Hegel also made this negation of the existing order the basis of their thinking. Stirner took his stand on "nothing." Feuerbach says that one has to be "absolutely negative" in order to be able to create new things. Bauer demands "feats of nothingness" as the foundation of new worlds.

If these are the three greatest turning points of history, when Socrates gloried in his not-knowing in the face of a theocracy; when Christianity, opposing the imperial powers, set the soul above everything else; when Descartes told us to doubt everything—if these feats of nothingness created new worlds, then the very final and most difficult resolve, namely, to will nothing, nothing of what has been, will give man complete mastery over the world.

The term "nihilism" changes its color from an expression of pessimism and weariness to an active destruction until Nietzsche reveals the European nihilism as a "logic" of decadence, i.e., as the necessary presupposition of a new beginning. By definitely turning the romantic nihilism of weakness into one of strength, Nietzsche drew those extreme conclusions from the experience of the last century which only now prove truly epochal and hold sway over us. He considered the pessimism of the "fin de siècle" merely a "precursive form of nihilism." Thus he set for himself the task of pushing the feeling of inanity and aimlessness of all existence to that extreme point where it should reverse itself into the will to new values.

In the first chapter of his last book, the *Ecce Homo*, Nietzsche explains to the world why he represents something decisive and fateful between two millennia, a person on the threshold. He knew himself as both decline and rise, as an end and a beginning. The same ambiguity which marks his existence also marks his concept of Europe. Europe is a world at once perishing and growing. But between these two processes there is no continuous transition, there is only a fateful act of decision. Nietzsche's ultimate goal is the spiritual and political mastery of the European over the globe. In order to force Europe into this "long range policy" [*Grosse Politik*] which is simultaneously a "war of spirits," Europe must overcome its nihilism by becoming ready to form again a decisive and purposive whole, beating out a new order of life. As a hammer for the will to power and life, Nietzsche regarded his doctrine of the eternal recurrence, because it bids man accept his life at every moment as though it would return through all eternity, a doctrine counterbalancing the inanity and aimlessness caused by a disease of the will. The infirmity of the will is at its worst where civilization has longest prevailed, as in France. It decreases as the barbarian still or again asserts his claims under the loose drapery of Western education, as in Russia, which is touched by European civilization, but only skin-deep. However, the more the threatening attitude of Russia increases, the more will Europe have to decide to become equally threatening by acquiring *one* will by means of a ruling cast that can set its aims thousands of years ahead and drill the democratic masses for this purpose. The time of petty-states is over. The twentieth century, Nietzsche prophesies, will, with the struggle for the dominion of the globe, bring the compulsion to great imperialistic politics. To this end, however, Germany will have to strive in all earnest for an "agreement" with England.

For nobody believes any longer that England herself will be strong enough to keep playing her old role even for fifty more years. . . . Nowadays one must be a soldier first, lest one lose his credit as a merchant. In brief, regarding these as well as other matters, the next century will be seen following in the footsteps of Napoleon, the most outstanding and anticipating personality of modern times.

The standing armies, permanent since the Napoleonic wars, are but the first sign of Europe's new military development.

Personal, virile and physical capacity recovers its value, valuations become more physical, nutrition consists more and more of meat. Beautiful men have once more become possible. Bloodless sneaks are a matter of the past. The savage, (even the wild animal), in every one of us is acknowledged. Precisely on that account, philosophers will have a better chance.

One must meet the alternative of perishing or of gaining a foothold.

A master race can grow up from terrible and violent beginnings only. Problem: where are the barbarians of the twentieth century? Obviously, only after tremendous social crisis will they loom and consolidate themselves. It will be those elements which are capable of the greatest rigor towards themselves and able to vouch for the longest and strongest will.

Nietzsche's faith in the future of Europe lies in its growing "more man-like."

This political program is not to be found on the periphery but at the center of Nietzsche's philosophy. It follows from his analysis of European nihilism and its counter concept of the will, which is to replace the "Thou shalt" of the Christian faith. Europe's fate is, in Nietzsche's consciousness, bound up with himself. An echo and outburst of this will to determine Europe's faith is manifested in the letters from the period of his mental derangement. He invites the European princes (*nota bene,* exclusive of the Hohenzollerns) along with the Pope to a conference to take place in Rome.

But his entire sane production, too—from the *Thoughts out of Season* to the *Antichrist*—is a continuous war on everything that has been believed in, demanded, and sanctioned through two thousand years. As immoralist and "destroyer *par excellence*" he taught that only by destroying could one create, true to the general description of the Germans given by Stirner in his review (1841) of Bauer's *Posaune* (trumpet):

> Only the German and he alone demonstrates the mission of radicalism in the history of the world; he alone is radical and he alone is authentically so. No one is so inexorable and inconsiderate as he; he overturns not only the existing world in order to remain upright himself, he overturns himself, too. Where the German pulls down, a God must fall and a world perish. With the Germans destroying is creating and the destruction of the transient is his eternity.

It is the decline of Christianity and its morals which Nietzsche wants to hasten, for "what is falling, should be pushed down." The positive element of this will to overthrow the existing order is the will to power as a "revaluation of all values," the first part of which is (according to a last draft of 1888) the *Antichrist*. Zarathustra is the "victor over God and Nothingness," namely, the nothingness proceeding from the death of the Christian God. The will of man, now godless, must learn to command itself. For this, the superlative energy of such a will is required. European nihilism, as Nietzsche sees it, is thus first a crisis of Christianity and lastly a decision to will and to create new, pagan Gods. In the meantime, however, the sole temporary truth can only be: "*Nothing is true any longer, everything is permitted.*" That the liberty to everything as well as to nothing is implied in this is "the advantage of our time." Morality and humanity are being replaced by the will to some aim and thus to its means.

From Napoleon and Bismarck, Nietzsche learned that the democratic leveling of Europe would some day culminate in dictatorial leadership. For "the same new conditions which as a rule will produce equalized and mediocre men, useful, industrious . . . and clever collective beings, are in the highest degree suitable to give rise to exceptional men of the most dangerous and attractive qualities. . . . The democratization of Europe is also an involuntary arrangement for the rearing of tyrants—taking the word in its full sense, even in its most spiritual sense." Nay, it might even prove for the emancipated masses themselves a kind of redemption and justification, if someone appeared who would use them as means to his ends. "The same conditions which tend to develop the gregarious animal also force the development of the leader-beast."

Nietzsche's ideas paved the way to the Third Reich. He did not himself walk that way, but like all pathmakers, prepared it for the others. The German *Aufbruch* or awakening, which is supposed to have made nihilism a matter of the past, is indeed the achieved logic of disintegration, a "Revolution of Nihilism" as Rauschning rightly has called it, though he underestimates the depth of its historical ramifications.

2 / Nature, History, and Existentialism

I

WE ARE ACCUSTOMED to confront nature with history and we do so in consequence of a definite historical situation which arose in the sixteenth century with modern natural science. The natural antithesis to nature would be not history, but art. In epochs when men were closer to nature than we are, as in classical antiquity, nature, or *physis*, was contrasted with art, or *techné*, that is, with the artificial, which is not "by nature" but is wrought by man, its artificer. According to the classical view, art can do no better than imitate nature. The seeming self-evidence of our familiar distinction between nature and history, and accordingly between natural sciences and humanities, has its origin at the beginning of modern times. Two sciences which characterized themselves as new ones gave the first philosophical expression to this distinction: the anti-Aristotelian natural science of Descartes, and Vico's anti-Cartesian *Scienza Nuova*. The criterion of this distinction, however, lies primarily not in the difference of the respective fields, but in the secondary distinction as to what can be known about nature and history scientifically. The priority of the problem of knowledge and method over the question of subject matter is again typically modern.

Descartes divided the whole realm of reality into two kinds of being: the *res cogitans* and the *res extensa*. From the principle of being-thinking, he constructed nature as the object of mathematical physics. There is a true and certain knowledge about nature; about history nothing can be known truly and with certainty. What we seem to know about history rests on mere tradition, opinion, and custom.

Against this philosophical foundation of modern natural science by Descartes, Vico asserted in his *New Science* the more authentic knowability and truthfulness of the historical sciences of man and his history. He tried to demonstrate that true and certain knowledge is possible only of things which we have made ourselves—that is, of the world of history, the *mondo civile,* where the true (*verum*) and the made (*factum*) convert. The world of nature is inaccessible to man because he did not make it. It is intelligible to God alone as its creator.

With regard to the fundamental division of the world into a natural world and a historical, or man-made, one, even Vico, Descartes' opponent, remains nevertheless a Cartesian—like Pascal, who likewise stated that the whole extended universe of corporeal nature, the stars and the earth, cannot counterbalance the smallest motion of a human mind. The human mind knows the whole universe and itself; the corporeal world is unaware of itself.

This distinction is still maintained on both sides—in the natural sciences as well as in the humanities. C. von Weizsäcker, in his *History of Nature,* epitomizes it by saying that nature is much older than man but only man knows what nature is, working out a natural science which is as such a historical one. Vico's way of posing the question, which was polemically conditioned by Descartes, has developed further with Herder, Hegel, Croce, Dilthey, and Collingwood. It still determines Heidegger's *Being and Time,* where the criticism of the Cartesian ontology rests also on the distinction of two kinds of being which are different in principle: human *Dasein,* which "exists" because it is spontaneously related to the world and to itself; and, on the other hand, beings which are not self-related. Further, only human existence is pervaded by "historicity." Heidegger's existential construction of history from the temporal finiteness of man's existing *Dasein* purports to radicalize the work of Dilthey. Actually, Heidegger achieved the self-redemption of modern historicism, as demanded by Dilthey, only through absolutizing historicity itself. In *Being and Time,* nature is conceived not as autonomous and creative, but as an element that we encounter only within our world—this "world" being an existential structure, that is, relative to historical human *Dasein.*

Only Schelling and Hegel have attempted to reduce the traditional distinction between nature and history, as fixed by Descartes as well as by Vico, though in opposite directions, to a comprehensive notion of nature and mind respectively. Impossible though it is to overlook Schelling's lifelong effort to understand nature spiritually and historically, one easily forgets that even Hegel's philosophy of mind and history is but the reverse of his philosophy of nature. The central notion of Hegel's philosophy of history, the "cunning of reason," is not at all restricted to the historical phenomenon of the dialectical perversion of human intentions to unintended effects and results. What Hegel presupposes in principle is not a particular reason in world history, but a reason that governs the universe, for example in the lawful motion of the celestial bodies, and is therefore discoverable in the historical world as well. The essential difference is that in nature, reason operates without consciousness. In both worlds, universal reason unfolds itself in a particular element. He says that one has to arrive at the insight that the purpose of eternal wisdom "manifests itself in the realm of nature as well as in the realm of the active mind." For Hegel, the historical world is a sort of "second nature" and a "second world" within the context of the one universe which is fundamentally determined by reason or, in Christian terms, of the one creation of the one God, who is spirit.

The question, however, is how universal necessity and rationality, in contradistinction to contingency, can determine the historical world if the freedom of human will, interest, and passion belongs to the proper character of the historical world in distinction to nature. To answer this question, Hegel introduces the "cunning of reason," which works, as it were, behind the back of all particular wills and interests, and brings it about that the egotistical will of individual persons must will what is universally necessary and rational, so that the subjectivity of willing receives a substantial content, superseding mere arbitrariness.

In consequence of this fundamental conception of the one world of spirit, Hegel's explanations of the working of the "cunning of reason" refer equally to quite different phenomena: to elementary natural processes, to the building of a house, to the world of history. Chemical and physico-mechanical process are made serviceable to higher biological ends through the cunning of reason. The flame absorbs the air but it is, at the same time, fed by wood which grows in the trees which are fed by the oxygen of the air. Thus the burning wood, while absorbing oxygen from the air, fights against its own source. A similar dialectic can be seen in the building of a house. The natural elements—fire to melt iron, air to stimulate fire, water to operate the mill which cuts the lumber—all help to build the house. And yet the purpose of the house is to protect us against fire, water, and air. Through a "cunning of reason," the elements are used against themselves. Similarly in world history, human passions and interests satisfy themselves egotistically, apparently for their own sake, but produce willy-nilly the edifice of progressive world history which is reasonable in the whole. Seen from a narrow and single perspective, human beings fight only for their particular rights and against a universal order. But within this struggle a new historical order comes about which determines all the particular wills. The cunning of reason, like divine providence, uses the particular passions and interests, thus bringing it about that human freedom organizes a historical world, instead of dissipating in anarchy.

Hegel's conception of spirit as comprehending nature and history and Schelling's spiritual philosophy of nature did not become productive. We are still thinking within the framework of Descartes and Vico. To overcome the dichotomy of Descartes and Vico, it would be necessary that our attitude toward the world, the natural as well as the historical one, be transformed. So-called historicism cannot be overcome without questioning its older counterpart, modern natural science. Our remoteness from such a radical revision becomes evident in the historical materialism of Marx. In his historical thinking, Marx was inspired by Hegel's immense historical sense, and on this basis he subjected the whole history of modern civilization to such a radical criticism that it became reduced to a mere "pre-history" of the future. But on the other hand, Marx accepted without criticism, together with the progress of capitalist industry, the methods and results of modern natural science and technique, considering them a marvelous progress. He took it for granted that nature is a mere means and material for the purpose of developing the historical forces of human production.

This way of thinking, however, is not specifically Marxist, but is generally modern and has prevailed since Bacon and Descartes, who proclaimed it the end of science to make man master over nature. The better man succeeded in this, the more could natural science be made serviceable to man's historical purposes and projects. Not only did the inventions of natural science expand the range of modern historical movements and accelerate their speed, but they also enlisted nature as never before in the service of history. So-called historicism would be harmless if it had merely historicized and relativized the so-called spiritual world. It made nature relative to us, with the effect that actually nothing natural was left over. In our scientifically organized world, naturalness is no longer the standard of nature. What still remains of natural things seems to be a mere leftover of that which has not yet been thoroughly subjected by man. This historical appropriation of the natural world is at the same time an estrangement from it. The earth has not become more familiar to us since we have become capable of covering immense distances in a short time. The more we plan globally and exploit the earth technically, the further nature recedes in spite of all our technical seizure of it.

II

IN CONSEQUENCE of this modern tendency to think and to act in terms of purposes, the quest for meaning has become focused in history, because only as history can the world be related directly to man and his purposes. If the world as nature, as *physis* and *cosmos*, ever became absorbed in the world of history, the question about the meaning of history would indeed become identical with the question about the meaning of the universe. But who would not feel that that cannot be so? The notion of a "world history" is actually a misnomer, for world history is universal in a very limited sense only. Our "world history" of a few thousand years vanishes in time and space if seen within the whole of the "history" of the universe, and the quest for its meaning can be raised meaningfully only in relation to this spurious segment. We neither ask for the meaning of heaven and earth, the stars, the ocean, and the mountains, nor for the meaning of vegetable and animal life. Our quest seems to be restricted to ourselves and to history as our history. But why do we not ask for the meaning of all that exists, not alone through us but without our devices, by nature? Why does the natural light of the stars mean less to us—almost nothing—than a traffic light? Obviously because the meaning of a traffic light is in its purpose, while the light of sun, moon, and stars has no human and artificial purpose.

Corresponding to the limitation of our so-called world history to our own historical world, the quest for the meaning of history is in itself historically conditioned. It is a specifically Western, even Christian, quest. It can be traced back to the Old and New Testaments' faith in a purposeful story of salvation. It is derived from the assumption that history is directed by a will and, therefore, toward a purpose and fulfillment. The end or purpose, and therefore meaning, was originally grounded in the providential will of God. Since the ancient theologies of history became superseded by the modern philosophies of history, the will of God became transformed into the will of man, who plans creatively his own historical destiny. Without a purposeful will, divine or human, and without a prevision, there is no what-for, no purpose and end as *telos* and *finis* which together constitute an *eschaton*.

The possibility of a philosophy of history and of its quest for an ulitmate meaning stands or falls with eschatology.

Classical antiquity and the Orient have never asked for the meaning of world history. Oriental thinking does not know the contrast between nature and history either with regard to world-historical individuals or with regard to the nations that suffer historical destinies. The ancient Oriental ruler rules "historically," inasmuch as he is the "Son of Heaven," and he is a good ruler if he follows the Tao or the "ways of Heaven." Though the Chinese and the Japanese notion of Heaven signifies more than the visible sky, it still comprises this natural notion, from which the cosmic title of Oriental emperors is derived. As for the mass of the people, Orientals still suffer historical catastrophes as natural ones. They submit to them in the same way as to a plague, a flood, or an earthquake. There has never been an Oriental Voltaire who proclaimed the historical progress of civilization against nature and therefore despaired of the meaning of history at the occasion of the great earthquake of Lisbon. For the Oriental mind, such events, whether natural or historical, are neither meaningful nor meaningless. They are overruling destinies to which one has to submit, instead of overstating them with the Western pathos of an "epochal" consciousness or an existential decision, in a unique historical situation.

Oriental wisdom never quested for a meaningful end of history. It did not combine world and history into one single compound. In comparison with this ancient wisdom, all the striving in America and Russia is but the extreme consequence of modern Europe. The ultimate aim of this Western will is the fulfillment of a historical purpose and therefore of historical meaning. The predominant philosophies of history in Europe, America, and Russia agree in the common will to achieve a meaningful aim. Aims can be reached only through progress—of whatever kind: progress toward the fulfillment of conscious freedom (Hegel), toward scientific positivism (Comte), toward a classless society (Marx), toward a conscious decline (Spengler), toward a universal religion as the creative escape from a declining civilization (Toynbee). All are directed toward an aim and are therefore progressive toward the fulfillment of a meaningful purpose.

One could, of course, object that Oriental thinking is foreign to the West and contend with Hegel that the Orient has not yet grasped the full meaning of spirit, freedom, and will, which manifested themselves first with the Greeks and then in the Christian era. But even classical Greek thought is no closer to our historical thinking. Greek philosophy and historiography never fancied that history has a purposeful and meaningful orientation toward a future fulfillment. No Greek philosopher ever thought out a philosophy of history. Aristotle, who dealt with everything—animals and plants, earth and heavens, politics and ethics, rhetorics and poetics—did not write a single treatise on history, though he was the teacher and friend of Alexander the Great and a contemporary of one of the greatest historical events. The Greeks asked primarily about the *logos* of the *cosmos*, but not, like Jews and Christians, about the Lord of History as a story of redemption. The Greeks were deeply impressed by the visible order and beauty of the universe, and the natural law of becoming and disintegrating determined also their vision of the historical world. In the eyes of the Greeks that which is always the same and everlasting, as it appears year after year in the "revolution" of the heavenly bodies, manifested a deeper truth and aroused a higher interest than any radical historical change. As for the vicissitudes of human destiny within this orderly *cosmos*, they trusted that man is capable of meeting every situation, even a hopeless one, with magnanimity.

Classical humanity never put itself into a vacuum with unconditional trust or faith, as Judaism and early Christianity daringly did. It is precisely such an adventure of faith which is demanded by the quest for an ultimate meaning of history, because the visible events do *not* show an ultimate fulfillment and do *not* give an answer to such a radical question. Christian trust in a future fulfillment has been abandoned by modern historical thinking, but the perspective toward the future as such has been maintained. It pervades all European thought and all our concern with the whence and whither of the historical process. Together with the horizon of the future, the quest for meaning as goal and purpose has persisted.

The future is the true horizon of history and historical thinking only if the truth rests in the Judaeo-Christian faith in a future redemption. And since the West is still a "Christian Occident," its historical consciousness is eschatological from Isaiah to Marx, from Augustine to Hegel, from Joachim to Schelling. This holds also for political history. The English, French, and Russian revolutions would not have taken place without the faith in progress, and secular faith in progress would hardly have come into existence without the original faith in an ultimate goal of human existence. "The revolutionary desire to realize the kingdom of God is the flexible starting point of all progressive thinking and the beginning of modern history" (Friedrich Schlegel). The significance of this eschatological orientation consists in this: that it was capable of conquering the ancient fear of fate and blind fortune. Comparable to the compass which gives us orientation in space and thus enables us to conquer it, the eschatological compass gives orientation in time by pointing to an ultimate goal and thereby to an ultimate meaning of historical vicissitudes.

III

THE IDENTIFICATION of meaning and end or purpose is not an arbitrary one, but neither is it absolutely required. The metaphysical place of ultimate "meaning" might be found precisely where no aim is willed. Then the relation of meaning and purpose would have to be reversed in the sense of ancient wisdom, according to which it is the end of man to contemplate the natural universe of heaven and earth, which is free of purpose.

The exclusive emphasis on our human existence and on the world as a historical one has a concomitant in the lack of sense for that which is natural. This denaturation of human life to a historical existence did not, however, arise with modern historicism and existentialism, but with modern natural science. It is against the background of nature as conceived by modern natural science that existentialism itself comes into existence, for its basic experience is not the historicity but the contingency of human existence within the whole of the natural world. If we reflect upon the history of Western thinking, a distinct turning point can be seen when the pre-modern concept of an essential human existence within an orderly *cosmos* changes into a chance-existence. The change occurred at the beginning of the seventeenth century, as a consequence of the astronomical discoveries of the sixteenth century. From then on, writers and preachers indulged in what may be called a cosmology of corruption. The universe seemed to have lost all its harmony and stability. Mutability extended from the earth to the heavens, and man was lost in an incoherent world. John Donne expressed this mood strikingly in his *Anatomy of the World* (1611), to which Burton's *Anatomy of Melancholy* (1621) is the counterpart. In the words of Donne:

> And new philosophy calls all in doubt,
> The element of fire is quite put out;
> The sun is lost, and th' earth, and no man's wit

Can well direct him where to looke for it.
And freely man confesse that his world's spent
When in the Planets, and the Firmament
They seeke so many new; and see that this
Is crumbled out againe to his Atomies.
'Tis all in pieces, all cohaerence gone;
All just supply, and all Relation:
Prince, Subject, Father, Sonne, are things forgot,
For every man alone thinkes he hath got
To be a Phoenix, and that then can bee
None of that kinde, of which he is, but hee.
This is the world's condition now.

What men need is a "new compass for their way."

It was Pascal who drew the philosophical and theological consequences from the impact of the "new philosophy" of nature upon the condition of man. He reset, as it were, the compass of Christian faith in accordance with a changed universe. His existential *pathos* and his insight into the "human condition," an expression which was thereafter to replace the "nature of man," cannot be separated from his new conception of the universe, the basic character of which is its infinity in time and space. We "exist" de facto, in the sense of existentialism, because we are lost in the infinite universe of modern natural science. This was clearly realized by Pascal when he compared the human condition with the zero point between the infinitely great and the infinitely small. With the mathematization of nature, man lost his own nature too. There is an intimate relation between the experience of a naked, factual, absurd existence, cast into the world, and the anonymity of the world itself in which we happen to exist.

A few instances may illustrate the rising experience of the contingency of human existence and its cosmological implication. I take them from Pascal, Kant, Kierkegaard, and Nietzsche. All of them illustrate the physical and metaphysical homelessness of modern man within the whole of the world.

In a fragment of Pascal's *Pensées* we read:

When I consider the short duration of my life, swallowed up in the eternity before and after, the little space which I fill . . . , cast into the infinite immensity of spaces of which I am ignorant and which know me not, I am frightened, and shocked at being here rather than there; for there is no reason why here rather than there, why now rather than then. Who has put me here? By whose order and direction have this place and time been allotted to me?

Like a quieting answer to Pascal's fear in face of the unfath-
omable infinities of objective time and space, sounds Kant's theory
of time and space as subjective forms of intuition. But Kant, too,
experienced the radical contingency of human existence, even of
the whole creation. The conclusion of his *Critique of Practical Reason* contains the well-known passage of the starry heavens above
us and the moral law within us. The two worlds, the outer one
of nature and the inner one of moral existence, are connected in
our consciousness, but in themselves they are completely dispa-
rate. In the face of the universe, natural man is nothing; in relation to himself as a moral person, he is all-important and the
natural world is nothing. In the *Critique of Pure Reason,* Kant
goes further. Like a radical existentialist, he realizes the impossibility of establishing the inner necessity of the whole creation.
To establish it we would have to know that there is an ultimate
principle of existence which exists necessarily or essentially. But
we cannot conceive of any existence, not even of that of God, as
necessary. This, says Kant, is a true abyss for human reason.

We cannot put off the thought, nor can we support it, that a Being, which
we represent to ourselves as the highest among all possible beings, should
say to himself: *I am from eternity to eternity, there is nothing beside me,
except that which is something through my will—but whence am I?* Here
all sinks away from under us, and the highest perfection, like the smallest,
passes without support before the eyes of speculative reason, which finds no
difficulty in making the one as well as the other to disappear without the
slightest impediment.

What remains is total and radical contingency of existence,
existence without support, a thought which Kant felt to be intolerable for human reason, while its opposite, inner necessity, is
undemonstrable. The difference between Kant and modern French
existentialists is that the latter seem to have managed to find radical contingency tolerable and even liberating, and the demonstration of an inherent necessity unnecessary.

Kierkegaard states that the interest in existence is wholly opposed to a possible interest in the laws of the natural world. For
an "existing thinker" neither the cosmic law nor the moral law
has a proper interest, but only the isolated human existence as
such, which is singled out religiously by its relation to God.
Shocked by the absolute contingency of our worldly existence,
Kierkegaard advanced the following questions: "Who am I? How
came I here? What is the thing called the world? How did I obtain
an interest in this big enterprise? And if I am compelled to take

part in it, where is the director? I should like to make a remark to him."

In spite of the literal resemblance of this passage to that of Pascal, there is a distinct difference of tone and intention. With Pascal, the frightful contingency of man's existence is apprehended within a definite frame of reference: the spatial and temporal infinities of the physical universe. For Pascal, the world is not a "big enterprise" but the majestic and overwhelming reality of the universe. With Kierkegaard and the existentialists, this physical universe, as conceived by modern natural science, is present only as the hidden background of man's forlorn existence. Insignificant though this natural background seems to be existentially, it is the reverse of existence as understood by existentialism.

From this cosmological nihilism of modern subjectivity, Nietzsche drew the last consequences in his attempt to recapture the lost world of the Greek *cosmos* for the existence of modern man. His starting point, to be sure, is the modern one, that is, the insight that since Copernicus man has been "falling from a center toward an x." In an early sketch "On Truth and Falsehood in a Transmoral (cosmic) Sense" he says that man is lost in some corner of the universe with its infinite systems of worlds upon worlds. He has no key to nature. To recapture the truth of the natural world, and thereby of human existence, Nietzsche ventured his great experiment of "re-translating man into nature" —into the *logos* of the *cosmos*, into the eternal recurrence of the same, namely, the everlasting process of becoming and disintegrating.

Accordingly, Nietzsche is also the modern philosopher who made an attempt to overcome the quest for a meaning as aim and purpose. He wanted to extricate himself from nihilism and to regain the natural truth of the universe as *cosmos* and *physis*. But how is it possible to will that which is what it is by nature? Willing aims necessarily at an end and where-to. A will without an aim would live in a *horror vacui*. Hence Nietzsche's insight that "we prefer willing nothingness to not willing at all." Nihilism means to Nietzsche that the ultimate aims, or values, devaluate, that man as will lacks an aim. To overcome nihilism, the boundless freedom of emancipated willing must ultimately be overcome. Man must learn to will "backwards," that is, to accept all that is already there, without his purposeful will; man must be willing to conform to the cosmic law of the world, which is "innocent" because it has no aim, no purpose, and no meaning. What at first seems to be extreme nihilism, a human existence without purpose and meaning, is thus reversed to the highest positivity: to coexist with the natural world of eternal self-creation and self-destruction, "without aim, unless there be an aim in the happy self-sufficiency of the circular movement, without a will—unless a circle bear good will to itself." The reason for Nietzsche's philosophical shipwreck was not that he revived the classical vision of the *cosmos* as an eternal recurrence of the same, but that he attempted to establish its truth by his own creative will, under the title of a "will to power."

Modern thought has in no way surpassed Nietzsche's attempt to restore the truth of all existence cosmologically. It is true, contemporary existentialism radically posits again the old question about Being and Nothingness, but it is caught in the contingency of human existence within the totality of the universe.

The world which is concretely analyzed by contemporary existentialism is neither a living *cosmos*, seen with Greek eyes, nor an order of creation, as understood by Christian faith; nor is it the world of mathematical physics. It is only our historical world of selfhood and interhuman relations, in short, a world without nature. In Sartre's *L'Être et le néant,* nature is an opaque *en-soi* over against the *pour-soi* of human existence. It is accessible only in natural appetites of the human body. In Heidegger's *Being and Time,* nature is comprised under the lowest category of the merely "extant," in contrast to human existence, which alone has a world and can have meaning. Kierkegaard is exclusively concerned with the inwardness of selfhood. He scorned the discoveries of telescope and microscope. A thoughtful person, he says, who wants to understand what it means to exist as a self before God cannot be interested in natural science, for it does not make the least difference to our moral and religious decisions whether the moon consists of blue cheese or of something else. To busy oneself with billions of years of cosmic history or with a few thousand years of Hegelian world history is, according to him, but an escape from authentic existence.

This completes the isolated contingency of human existence, its total homelessness. And indeed, how can one feel at home in a universe which is conceived as the chance result of statistical probabilities and which is said to have come into existence through an explosion? Such a universe cannot inspire confidence or sympathy, nor can it give orientation and meaning to man's existence in it. We are then indeed "cast" into this world, and have therefore to "project" ourselves. Even the most recent conception of time and space, and the assumption that beyond certain limits the concepts of time and space cease to be applicable at all, cannot restore the universe as an encompassable world order into which man fits. Such a universe can perhaps be figured out, but it is no longer imaginable, and the scientist who calculates it does not live in it as a human person.

Neither classical philosophy nor Christian theology understood man's position in the world in this way. To Aristotle, existence meant an unquestionable element within the essential structure, order, and beauty of a dependable and clearly defined *cosmos,* which includes the existence of rational animals called men. As an animal, man shares in the natural character of nature; as a reasoning being, he has the privilege of contemplating and investigating the perfect hierarchy of all essential existences. To Augustine, man and universe were both contingent existences, but created by God. Though only man was created in the image of God, therefore surpassing the animal world, the uniform conception of creation nevertheless affects world and man alike. The Christian God, it is true, does not reveal Himself in the heavenly bodies or in a holy animal, but exclusively in mankind and thus in "history." But Jesus Christ redeems not only fallen man but, with him, the whole of a fallen creation.

With the dissolution of these two ancient convictions—the classical and the Christian—historicism and existentialism came into being. If the universe is neither eternal and divine (Aristotle), nor contingent but created (Augustine), if man has no definite place in the hierarchy of an eternal or created cosmos, then, and only then, does man begin to "exist," ecstatically and historically.

This explains also the boundless intensity of modern history. Our extreme concern with the historical world as the only scene of human destiny is the result of our estrangement from the natural theology and cosmology of antiquity and from the supernatural theology of Christianity. Both offered a frame of reference for the experience of history and a horizon for its understanding. The loss of this delimitation by and foundation in classical cosmology and Christian theology has created that absolute relevance of history which we are now inclined to take for granted.

3 / Heidegger: Problem and Background of Existentialism

*Die Heimatlosigkeit wird ein Welt-
schicksal. Darum ist es nötig, dieses
Geschick seinsgeschichtlich zu denken.*
—Martin Heidegger

THE BASIC WORKS of existentialism have not yet been translated.[1] What is generally known about the subject is derived from many secondary channels and from articles about a new philosophy, allegedly of "nihilism," but not from a knowledge of the sources. Moreover, political circumstances play such a role in the selection of, and attention to, contemporary literature and philosophy that the average American student knows more about Jean-Paul Sartre than about Karl Jaspers, and more about Jaspers than about Martin Heidegger of whom Sartre was a pupil. This sequence in the degree of familiarity is politically conditioned, for Sartre is a Frenchman who was engaged in the resistance movement, and Jaspers a German who for ten lonely years was barred from academic activity by the Nazis, while Heidegger, who supported National Socialism in 1933, neither resisted the regime subsequently nor was dismissed from his post during its period of domination.

Since 1945, the fortunes of Jaspers and Heidegger have changed considerably. Jaspers has for the time being the unenviable distinction of being placed in the limelight of the German academic scene, while Heidegger has had to retire into privacy and now enjoys the privilege of being spared such exposure and public responsibility.

I shall not enter here into the discussion of Heidegger's "Nazism" nor into the more comprehensive and intricate question of a

1. A translation into English of Heidegger's *Sein und Zeit* has been published since this sentence was written.—ed.

philosopher's social responsibilities.[2] Whatever one may think about these matters, the sequence derived from political circumstance—Sartre, Jaspers, Heidegger—must be reversed with regard to philosophical priority and significance. For Heidegger's *Sein und Zeit* appeared in 1927 (Halle), Jaspers' *Philosophie* in 1932 (Berlin), and Sartre's *L'Être et le néant* in 1943 (Paris). Sartre is Heidegger's most original and creative pupil; Jaspers and Heidegger worked out their respective philosophies independently and simultaneously in their lecture courses after the First World War. All three of them exert an influence that can hardly be overestimated. In spite of the many attacks on existentialism, inside and outside Germany, before and after Hitler, existentialism holds its own and for the past twenty years has colored every Continental discussion in philosophy as well as theology. It is the philosophy which seems to express in Germany, France, and Italy the real problems and issues of our historical situation. The only powerful competition existentialism has met so far comes not from other academic schools of philosophy, but from the Catholic church and from Marxism. I venture to say, and I shall presently try to substantiate my thesis, that the fashion of existentialism is indeed more than a fashion, for it is shaping, with ultimate logic, the basic mood of modern man's worldly existence. We are all existentialists, some consciously, some willy-nilly, and some without knowing it, because we are all more or less caught in the predicament of being "modern" by living in an epoch of dissolution of former beliefs and certainties. Even those who have never read a line of Heidegger, Jaspers, or Sartre are so familiar with such typical categories of existential philosophy as "contingency" and "finiteness" of our existence, "anxiety" and "care" and all that which Jaspers calls "extreme situations," that they can hardly imagine a normalcy apart from mediocrity.

And yet it is very difficult to say exactly what this "modernity" is and when it began to appear. Goethe thought that Balzac was abominably modern and "ultra," presenting in his novels "the ugly, the hideous and depraved" instead of the wholesome. Baudelaire thought that Flaubert's *Madame Bovary* was "profoundly modern." Our grandfathers thought that impressionism was terribly modern and our fathers that Van Gogh was ultramodern. Now, for us, the human comedy of Balzac has become rather antiquated in comparison with the human hell in Dostoevski's

2. See my article, "*Les Implications politiques de la philosophie de l'existence chez Heidegger*," in *Les Temps modernes* (November, 1946), and the critical response to my thesis in the issue of July, 1947.

novels; poor Madame Bovary's problem no longer impresses us as profoundly modern; impressionism is surpassed by expressionism, and Van Gogh's paintings are realistic compared with those of surrealists. But in spite of the relativity of what a generation feels to be "modern," all these writers and artists still have something in common that distinguishes them sharply from a seventeenth-century man. They are all, to use Goethe's phrase, ultra, beyond, or "ecstatic." They do not represent a human cosmos in their works, but fragments of an uncertain frame of reference. Perhaps one could say that modernity begins with the dissolution of a natural and social order in which man was supposed to have a definite nature and place, while modern man "exists," displaced and out of place, in extreme situations on the edge of chaos. Present-day modernity is therefore vastly different from what was debated under this title in the seventeenth century with regard to the relative merits of the "moderns and ancients." The comparison with the ancient classics was a comparison with works of the same kind. Milton, for example, was compared with Virgil, Corneille with Sophocles.[3] Our modernity, which came of age with the industrial revolution of the nineteenth century, is not comparable with what has gone before because it has changed the very standards of comparison. Hence the many prognostications of a decisive change in the constitution of European life and thought during the nineteenth century by men like Goethe, Baudelaire, Proudhon, Kierkegaard, Marx, Nietzsche, and many minor figures. This change has eventually found its precise philosophical expression in the term "existence" and its altered relation to "essence." To elucidate the problem involved in and the background behind those two concepts, we shall first have to explain Heidegger's concept of existence; second, the relation between essence and existence in the thought of Aristotle, Thomas, and Hegel; and third, the reaction against Hegel's philosophy of essential existence by Schelling, Kierkegaard, and Marx.

HEIDEGGER'S CONCEPT OF EXISTENCE

WE SHALL CONFINE THE DISCUSSION of existentialism to Heidegger's concept of existence as presented in *Sein und Zeit*,[4]

3. See W. Barrett, *What Is Existentialism?*, Partisan Review Series II (New York, 1947), p. 54.
4. Occasionally we shall also refer to *Was ist Metaphysik?* (Frankfurt-am-Main, 1929); *Vom Wesen des Grundes* (Halle, 1929); and *Vom Wesen der Wahrheit* (Frankfurt-am-Main, 1943).

passing over Jaspers' philosophy because Heidegger is more modern and radical. He is more radical because his analysis of Being within the horizon of Time does not, like the "elucidation of existence" by Jaspers, *presuppose*, and then relativize, the objective knowledge of positive science and *aim* at a traditional though relativized metaphysics of objective transcendence. Accordingly, Heidegger's existential introduction to the interpretation of Being as such presents an unbroken unity of thought, starting from the fundamental analysis of man's existence, while Jaspers' philosophy consists of three parts: (1) orientation in the objective world; (2) appeal to existence; (3) search for transcendence. The two latter concepts reflect the traditional ideas of a human "soul" and its relation to "God." What Heidegger calls "world," "existence," and "transcendence" are entirely different. His interpretation of the phenomenon "world" does not presuppose the scientific understanding of the world, for the scientific understanding of Being, as applied to man and the world, is philosophically a problem and not a possible starting point. Likewise, Heidegger rejects the whole enterprise of "metaphysics" in the traditional sense of this word where it indicates something eternal, infinite, perfect. Instead, he proposes to understand man's being in particular and Being in general within the horizon of Time. What Heidegger calls metaphysics is bound up with the structure of man's finite existence in the world. It is metaphysics in an entirely untraditional sense, namely, a "finite metaphysics of finiteness." And since Heidegger neither starts with positive science nor aims at positive metaphysics, the middle concept of Jaspers' philosophy, "existence," also has a different meaning for him. It is true that human existence as understood by Heidegger also oversteps or "transcends" itself, but not toward a perfect Being. Existence transcends itself toward its own world and nothing else. Heidegger's existentialism is uncompromisingly "worldly," not even this-worldly but simply worldly, without any positive or negative concern about a beyond; and yet it is not at all a positivistic secularism. In the last analysis, the religious positions of Jaspers and Heidegger are even strangely inversed: the intellectual background of Jaspers, who has a certain leaning toward religion and a definite affinity to liberal Protestantism, is positive science,[5] while Heidegger, from whose philosophy Sartre has drawn atheistic conclusions, was nurtured by theology and still retains much more of a religious pathos than Jaspers' "philosophical faith," which is no more than a last echo of secu-

5. See J. Collins, "Philosophy of Existence and Positive Religion," in *Modern Schoolman* (January, 1946), p. 89.

larized Christianity in German idealism. Finally, with regard to
their styles of thinking: Jaspers retains the Hegelian ambition of
embracing the totality of possible levels and attitudes. He built
up a system which is, in principle, finished, though fluid and un-
dulating. Heidegger is cutting through and digging in, and the
apodictic form of his diction should deceive no one about the unresolved tensions of an unfinished and still maturing conception.

The following is a bare outline of Heidegger's concept of
existence, leaving aside the more appealing and popular aspects
of his philosophy, that is, all the concreteness, plenitude, and
suggestiveness of its phenomenological analyses. I shall concentrate on the bare notion of existence in its relation to essence.
Heidegger's startling thesis is that man's nature or essence is
nothing else but "existence." What does this mean and imply?
Heidegger begins his great work with a quotation from Plato's
Sophist: "Since, then, we are in a difficulty, please tell us what
you mean when you speak of being; for there can be no doubt
that you always, from the first, understood your own meaning,
whereas we once thought that we understood it, but now we are
in a great strait." Out of this embarrassment that we are constantly handling and apparently understanding Being, but are
ignorant of its meaning, Heidegger made the effort of beginning,
as it were, from scratch. Several prejudices with regard to the
notion of Being obstruct such an attempt. The chief prejudice
is that Being is the most general, abstract, and empty of all
notions. For there is indeed nothing of which we do not predicate
that it "is." God, we say, is; the world is; man is; values are; prop-
ositions are true or false. Today is the twenty-first of January,
this is a classroom and this is a lecture—and there we are. In
each of these different apprehensions of something which "is"
we vaguely coapprehend a general character of Being as such.
But this general character is not the generality of a genus under
which more specific sorts of beings are subsumed. For Being, in
its universal and abstract sense, surpasses all the different kinds
of real or ideal beings. It is not a particular though more general
kind of something real. It seems rather to be nothing. Being as
such, therefore, is undefinable by *genus proximum* and *differentia
specifica*. The question, "What is Being?" or "What is the meaning of 'is'?" seems to be an impossible and insoluble problem for
the question already implies what is asked for, namely, an "is."
How and from where can we then approach Being as such?

We can approach it only if pure Being, or Being as such, is
in some way related to a concrete being, though surpassing it.

Perhaps Being is not only the most general and empty notion, but also something quite individual. This is indeed the case. For there is among all beings a unique being which alone can question Being as such and thus make ontology possible. A house or a plant or an animal has never asked, "What is Being?" It is man alone who can ask such an extravagant question. And why can he and does he ask it? Because he is an exceptional, fatally privileged being, or in Heidegger's ontological term, a *Dasein,* a being-there. He is in his real being an ontological being, that is, a being capable of transcending his own and every other concrete being toward Being as such. As a self he can relate himself to other beings, to everything in the world, and to his own being in it, and thereby surpass all these kinds of concrete beings. With the emergence of man or *Dasein* amidst all other beings there occurs an "inroad" into the totality of beings, which opens the view on Being as such. Man can surpass or transcend every particular being and ask about Being as such because he is the only being which, *in* his being-there, is concerned *with* his being and is thereby open for its possible comprehension.

Despite the sheer factuality of our "being-there" we are not simply extant [*vorhanden*], like a stone, nor are we determined by an alien purpose [*zuhanden*], like a hammer which is what it is as something "to hammer with" and which only man can handle, for the hammer itself has no self and cannot enjoy its own purpose. In distinction from these two other ways of being, the merely extant and the functional being, man has the privilege of being in such a way that he is thrust upon himself as a self, and yet owns his own being. He can, therefore, also withdraw from it, in suicide and sacrifice. Animals which are possessed by their natural being cannot transcend it, neither by taking possession of it nor by withdrawing from it. This kind of Being or rather to-be, which is peculiar to human *Dasein*—that is, responsibility *to* one's own being, without, however, being responsible *for* being there—Heidegger calls existence. It is man's way or manner of being-there. Existence is, however, not a fixed quality like being tall or short. It is a constant possibility. We *can* exist in this or that manner, authentically or unauthentically, in an individual or in an average way. However we choose to be, these possibilities remain inevitably *each one's* own possibilities. Man's *Dasein,* which chooses and pursues one of his possibilities, is always *my* personal or *your* personal existence, amidst and in spite of all sociality. In all his taking care of something and caring for others, man is ultimately concerned with his own being and possibilities, which rest, however, on the sheer fact of his being-there. As such a being he can reflect upon and ask about Being as such and elaborate a philosophy of Being, or ontology.

Thus we can now understand why the most abstract, impersonal, and general question of ontology is intimately bound up with a most concrete, personal, and specific being. A philosophical analysis of Being can only be worked out on the basis of an existential analysis of man's being; it has to start from a "*fundamental* ontology." It is true that the universal concept of Being transcends every concrete being, but it cannot be grasped unless we methodically reduce the ontological problem to man's existence as the ultimate *source* and also *end* of the ontological interest. To answer the universal question of Being, we have to concentrate this transcendent quest in a most singular being, namely, that of the questioner. The claim of beginning without any such presupposition—"standpointless," as it were—is an illusory pretension.

After these preliminary statements, Heidegger proceeds to a more detailed analysis of man's being. Man's being, which is concerned with his own being, has *to-be*—that is, he must be; he cannot surrender his being-there to some other being and get rid of it. He is, rather, surrendered or delivered up to himself. He has, therefore, to bear, as long as he exists, the "burden" of existence as an essential character of his being-there. If, says Heidegger, one can speak at all of man's essence, then this so-called essence is implied in the fact that he has to-be; in other words, man's essence has to be understood from his existence. It may or may not be correct that man is a rational animal (Aristotle) or an *ens creatum* (Thomas), a creature in the theological sense, or a compound of spirit, soul, and body—whatever his essence may be, first of all he is there, as a self-concerned existence. "The Essence of (man's) *Dasein* is his Existence." While essence refers to the conceivable *what* I am, existence refers to the factual *that* I am and have-to-be. This *that* in man's existence precedes whatever he is, biologically, psychologically, socially.

Man's existence implies further that he is *in the world*. But the "world" is not an external sum total of all extant beings, nor is it a system of merely functional beings. It is a universal and yet existential structure. Man is not like a stone in the world, but is essentially relating himself *to* "his" world. He is constituting and "projecting" the world into which he is thrown and by which he is swayed and permeated. He is from the very outset of his human existence a worldly existence. "To-be-in-the-world" is a fundamental character of man's existence. To have a world means more than to behave within a given environment. It means, rather, to be open for the manifestation of Being as such by "ek-sisting," that is, by being exposed to the totality of being and having to stand such an exposed or "ecstatic" existence. Organic and inorganic nature is alive or lifeless, respectively, but does not exist in the human dimension of a self- and world-transcending existence. And the world itself is not a blind mass of being but a way or state of being. "Cosmos" in Greek philosophy means not simply *physis* but a specific constitution of the natural world, an orderly totality as distinct from a disorderly, chaotic totality of the same beings which, as cosmos, are *kata kosmon,* cosmos-like. And this total state of being is further related to human beings; only to human beings who are awake is the cosmos a "common" world, while in the state of sleep each individual has his own world. The emphasis on the relatedness of world to man became accentuated in the Christian understanding of the world. For St. Paul, cosmos is not primarily a cosmic state but directly a state of man—humanity in the state of alienation from God. In both traditions, classic and Christian, cosmos or world transcends the concept of nature. Nature, says Heidegger, cannot elucidate the ontological character of world and of our being in it because nature is only a kind of being within our world and we encounter it therefore within the analysis of man's being-there. Thus the initial definition of the fundamental being whose essence is absorbed in existence seems to stand firm.

As a pure factuality of worldly existence, man has no wisdom about his whence and whither. For this very reason, he feels all the more intensely the pure fact of his being, the factuality that he is, no matter how much he may try to surrender himself to some busyness in order to evade the uneasy consciousness of being ultimately nothing else than a factual self or existence. Heidegger calls this factuality of one's own existence *Geworfenheit,* "being-thrown" into existence. No human *Dasein* has ever freely decided whether it wants to come into existence. Hence, it is utterly unintelligible why we have to be. Out of this experience, man makes many attempts to throw himself out of his being thrown into existence by projecting this and that. The ultimate project [*Entwurf*] which man can and ought to project is, however, the anticipation and appropriation of his death. For only by anticipating and facing resolutely the end of a still unfinished existence can a human existence become "whole" and wholly intense. By anticipating death as the final end, man acknowledges his final finiteness and ultimate nothingness.

This nothingness of our being-there is revealed primarily in indefinite anxiety. Anxiety is distinct from definite fear of this and that. It is concerned not with particular objects in the world, but with the whole of our worldly being-there. In such an anxiety, which may emerge on quite trivial occasions, man suddenly loses his customary hold on the world. The whole of Being seems to drift away into nothing. But this experience of stretching out into nothingness is in itself a positive one, for it gives us the necessary background against which we become aware of Being as such— of the amazing fact "that there is something" and not nothing, "the wonder of all wonders."

Being open-minded to this anxiety and advancing freely toward the inevitable end is the highest test of man's freedom from contingency. Just because factual existence does not rest upon anything but itself, it is the factual source of a radical freedom, of the freedom to will one's own finiteness and to assent to that fundamental nothingness which pervades all Being for us. Radical freedom, that is, freedom in regard to being as such, and not only from certain conditions of life, is bound up with the manifestation of nothingness.

This is, very briefly and roughly, the outline of Heidegger's concept of existence. I think it would be very difficult to refute the so-called "nihilism" of existential ontology, on theoretical as well as moral grounds, unless one believes in man and world as a creation of God or in the cosmos as a divine and eternal order —in other words, unless one is not "modern." This does not mean that the problem of nothingness is an invention of existentialism. Like "existence," the "nothing," too, has always been a problem, but in very different contexts.

In Jewish-Christian theology, the nothing is an absolute void. It is conceived as the empty and powerless opposite to the omnipotence of God, who creates being out of nothing. In classic philosophy, the nothing is the negative borderline of being; it is not positive but merely absence of being or, more precisely, of being-formed or being-shaped. In modern existentialism, nothingness is not merely absence of, or contrast to, Being, but belongs essentially to Being as such. Moreover, it is the ontological condition of freedom. Thus Heidegger ventures to reverse the classical saying, *ex nihilo nihil fit* (out of nothing, nothing can emerge), into the opposite thesis, *ex nihilo omne ens qua ens fit* (out of nothing—that is, from possible nothingness—all being as such emerges). This proposition is anticlassic because it endows the nothing with a creative significance, and it is anti-Christian because it applies the doctrine of divine creation out of nothing to a finite existence. For a finite existence like man, the meaning of Being as such becomes manifest only in the face of nothingness. The experience of it reveals the amazing strangeness of Being as such. On account of this experience of Being in the state of slipping away the question can arise, "Why is there anything at all rather than nothing?" This quest for an ultimate "why" of Being as such also motivates all our secondary questions about the particular causes or reasons of this and that.

The logical evidence of the traditional proposition that "nothing is without cause," the "principle of sufficient reason," rests on the translogical fact that man can ask about the "why" of his own and every being. The possibility, however, of asking "why" rests on the fact that man's existence is not bound up with and contained in itself but is removed from it. Man is a self-transcendent existence which has a certain free play and is therefore capable of thinking and acting in possibilities, in projects, instead of merely accepting given realities. Hence we can ask: why this and *not* that? why thus and *not* otherwise? why is there anything at all and *not* nothing? The possibility of asking "why not" refers to our freedom as the ultimate ground of these transcending questions. But this freedom has a radical limitation. It is the freedom of a contingent and finite existence and therefore finite in itself. The freedom of overstepping or transcending all particular kinds of being, which enables us to ask "why not" is, together with man's existence, an enterprise or "project" which is thrust upon us. We are, as Sartre says, "condemned to freedom." The ultimate ground of our causal question, that is, our freedom, is in itself groundless—or bottomless [*Abgrund*], incapable of freely grounding itself.

All this is certainly modern, but neither classic nor Christian. Heidegger's *Sein und Zeit* leaves no doubt that Christian and Greek ontology are no longer acceptable to him. His whole work is intended as an introduction to the "destruction" of the ontological tradition, that is, to a critical reexamination of the original foundations and limitations of the Greek and scholastic notions of Being. The fundamental limitation of Greek ontology is, in regard to the problem of Being, that it understands man's being and Being in general in orientation to the *world* as cosmos and *physis,* and in regard to the problem of Time, that it takes its orientation from what is *present* and *always present* or eternal.[6] In other words, Greek thought has no sense for man's exceptional, "ecstatic" existence, and therefore no sense for the future as the primary horizon of all human projects.

The fundamental limitation of medieval ontology is that it has taken over the results of Greek thought without their original motivations and transplanted them into the basic doctrine of creation, according to which all finite being is an *ens creatum* as opposed to God's *ens increatum.* On this theological basis, man's essential existence consists in transcending himself toward his creator. This idea of transcending toward a perfect and infinite being subsequently became diluted and secularized. It pervades the whole transcendental philosophy of German idealism and also Jaspers' semi-Christian existentialism.

Against this whole decaying tradition, Heidegger ventured to reexamine anew the problem of Being. He nowhere pretends to have solved it, saying explicitly in the last paragraph of *Sein und Zeit* that its only purpose is to kindle the question and to bring into motion what has become stalemated. He concludes his work not with a ready-made answer, but with a series of open questions, and he is still on the way—away from the initial pathos of resolute "existentialism"! This "being-on-the-way," which is the strength and honesty but also the weakness and hypocrisy of modern thinking, is not a Christian pilgrimage toward a definite goal but, as with Nietzsche, an adventurous wandering where the wanderer is afraid but also proud of not knowing whither the adventure might lead him.

In view of the earnestness and radicality of Heidegger's enterprise, it was a strange mistake when in the twenties, those who disliked existentialism thought that they could dismiss it as a "philosophy of inflation." But even twenty years after the publication of *Sein und Zeit* one could still read in an article in the *New York Times* (July 6, 1947) the following definition of existentialism: "It was invented by a Nazi, Heidegger; it is a philosophy of nihilism like Nazism, appropriate to the vacuity of German life." Unfortunately, for this definition, existentialism was invented during the Weimar Republic (which offered Heidegger a chair at Berlin University) when the vacuity of German intellectual life was still pretty well filled by a host of other philoso-

6. See Helene Weiss, "The Greek Conceptions of Time and Being in the Light of Heidegger's Philosophy," in *Philosophy and Phenomenological Research* (December, 1941), pp. 173ff.

phies of "life," "culture," and "values." Existentialism has outlived not only the Weimar Republic but also the Third Reich. It has even gained ascendancy and has its strongest support now in France, the classical country of Cartesian rationalism. The German climate after the First World War did perhaps stimulate, but it could not cause, the rise of existentialism, the germ of which was planted long ago.

THE RELATION BETWEEN ESSENCE AND EXISTENCE IN THE THOUGHT OF ARISTOTLE, THOMAS, AND HEGEL

To ESTIMATE the significance of the existentialist innovation in the understanding of existence, one has to contrast it with the relation between essence and existence in the philosophical tradition. In some way, existence has always been a fundamental problem in man's thought about Being. The real issue is not the birth of an entirely new problem, but a new way of posing the same old problem within a different context. What is new in modern existentialism is that the traditional reference of existence to essence is replaced by the absorption of essence into existence.

Aristotle, in Book VI of his *Metaphysics,* discusses the several meanings of Being. All sciences, he says, mark off some particular realm of being without inquiring into Being simply as Being. For example, the science of building presupposes the existence of certain building matcrials without inquiring into the creativity that brings a building, through the mind of an architect, into existence. Metaphysics, however, seeks the principles and causes of all beings "in so far as they are or exist," while sciences take existence for granted. They also neglect the inquiry into the conceivable essence of their particular realms of being. So far, Aristotle sounds much like Heidegger, or rather, Heidegger seems to have restated Aristotle. But then Aristotle goes on to say that the neglect of existence and essence are only two aspects of "one and the same omission" and that "the one goes along with the other" for, he says, the inquiry into *what* something is (its essence) also decides *if* it is (its existence). Essence and existence are both manifest to "the same kind of thinking."

These few sentences indicate the limitation of classic ontology. They show that Aristotle, in spite of his emphasis on Being as Being, is not concerned with the sheer factuality of existence in general or with the contingency of human existence in particular, but with essential existence, because "whatness" and "thatness" are inseparable and neither precedes the other. It is true that over against Plato's "idea," Aristotle asserts that the *ousia* or essence is a real substance, but just because he defines it in opposition to Plato, his own concept of Being is that of being-something and in its full sense, it is the being of something which has the reason or ground of its being in itself. Accordingly, Aristotle explicitly excludes from his considerations whatever is by accident or chance. For, he argues, an accidental or inessential existence cannot become the subject of a rational science. Accidents are innumerable and incalculable; the fortuitous, he says, "is practically a mere name." As an illustration, he points out that a spacious house may be comfortable for a large and rich family but inconvenient for a small and poor family. This is, however, accidental to the essential character of a house. This illustration shows again that the "accidental" which Aristotle has in mind is not the principal accidentality of a whole existence as such but only the particular accident that may occur to something which already exists essentially. All serious philosophy, he concludes, is either of that which is always what it is, or at least for the most part and as a rule.

Within this sound limitation of Aristotle's thought, the existentialist question, "Why is there anything at all rather than nothing?" and the corresponding emphasis on the contingency and factuality of existence could not emerge. It could not, not because Aristotle was a modern positivist, but because he was a Greek thinker for whom existence as such—that there is something—was an unquestionable element within the essential structure, order, and beauty of an always existing cosmos without beginning and end, including the existence of rational animals called men. They are distinguished from other beings not by the irrational freedom of sheer willing and projecting, but by the freedom of disinterested contemplation. The highest distinction of man is that he is capable of contemplating this perfect hierarchy of an imperishable universe within which each being has its definite properties, place, and degree of perfection. For Aristotle, the ultimate source of philosophical research is "amazement"—not, however, about the strange factuality of Being as such but about the hidden principles of the orderly changes in the visible universe.

The Aristotelian view of the world was taken over by Thomas, but with some important modifications.[7] For Thomas, as a Chris-

7. See E. Gilson, *Le Thomism*, 5th ed. (Paris, 1945), pp. 42ff. and 511ff.

tian theologian and believer, all being is primarily *ens creatum,* brought into existence out of nothing by the absolutely free will of a transcendent creator. Accordingly, within Christian thought the concept of existence has a definite priority to that of essence, and to that extent, Thomas is an "existentialist" or, rather, existentialism is derived from Christian thinking. Its quest for an ultimate why of existence as such, as expressed in Heidegger's question, "Why is there anything at all rather than nothing?" was not asked by Greek philosophy, but is implicit in the story of creation and explicit in existentialism, though apart from creation.

Thomas distinguishes between *ens* or a being and *esse* or to-be, the latter meaning the act of existence. To accentuate existence he speaks of *ipsum esse,* of the very existence of a being. This *esse* or to-be is the verb root of *ens* and *essentia,* of being and essence. An existing being is a *quidditas* or essence, in so far as it is conceivable and definable in regard to what it is. For everything is known by what it is, its essence. But of all created substances nothing is what it is by itself [*ens per se*]. Only God is without a cause because he alone exists essentially; his very essence is to-be. Seen in this Christian perspective of creation, Aristotle's analysis of the various reasons why a certain being is what it is is insufficient. For what Aristotle demonstrates are only the inherent principles of an existing something, but neither does he ask nor can he answer why something is at all. He is not radical, as Thomas and Heidegger are. Prior to a formative principle is the beginning of existence as such. Aristotle's actualizing form is not the first principle of existence; it determines only the completion of a potential existence. On the level of Aristotle, one can only inquire into the existence of something already existing. But the first principle of Being is *ipsum esse,* the very to-be, and this is for Thomas not only a most *strange* factuality (as it is for existentialism) but also the most wonderful and *perfect* actuality. To-be is already an indication of perfection, in accordance with the biblical saying that all created things are as such good and perfect, simply by being endowed with existence. This is, of course, the very opposite of the mood of modern existentialism and yet comes very close to it. For if we abstract from God as the only essential existence, modern and Christian existentialism agree in this that all *finite* existence is *not* an essential existence, existing necessarily by itself. For Thomas, too, existence is an exceptional category, undefinable by a "what" or essence. The knowledge of what something is does not yield anything for demonstrating that it is. Thus existence seems to be entirely adventitious, coming from outside, and hence we might conclude—not only with modern existentialists but also with the Arab and Jewish Aristotelians of the tenth and twelfth centuries (Al-Farabi, Algazel, Avicenna, Maimonides) [8]—that existence is a pure accident. Thomas often seems to be of their opinion and yet he criticizes them severely because to him this apparent accident of existence is the very heart of being. It appears as an accident only if one starts from essence, but if one starts from the whole existing being, then existence reveals itself not only as a different order from essence, but also as a far superior order, for without it no *ens* and essence would be. The fact of existence is for Thomas the most "intimate," "profound," and "perfect," though undefinable, determination which includes all the rest.

Thus the existentialist thesis that existence precedes essence can be traced back to Christian thinking from which, however, it is strictly separated by the doctrine of creation. Existentialism is creationism without creator. On the other side, in the perspective of creation, finite existence is not only contingent and unjustifiable by itself, but the contingent and finite aspect of existence emerges only within such a transcendent perspective toward a necessary, infinite, and essential being.[9]

This idea of an essential existence persisted in the form of the ontological argument for the existence of God from Anselm

8. See Emil L. Fackenheim, "The Possibility of the Universe in Al-Farabi, Ibn Sina, and Maimonides," in *Proceedings of the American Academy for Jewish Research*, XVI (1946–47).

9. Sartre, in *L'Être et le néant* (Paris, 1943), pp. 653, 708, 713ff., 717, 721, draws indeed the ultimate conclusions from the premises of radical existentialism when he asserts that the ideal of pure existence is to become—God! The *pour-soi*, he argues, is always its own deficiency, for it lacks the solid self-sufficiency of an *en-soi*. The *pour-soi* emerges only through the appropriation and annihilation of an *en-soi*. But through this assimilating annihilation of an alien world *en-soi*, the *pour-soi* projects itself toward the ideal of becoming eventually an *en-soi-pour-soi*. In other words, the groundless freedom of projecting wants to transform itself into a being which is the ground or reason of itself, that is, it projects ultimately the idea of God as *ens causa sui*. But this idea and that project are, according to Sartre, an impossible project and idea. "The fundamental passion of man" is therefore "in vain" and thus it happens that men escape from the absolute and yet bottomless responsibility of their chance-existence "into solitary drunkenness or to the leading of nations." It is true, Sartre says, that man can essentially *ask* for a reason of his contingent existence, but this quest implies the perspective toward an essential existence which is the reason of its own being. What man actually experiences is the constant and inevitable failure of his attempt to surrender his contingent and bottomless existence to something necessary and grounded in itself. Compare H. Marcuse, "Remarks on J. P. Sartre's *L'Être et le néant*," in *Philosophy and Phenomenological Research* (March, 1948), p. 315.

to Descartes, Spinoza, Leibniz, and Wolff. Only Kant destroyed it. He argued that in no case can existence be "picked out" from essence. A real God or one hundred real dollars and an imagined God and one hundred imagined dollars are essentially—that is, as to *what* they are—the same. What distinguishes them is not their conceivable essence but the nonrational positivity of existence which is external to essence.

One may doubt whether Kant's criticism of the ontological argument really meets the point of Anselm's demonstration. But the distinction between existence and essence is valid with regard to all finite beings, since the difference between essence and existence is the very mark of finitude, as was already urged by Thomas. After Kant and against him, the ontological proof for the existence of God became reestablished by Hegel, on the basis of Aristotle, though in the service of a Christian philosophy of religion. Like Aristotle, Hegel starts from the identity or, rather, the togetherness of factual existence and conceivable essence, of Being and Thought, excluding therefore, as did Aristotle, the accidental, the chance-existence from the interest of metaphysical science. He defines the real as the result of a dialectical "unity of essence and existence," of the "inner" essence and "external" existence. Beings which do not attain to such a congruence are, according to Hegel, "insignificant," "trivial," "casual" existences about which philosophy need not trouble itself. Having thus excluded the contingent from the interest of knowledge, Hegel extends his definition of reality to all beings which have a "true" or "real" existence in the emphatic sense of this word. There is, according to Hegel, no real existence which is not essential and necessary: there is no reality—neither in nature nor in history—which is not reasonable, and no reason which is not real. Hence his bold confidence that philosophical reason can penetrate the whole universe and make it intelligible to us. This extension of the unity of reality and reason, of being and thought, of existence and essence, to every "true" being implies that nothing in this world is absolutely finite and thereby split into existence and essence. Everything real participates on different levels in the infinite, and absolute, the divine.

On the basis of the Judaeo-Christian distinction between created and uncreated being, between the finite and the infinite, but with the conceptual means of Aristotle, Hegel overdid what was sound in classic philosophy and perverted what was genuinely Christian. For the thesis of the structural unity of essence and existence serves him as a theodicy, as a justification of God in the world of nature and history. What, according to Thomas and Christian theology in general, is an ontological privilege of God —namely, to have an essential existence—is, according to Hegel's confusion of Aristotelian metaphysics and Christian theology, valid for every being which can reasonably and emphatically be said "to be." Reality is everywhere the manifestation of an existing "*logos*," a concept in which the Greek *nous* is inextricably confounded with the *logos* of the New Testament.

Opposed to this Hegelian "reconciliation" of conceivable essence and factual existence, of reason and reality, thought and being, there emerged in the 1840's the many-sided attacks on Hegel's philosophy and on philosophy as such by Schelling, Kierkegaard, Feuerbach, and Marx. All of them were anti-Hegelians. They insisted, with different aims and in opposite directions, on the factual, naked, "unforethinkable" positivity of sheer existence as opposed to Hegel's philosophy of rational reality or essential existence.

SCHELLING, KIERKEGAARD, AND MARX

WHEN SCHELLING in his later period distinguished between positive and negative philosophy, claiming the positive one for himself and accusing Hegel of having been negative, he meant that reason can only reach the ideal essence of things, their possibility or that which can be, but never any positive, that is, positively posited, existence. Hegel, he says, hypostatized the rational concept of what something is to a fake-existence, simulating in his dialectical movements of thought the real. He has thus transformed all living reality into a "desert of Being." Rational philosophy is negative with regard to existence because reality cannot be anticipated by thought. It is "unforethinkable"; it can be grasped only "empirically" by metaphysical empiricism. A true philosophy of reality has to begin with the presupposition of accidental existence, the *geradezu Existierende,* the *ipsum esse* of Thomas. Reality cannot be thought out; it comes into existence and to reach a philosophical understanding of it, it is first of all necessary to "tear oneself away" from the blind fact of existence. "The whole world is such an unforethinkable, blind existence."

The pupils of Hegel who listened to Schelling's Berlin lectures in which he announced his program of a new age of philosophy, even of religion, were as much impressed as the pupils of Husserl who listened, thirty years ago, in Freiburg to Heidegger and turned

away from Husserl's theory of *epoché*, of "bracketing" real existence in order to grasp the pure essence of things. In Schelling's
audience were Russian and German Hegelians, and society;
among them were Kierkegaard, Friedrich Engels, Bakunin, and
Jacob Burckhardt. Since most of the audience expected a revolutionary tendency, they were disappointed when Schelling developed his scholastic doctrine of *Potenzen*, aiming at a philosophy
of mythology and revelation. Schelling's last academic activity
was the first important step toward a break with Hegel's reconciliation of reason and reality, of essence and existence, and a new
beginning after Hegel's conscious consummation of "history of
the concept," that is, of the whole European philosophical tradition.

The most important and influential "existentialists" among
the next generation were Kierkegaard and Marx. Neither of them
directed the philosophical tradition into new channels, as did
Schelling, but they opposed, together with Hegel's system, the
metaphysical enterprise as such. If modern philosophers have a
bad conscience in the pursuit of their theoretical profession,[10] it
is mainly due to Kierkegaard's and Marx's radical criticism of
philosophy as such and to their practical tendencies. We have
lost Hegel's confidence that reality cannot resist the power of
thought and concept.

What Kierkegaard and Marx were concerned with was not
disinterested speculation about universal structures, but rather
individual and social practice, or, more precisely, ethical and
political action with regard to the religious and political conditions of contemporary human existence. For Kierkegaard, philosophy became reduced to the psychological analysis of the inner
stages of life, for Marx to the social-economic analysis of the
external conditions of production. Both emphasized, though in
opposite directions, the naked fact of our personal and social
existence. They understood the human world of the nineteenth
century as determined by commodities and money (Marx), and
the individual of the *fin du siècle* as permeated by irony, boredom,
and despair (Kierkegaard). Hegel's consummation of the history
of the spirit became for both an end, preparatory to an extensive social revolution and an intensive religious reformation, respectively. Hegel's "concrete mediations" turned for both into
abstract "decisions," either for the old Christian God (Kierkegaard) or for a new social world (Marx). Hence a theory of social

10. See H. Arendt, "What Is Existenz Philosophy?" in *Partisan Review* (Winter,
1946), p. 40.

practice and a reflection upon inner action replace Hegel's Aristotelian belief in the supreme dignity of pure contemplation. Kierkegaard and Marx both turn Hegel's reconciliation of state with society and church into a radical criticism of the capitalist world and of secularized Christianity, thus destroying together from two opposite ends the world of the Christian bourgeoisie of the nineteenth century.

The philosophical foundation of their radical criticism is to be found in their relation to Hegel's basic concept of reality as "unity of essence and existence." Protesting against the chapter on "Reality" in Hegel's *Logic*, Kierkegaard, like Schelling, contends that real reality is inseparable from that which is by accident and therefore cannot be assimilated and comprehended by an ontological logic. The most intimate character of reality is its contingency or, in religious terms, existence as such is a "miracle," the inexplicable miracle that there is something, in particular that I am there, here and now. This fact is, according to Kierkegaard, the only real "interest" of metaphysics and upon this interest speculative metaphysics cannot but wreck itself. Logically, Hegel might be right in asserting that the pure, abstract concepts of being and nothing are identical; in reality they are, however, totally different. The real reality, says Kierkegaard, and Heidegger followed him in this, is "to be interested in or concerned with factual existence." Existential reality is an *inter-esse* or in-between the hypothetical unity of being and thought. The fundamental question, therefore, is not *what is* but *that* I am.

My life has been brought to an impasse, I loathe existence, it is without savor, lacking salt and sense. . . . One sticks one's finger into the soil to tell by the smell in what land one is: I stick my finger into existence—it smells of nothing. Where am I? Who am I? How came I here? What is this thing called the world? What does this world mean? Who am I? How did I come into the world? Why was I not consulted, why not made acquainted with its manners and customs . . . ? How did I obtain an interest in this big enterprise they call reality? Why should I have an interest in it? Is it not a voluntary concern? And if I am to be compelled to take part in it, where is the director? I should like to make a remark to him.[11]

Marx's criticism of Hegel's reconciliation of essence with existence is very different from that of Kierkegaard. Even as a "materialist" Marx remained a Hegelian idealist, for his ideal of a communist society in which freedom is realized is, in principle, nothing else but the "realization" of Hegel's principle of the unity of essence and existence. The communist society, as conceived

11. Kierkegaard, *Repetition* (Princeton, 1941), p. 114.

by Marx, realizes the unity of reason and reality, of general essence and individual existence. In a perfect communist commonwealth, each individual has his human essence realized as a common existence. In consequence of his acceptance of Hegel's principle, Marx could say that Hegel is not to blame for having asserted the reality of reason, but rather for having neglected the practical task of its realization through change and criticism. Instead of criticizing theoretically and changing practically the whole established reality of servitude and unreason for the sake of freedom and reason, Hegel accepted the results of our political, social, economic, and religious history as reasonable in themselves. From the critical and revolutionary standpoint of Marx, such acceptance of the existent is "crassest materialism"—and Marxism purest idealism! And since Marx believed in the possibility of an empirical unity of essence and existence, he is not in the line of modern existentialism which has its name from the reduction of essence into existence.

With this rebellion of Marx and Kierkegaard against Hegel's synthesis, modern existentialism begins, so far as an immediate historic filiation can be traced. Actually, modern existentialism began as early as the seventeenth century, with the Cartesian revolution in the conception of the world and its impact upon Pascal's thought about man's condition in it.

Considering the long and laborious historical process that was required to produce eventually those terms which are now popular slogans, it would be extremely superficial to think of modern existentialism as the mere product of a particular German situation.

If there is a historical and theoretical alternative at all to modern existentialism, one has only the choice of understanding the world and man's place in it either as an immutable natural order —that is, with the eyes of Greek contemplation—or as divine creation—that is, with the eyes of Jewish and Christian faith. Either choice would be indeed persuasive since one cannot wish to remain forever nailed on the cross of contingency, absurdity, and total displacement. But choosing between the one or the other "project" or *Weltentwurf* would still be an existential attitude and decision and therefore contradictory to the nature of the chosen world-view. For neither of them is a mere project of human choice and decision. The one is revealed and intelligible only to faith; the other, too, is revealed, though not by historical revelation but in and by nature itself to the nature of man. We cannot choose not to be modern, if it is true that modernity has, since Descartes, rested on the choice of a standpoint and viewpoint. We would have to overcome in principle the modern attitude as such toward the whole of Being if we are to overcome existentialism. This is precisely the direction in which Heidegger is now transforming and reversing the problem of "Being and Time" and the reason why he rejects, together with the traditional distinction of essence and existence, Sartre's existentialism, his own, but natural, child.[12] As long as we do not even intend to subject modern man and the modern world to a radical criticism, that is, to one affecting their coordinate principles, we remain existentialists, capable of asking the most radical question, "Why is there anything at all rather than nothing?"—but constitutionally incapable of answering it.

12. Heidegger, *Platons Lehre von der Wahrheit* (Berne, 1947), pp. 72f.

4 / M. Heidegger and F. Rosenzweig:

A Postscript to *Being and Time*

Introduction

WHEN I BECAME A LECTURER under Heidegger at Marburg University in 1928, there lived in Frankfurt, at a distance of but two hours' train ride, a man named Franz Rosenzweig. His name was known to us through a book that he had written on Hegel.[1] We did not know that at the same time he had also published a book entitled *The Star of Redemption*. Unnoticed amid the academic trade and bustle, Rosenzweig died in 1929, after having been in ill health for eight years: his body fell into a progressive paralysis which soon deprived him even of the faculty of speech. At the end, he could only lift a single finger, by which he gave signs and moved the keys of his typewriter. His mind, however, remained bright and vigorous until his death, which he called, a few hours before it came to pass, "the point of all points" that the Lord vouchsafed to him while he was asleep.[2]

When I left Europe in the fall of 1936 in order to go to Japan, Rosenzweig's *Letters* were among the books I brought there. They had appeared in 1935 and had been pointed out to me by a friend, but it was not until 1939 that I felt the urge to read those 700 pages.

1. *Hegel und der Staat* (1920).
2. Rosenzweig's personal data are briefly as follows. He was born in 1886, studied medicine for five semesters beginning in 1905, studied history and philosophy in 1907–8 in Freiburg under F. Meineke, and later in Berlin under H. Cohen. He graduated in 1912, having written as a thesis a part of the work on Hegel referred to above. He was a soldier from 1914–18, serving in the field during the last year of the war. At that time he also outlined the *Stern der Erlosung*. After the war, he finished the book on Hegel and the *Stern der Erlosung*, both of which came out at nearly the same time. He participated in the founding of a Jewish Academy in Frankfurt in 1922 and translated the Bible in collaboration with M. Buber, composing at the same time accompanying essays on the problem of translation.

The impression Rosenzweig's personality made upon me was so strong that I immediately procured also his principal work in philosophy, *The Star of Redemption,* and his collected essays, *The Shorter Writings.* I read all of the latter, which came to more than a thousand pages, at one sitting.[3] In part, my interest was aroused by the striking similarity between Rosenzweig's philosophical starting point and that of my own teacher, Heidegger. The thoughts which this similarity awakened in me are presented in this essay.

If Heidegger ever had a "contemporary" who deserved the name in more than a temporal sense, it was this German Jew whose major works, published six years before *Being and Time,* were not even remotely known to Heidegger or his pupils. The similarity in origin between the "new thought" of Heidegger and that of Rosenzweig, although it did not become common knowledge, was apparent to Rosenzweig. From a critical standpoint, this similarity consisted in the fact that each man directed his thought away from the metaphysics of consciousness of German idealism while at the same time each one avoided positivism. Positively viewed, each took the "facticity" of human *Dasein* as his common starting point. The same spirit of the age produced the first writings of E. Rosenstock, M. Buber, H. and R. Ehrenburg, C. von Weizsäcker, and F. Ebner. The beginning of "dialectical theology" also belongs to this historical period that followed the First World War. This was also the last period during which German philosophy was productive and had a definite viewpoint, and was not just an expression of the talent of individuals engaging in monologues. In this discussion, we shall limit ourselves to a critical comparison of *The Star of Redemption* with *Being and Time,* and in particular to the question of the *eternity* of time in contrast to its *temporality.*

In the shorter writings of Rosenzweig there are two pages which are entitled: "Exchanged Frontiers." These pages were written as a book review of the second edition of Cohen's *The Religion of Reason in Judaism.* Furthermore, they are a record of the impression made upon Rosenzweig in the spring of 1929 at a university conference that was held in Davos, the high point of which was a critical debate between E. Cassirer and Heidegger. Rosenzweig's remarks on that discussion were published posthumously in a periodical. Their tenor is as follows.

Cohen's work had a strange fate: those books which he had

3. *Stern der Erlosung,* III, 1921, 1930 (Tel Aviv); *Letters* (1935); *Shorter Writings* (1937), which contain also the preface to Cohen's *Jewish Writings.*

written as an apprentice in Kant's workshop (*Kant's Theory of Experience, Kant's Foundation of Ethics, Kant's Foundation of Aesthetics*) revolutionized the scientific philosophy of their time and were the foundation stone of the "School of Marburg." His masterpieces, the works of his mature period (*The Logic of Pure Reason, The Ethics of Pure Will, The Aesthetics of Pure Feeling*), were hardly noticed outside the Marburg School, his own system remaining the ill-timed opus of an intellect apparently out of tune with its own times. Finally, the aged Cohen outlined an annex and a new construction on the basis of his system, *The Religion of Reason*,[4] which was published posthumously and remained nearly wholly unknown, although this was the very work which undermined idealism as did no other, through its main concept of "correlation"—between man and God, man and man —and anticipated, as Rosenzweig puts it, the "new thinking of our times." [5] "The exchange of frontiers" in the discussion between Heidegger and Cassirer, according to Rosenzweig, consisted in the fact that Cassirer represented the "old thought" of Marburg Kantianism, whereas Heidegger—de facto, though not consciously —represented the "new thinking" of the old Cohen while opposing Cohen's legitimate disciple, Cassirer. Moreover, this made Heidegger the rightful successor to Cohen's chair, however paradoxical this must have seemed to every old "Marburger."

In order to establish his claim that Heidegger's thinking

---

4. This work, one of Cohen's most unique productions, remained, like Rosenzweig's *Stern*, almost unknown to the German academic world. Heidegger, for example, in his report on the "History of the Philosophical Chair at Marburg University," did not mention Cohen's *Religion of Reason* in his discussion of Cohen's works.

5. Cf. H. Herrigel, *Das neue Denken* (1928). Cohen's concept of correlation (in the eighth chapter of *Religion of Reason*) was unknown to me, also, when I discussed the relationship between man and fellow man in *Das Individuum in der Rolle des Mitmenschen* (1928).

The "new thinking" centered at first in the rediscovery of Feuerbach's "Principles of the Philosophy of the Future" and in its thesis that the basis of truth is not the self-consciousness of an Ego, but the interrelationship between Thou and I. Contemporary representatives of this new orientation were, among others, F. Ebner (*Das Wort und die geistigen Realitäten*, 1921), H. Ehrenberg, who in 1922 reedited Feuerbach's *Principles* and reexamined German idealism (*Disputation*, 1923), M. Buber (*Ich und Du*, 1923), and last but not least, E. Rosenstock (*Angewandte Seelenkunde*, 1924). On the other hand, it was the influence of Kierkegaard which shaped to a great extent the revolutionary turn of the dialectical theology of K. Barth and F. Gogarten as well as the existential philosophy of K. Jaspers, E. Grisebach, and Heidegger. The "new thinking" was a phenomenon characterizing a whole generation deeply impressed by the bankruptcy of the bourgeois-Christian world and the emptiness of the academic routine. Maliciously, one could call it a philosophy and theology of "inflation," as R. Otto once put it to me.

moves along the road taken by Cohen, Rosenzweig compares Heidegger's starting point from man as a finite essence whose existence, despite its freedom, is a "projected facticity" [*geworfene Faktizität*], with one of Cohen's utterances,[6] which emphatically stresses the "individual *quand même*" over against the academic-bourgeois idea that the real value of the human being consists of the "intellectual amount carried over to the eternity of culture," whereas it is just the passing of moods and attitudes that is lastingly human. Moreover, when Heidegger says in one of his lectures that man must be called back from the lazy enjoyment of so-called cultural values to the sternness of his fate, this accords well with Cohen's ironic remark when he says: The "ruins of a quondam reason" and the "scarecrows of the moral laws" could be left to their own fate! The "reason" left behind by the elderly Cohen was the "productive" reason of idealism: in its place he put the God-created reason of the creature—Heidegger would say: the reason which is inherent in the fact of our existence. The difference between Heidegger's and Cohen's return to the concrete individual, however, is this: Cohen, in stressing the "individual *quand même*" as it exists previously to all idealistic interpretation, quite simply wants to revive religious idealism, "adorning the vanity of the earthly with the glory of the eternal." In contrast, Heidegger no longer wants to have anything to do with eternity and interprets the individual life through its own temporality.

[I] THE COMMON STARTING POINT OF HEIDEGGER AND ROSENZWEIG

THE SAME SORT of difference can be found by comparing Heidegger with Cohen's pupil, Rosenzweig. Their starting point is the same: the naked individual in his finite existence, as he is previous to all cultural determination. Their desire to go back to the primary and essential things which belong to a genuine experience of life is a result of sharing the spirit of the times, namely, the times during and after the First World War, when everything superficial was necessarily swept away. However different Heidegger's academic sobriety may be from Rosenzweig's language and cultural background, both speak with a radical and passionate earnestness. In place of the many, both want the "one" again, i.e., the "One that is necessary" for a period that was

6. Letter to Stadler in 1890 on the occasion of G. Keller's death, now printed in Cohen, *Letters* (1939).

oppressed by the need for decisions, because the traditional assumptions of modern civilization no longer proved indisputable. Both want to make out the truth of human existence, both treat of man and the world, *Logos* as language, and time. Both develop their thought, with characteristic sharpness of intellect, primarily on the basis of a language which is handled by both in masterly fashion. They philosophize in opposition to their academic environment—"*in philosophos*"—as the motto of the first volume of *The Star of Redemption* reads, and at the same time "*in theologos*" —which is the motto of the second volume—because they themselves are both philosophers and theologians simultaneously. Philosophy, says Rosenzweig, today demands that theologians philosophize. Philosophy and theology depend on each other and together produce a new type of theological philosopher. Theological problems need to be translated into the human and the human problems pushed forward into theological ones [7]—a characterization of the "new thinking" which can be applied to Heidegger as well as to Rosenzweig, although Heidegger's attitude towards Christianity is that of an estrangement, while Rosenzweig's attitude towards Judaism is that of a return. The newness of their way of thinking implies the death of the old way. The latter has come to an end as a result of the incorporation of the whole history of the spirit in Hegel's system and its sham reconciliation of Christian theology with Greek philosophy. Hegel's system comprehends the whole of historical being, presupposing nothing other then a pure unity of self-sufficient thought.[8]

However, is this all-embracing, all-comprehensive thinking really self-sufficient? Is it not necessary to have some empirical foundation in order to be able to start at all, as Schelling and the left-wing Hegelians argued in their revolt against Hegel? And what else does the revolt against Hegel's system and the whole idealistic philosophy mean—on the part of Kierkegaard, Marx, Schopenhauer, and Nietzsche [9]—but a rehabilitation of man who is in "need" of and "interested" in Being, for whom, as Heidegger puts it, his own existence is "at stake." The real starting point for the knowledge of the whole or of Being in general is, according to Rosenzweig, not a superabundant, excessive mode of thinking, but something real and actual: "Man in the plainest sense as he still exists," a concept of pure "factuality" [*Tatsächlichkeit*],[10]

7. *Stern*, II, p. 24; *Kl. Schriften*, p. 389; cf. Herrigel, *Das Neue Denken, l.c.*
8. *Stern*, I, pp. 11ff.; II, pp. 21f.; *Briefe*, pp. 264, 645; *Kl. Schriften*, pp. 358f., 370.
9. *Stern*, I, pp. 12ff.
10. *Kl. Schriften*, pp. 363, 369.

meaning something definite and individual, not an idea or essence. "I, a rather ordinary individual with a first and last name; I, dust and ashes, I still exist and philosophize" [11]—these remarks apply even to that philosophy which believes that it can disregard the mere accident of my existence.

The affinity of this view to Heidegger's thesis that the one and indefinite Being in general is only approachable from the radically isolated, definite, and distinctive being which is my own self,[12] and therefore that a universal ontology requires a "fundamental" one, that is to say, an analysis of actual existence, is quite obvious. Furthermore, both men develop the meaning of "is" in opposition to the traditional concept of essence,[13] for the question of what the universe is concerns only a conceptual generality, whether this be "water" (Thales), or "spirit" (Hegel). It does not concern a reality that can be experienced and the peculiar "happening" that I alone can know about because it happens to me and makes up my own historical existence.[14] Essence, according to Rosenzweig, does not have anything to do with time; reality, however, can be grasped only in temporal terms. What happens does not happen in time, but time itself happens in what I do and suffer.[15] The "new thinking" knows that, like everything else at every moment, it is time-bound, involved in its own past and future, whereas the old philosophy endeavored to think timelessly.

This temporality innate in real Being requires a new method of expression. Thinking, Rosenzweig says, must become a "thinking from language," because speaking alone is temporal whereas thought as such deliberately disregards the time of discourse— of speaking, being silent, and listening. Thinking which is thus guided by language is not merely logical, but also "grammatical." Only thinking that is bound up with language takes time seriously in the various tenses of the *Logos*.[16] Such grammatically determined thinking characterizes Rosenzweig's *The Star of Redemption* no less than it does Heidegger's *Being and Time*, whose revolutionary originality consists above all in making the words of ordinary speech a philosophical terminology (words such as: *"alltäglich"—daily; "jeweils"—for the time being; "zunächst"—first of all,* and *"zumeist"—mostly, now and then, to be present at; "schon immer"—already and always; "im voraus"—beforehand;*

11. *Ibid.*, p. 359.
12. *Sein und Zeit*, pp. 3, 38ff.
13. *Ibid.*, §9.
14. *Kl. Schriften*, pp. 365f., 377f., 383; *Stern*, III, pp. 156, 161f.
15. *Kl. Schriften*, p. 384.
16. *Stern*, II, pp. 68ff.; *Kl. Schriften*, pp. 383f., 386f.

"um-zu"—*in order to,* etc.). On the other hand, what Rosenzweig says about the word "already" could easily have been found in *Being and Time,* if one disregards the fact that Rosenzweig's analysis does not aim at the mere *"Faktizität,"* but at man's being a creature. He develops the "logic of creation" that is based upon the "in the beginning" of *Genesis,*[17] as follows: the world is above all already there, simply there [*da*]; the being of the world is its "already-being-always-in-existence." Because we understand the world as such an already-existent being, we can grasp the meaning of created being and along with that the power of creation that makes both the world and man exist. It is no mere chance, therefore, that all German words which mean something referring to first and last have the form of the *past* tense: *"Grund"* and *"Grundlage," "Ursache"* and *"Ur-sprung," "Voraus-setzung"* and *"Ge-setz"* (that is: *im voraus fest-Gesetztes*).

By adjusting in this way to the reality of experience, the philosophy of both men becomes an "experiencing philosophy" or an "absolute empiricism," [18] a philosophy of "revelation," in Schelling's use of that phrase: each wants to reveal the reality of things, their "positive" character that is always presupposed, but for this very reason is also mere "existence." But whereas Heidegger empties the concept of revelation of its theological sense by formalizing it into the "unveiling" of veiled things, in accordance with his concept of truth [*a-letheia*] as the mere state of being unveiled,[19] Rosenzweig interprets the biblical concept of revelation in conjunction with that of creation and redemption.[20]

That reality which makes it most manifest that I am "still there" is for both—death, as the nothingness of our existence, which is not diluted by them in any idealistic manner. Death is the center of Heidegger's *Sein und Zeit* as the "highest instance" of our existence and is also the starting point of *The Star of Redemption.* Both see death as an affront to the philosophy of "pure" ego and consciousness that knows nothing about this empirical end of existence. Rosenzweig says that all knowledge begins with death. But the old philosophy disavows this fear of the earthly by confining dying to the body and keeping soul and spirit aloof from it, although the real fear of death knows no such distinction. So long as he lives, man is unable to shake off this fear of the earthly, nor should he. He should rather learn to live in the fear of death.

17. *Stern,* II, pp. 56f.
18. *Kl. Schriften,* pp. 379, 398.
19. *Sein und Zeit,* §44.
20. *Stern,* II; *Kl. Schriften,* p. 357.

"Philosophy cheats us of this task because it covers up the earthly with its humbug about the universe as a whole. Of course, the universe as a whole cannot die. Only the individual is capable of dying and all dying is lonely." [21] However, because philosophy conceives the "is" as a universal essence and denies death, that "dark presupposition," it looks as though philosophy were presuppositionless. In opposition to this kind of thinking, which is a fleeing from death, Rosenzweig consciously starts out with a fundamental presupposition, namely that of a life which is essentially doomed to die. In this, he is not different from Heidegger, who likewise insists on the necessity of some presupposition if we are to make "is" comprehensible at all.[22] The essential difference between the two, however, is that Rosenzweig, through the beginning as creation, the middle as revelation, and the end as redemption, travels the road to the "eternal life" to which corresponds an "eternal truth," namely the "Star." Whereas Heidegger characterizes the belief in eternal truths as a "relic of Christian theology which has not yet been cast out," and recognizes only "existential," that is, temporal truths. For, he said in an unprinted lecture, "we know nothing" of God as the Eternal, a view also found in Rosenzweig, but with the supplementary remark that this is a "not-knowing" *of God* and as such is the beginning of our knowing Him.[23]

Both philosophies are a "philosophy of standpoint," a *Weltanschauung* and an attitude towards life in the sense that they are based on a mode of thought which presupposes the factual standpoint of man as a creature of earth. This, however, is not to be understood in the manner of Dilthey's historical relativism, but in an *absolute* historical sense.[24]

Actually, my viewpoint is that philosophy must be philosophized out of the standpoint of the philosophizing person if it is to be true. There is no possibility here of being objective except by starting honestly with one's own subjectivity. The obligation to be objective requires only that the entire horizon really be considered, but not in the sense that things are to be looked at from a standpoint that is not one's own or from no standpoint at all. One's own eyes are certainly only one's own eyes. But it would be stupidly bourgeois to believe that they must be plucked out in order for one to be able to see correctly.[25]

21. *Stern*, I, p. 8.
22. *Sein und Zeit*, pp. 227f., 310.
23. *Stern*, I, p. 33.
24. *Kl. Schriften*, pp. 511f.
25. *Briefe*, p. 597.

But is this still "science" and knowledge of the "thing itself," if that only which falls within the limited horizon of our own accidental range of vision is what is seen and acknowledged?

We too raise this question and so does everybody else who in bewilderment regularly saw in the philosophical publications of the twentieth century the shortcomings of both the philosophical and scientific productions. Thus a want has made itself felt which obviously philosophy cannot supply by its own means. If it is not to give up its new concept again—and how could it do that, as it is only to this concept that it owes its survival beyond that critical stage where it solved its original task?—then support has to be rushed in from somewhere else, especially as far as the question of its scientific character is concerned. It has to retain its new starting point, the subjective, even extremely personal and—more than that—the incomparable self, which is plunged into itself and its viewpoint; and yet it must attain the objectivity of science. Where is to be found that connecting bridge between extreme subjectivity, between—I should like to say—deaf and blind selfhood, and the luminous clearness of infinite objectivity.[26]

Rosenzweig's answer to this is that the bridge between the greatest subjectivity and the greatest objectivity is exclusively formed by the theological concept of revelation, for only man as receiver of revelation has *both* in himself. The philosopher must at the same time be a theologian in order to be capable of understanding eternal truth, both as it is in itself and as truth for us.[27]

In Heidegger, the basis for any inquiry into the objective truth of his viewpoint is eliminated by ontologically formalizing [28] his own concept of "deaf and blind selfhood," so that it often looks as though we were no longer talking about real life, anxieties, and death, but about some pure "existence" in man,[29] the "being mine" which at any time [*Jemeinigkeit*] is mine only in the same sense as the "this-there" [*Dies-da*] [30] in Hegel's dialectic of sensory certainty is a *this*—namely, a formally general one, adequate in any case and at any time. Nevertheless Heidegger, too, feels the need of justifying his presupposition of that being which is "always mine" and his idea of existence. The manner, however, in which he brings this about does not lead out of selfhood, as the understanding of revelation does: it rather incloses this selfhood even more radically within itself, within a *circulus* that Heidegger deprives too rashly of its predicate *vitiosus*. For the question, as he holds, is not how to get out of the circle in which all understanding

26. *Stern*, II, pp. 23f.
27. *Stern*, II, p. 24; III, pp. 172f.
28. Misch, *Lebensphilosophie und Phänomenologie* (1931).
29. *Kant und das Problem der Metaphysik* (1929), §41.
30. Feuerbach, *Grundsätze der Philosophie der Zukunft*, §28.

and thinking is enmeshed, but to get into it in the right way, that is to say, so that whatever is fixed in advance, what neither can nor shall be removed, becomes explicit as such.

The task of a philosophical interpretation of Being is nothing else than to secure the "before-structure" [*Vorstruktur*] of all understanding of existence and thereby ascertaining its fore-having [*Vor-Habe*], its fore-sight [*Vor-sicht*], and its fore-conception [*Vorgriff*].[31] Bluntly expressed, this means that man can do no better than exist as decidedly as possible, wholly actualizing his potentialities by asserting himself in his own proper being. Or as Luther said, "*unus quisque robustus sit in existentia sua,*" i.e., anyone who is strong may be so in his existence. The ontological formulation of the latter is as follows: "Being, for whom its being-in-the-world is a concern about its own being, has an ontologically circular structure." *Dasein* and its understanding of being must move in a circle because it is always "in advance" of itself and in this way alone can it return to itself. In the Introduction to *Being and Time*,[32] existential ontology is said to have "fixed the end of the guideline to all philosophical inquiry at the point from which it *originates* and to which it *returns*," i.e., the *Dasein* of *Being and Time* is in all its temporal "ecstasies," always and only with itself.[33] To use Rosenzweig's words, it is "blind and deaf" to every light that does not burn in its own surroundings and to any voice that is not its own. It is and remains a cave dweller who knows neither the Platonic sun nor the Christian re-birth nor the Jewish vigil for the day of redemption. Thus, the basic concepts of Heidegger and Rosenzweig differ in terms of the above contrast, not in procedure, but in purpose—and to that extent then they differ also in the intention which each chiefly has in mind at the beginning.

II

BOTH HEIDEGGER AND ROSENZWEIG start out with the "facticity" or the "factualness" of one's own *Dasein* as always being there. In this way they deny the starting point which Descartes established, i.e., beginning with an ego or self-consciousness that is emptied of all its empirical reality. The meaning and the being of "I am" does not result from the ego in general but

31. *Sein und Zeit*, pp. 153f., 314ff.
32. *Ibid.*, p. 38.
33. Cf. A. Sternberger, *Der verstandene Tod* (1934).

from the personal pronoun of the first person which I alone always am. *Dasein,* Heidegger says, is always mine and "the mentioning of *Dasein,* in accordance with this character of the 'mineness' of being, must always add the personal pronoun: *I* am, *you* are, . . ." [34] So far Rosenzweig and Heidegger concur. Their paths diverge from one another in regard to the being of the "second" person, or "other," whereby the being of the "first person" then also acquires a different meaning. In his analysis, Heidegger recognizes the second person only in the leveled form of the *other* person, as *my* partner, or as the "thou" belonging to an "I." The *Dasein* that is always my own is defined, of course, as a "being-with" others,[35] but the being of these others is also one that is always my own and in consequence a mere "being-with" with me. It is not a being-with-one-another in which each, by mutually giving and taking, defines the other. The mere togetherness does not alter the fact, which is decisive for Heidegger's entire analysis of existence, that this "also-being-there" of the other does not constitute a reciprocity of behavior. Thus, if the relation [*Verhaltnis*] between two first persons, so to speak, is one-sidedly determined by *my* relation [*Verhalten*] to the second person as an other, then *Dasein* only "meets" itself again despite its "being-with" the other.[36] The "one-sidedness" of Heidegger's analysis cannot be supplemented by completing it with the other side that it lacks, because this one-sidedness is the distinctive quality of Heidegger's philosophical foundation. At best it can only be breached by means of the experience of and insight into the other as an *alter ego* or *secundus,* whose own peculiar being is no less his own and yet completely different, not only from my self, but also from every other, i.e., a "thou" in whom I recognize my own self.[37] A real "thou" is not a second person *among other persons,* but that fellow human being who above all reveals to me that I, myself, am an "I," who—in speaking and answering, in talking and listening —becomes aware of what the other's attitude implies and demands.

Primarily, the meaning of the rightly conceived "thou" is not restricted to the relationship between man and his fellow men. It comes into its own more particularly with regard to God. For it is only through God's calling Adam: "Where art thou?" that his "Here am I" reveals to man, by this answer, his being as related

34. *Sein und Zeit,* §9.
35. *Ibid.,* §26.
36. Cf. Löwith, *Das Individuum in der Rolle des Mitmenschen,* §§9–15.
37. Cf. H. Cohen, *Der Nächste,* ed. M. Buber (1935). Rosenzweig, *Stern,* II, pp. 168f., 190, 196; *Kl. Schriften,* pp. 364, 388.

to God. The ego at the outset is wrapped up in itself; dumbly, it waits for its being called—directly by God and indirectly by a neighbor. A person's ego does not exist as an ego from the very beginning; it requires the call by a second person whom it has to answer. Only then does it become real. Rosenzweig develops these relationships in terms of a "grammatical" interpretation of the biblical story of creation,[38] for *The Star of Redemption* is, in general, an anticipated commentary to his translation of the Book of Genesis.[39] In his interpretation of the story of creation, the "being" that Rosenzweig is concerned with understanding is disclosed first and last not as *mine*, but as *His* "being," i.e., as the being of "the Eternal" by means of which all temporal things exist. Against this view, Heidegger's analysis, despite its starting point in facticity, still moves within the idealistic framework. The latter is true even though Heidegger interprets existentially and concretely the idealistic concept of "productivity," which is the secularization of the theological concept of creation.[40] The *Dasein* of *Being and Time*, which is always "concerned with its own being," is hopelessly confined within the decision to be itself. Neither God nor its fellow man can answer the question of the meaning of being for it.

Since Heidegger defines the existing *Dasein* as "always mine," the world in which it exists is also always *its* world, an "Existenzial," i.e., a being that is of the same sort as I myself. Man is neither "present at hand" like a stone nor "ready at hand" like a tool. He also does not live like a natural creature in a natural world; rather, stones, plants, and animals confront him "in" the world because his own being is an *a priori* "being-in" in which something can confront him. The world is a "constitution of being" and a "structural moment" of *Dasein*. The *Dasein* of man and the *Dasein* of the world is therefore a "unified phenomenon." [41]

There are three things to pay attention to in this characterization of the world as an "Existenzial." First, there is the differentiation between *things* [*Seienden*] which are "ready at hand" in the world and the *being* [*Sein*] of worldliness [*Weltlichkeit*]. Secondly, Heidegger's view is opposed to the understanding of the *Dasein* of both man and the world as something *present to hand* in the world. The second point leads to the third which is that Heidegger's view is opposed to a characterization of the world as *nature*.

38. *Stern*, II, pp. 110–120.
39. *Briefe*, pp. 618f.
40. *Stern*, II, pp. 6of.
41. *Sein und Zeit*, §12, §28.

Nature is but "a limiting case of the being [*Sein*] of things in the world." [42] In fact, the entirety of natural being is of no importance in Heidegger's ontology. It is dissolved, so to speak, in the privative concept of that which is only "present to hand," a concept that includes all things [*Seienden*] that do *not* "exist" and are only "ready at hand." In *Being and Time,* nature has no autonomous existence. Heidegger can, however, answer the objection that this existential conception of the world is unnatural. From Heidegger's standpoint, it is all too natural for *Dasein* to run up against the "present at hand" and "the ready at hand" in providing for its world and in this way to understand itself "unauthentically" in terms of the world. But this self-justification of the existential and ontological analysis does not change the fact that Heidegger's concept of the world is contrary to the natural view of the world. The viewpoint of the natural consciousness finds its naive as well as its lofty expression in the biblical account of creation which relates how man awakens to himself in a world that is already created and "present to hand." Man names everything that exists in this world and by virtue of his naming power becomes the master of all the dumb creatures of the natural world. Heidegger, however, shows the unnaturalness of his concept of the world in that the so-called "unified" phenomenon can only be put together by means of three hyphens (being-in-the-world). But whoever trusts language and thinks in terms of it must become aware that it is no mere accident that language lacks a common word for the *Dasein* of man and the being of the world. The attempt to unify the world and man must presuppose for its success that man also exists by nature and has a human nature which is not essentially different from the nature of all other things. Heidegger's existential ontology of nature is neither able to restore the natural philosophy of the ancients, nor to reject the Christian distinction between the born and the re-born man, authentic and in-authentic *Dasein.* The upshot of this dual impossibility is Heidegger's concept of "worldliness" and "world-time," which are implicitly nourished by the Christian notion of *"saeculum"* that Heidegger's philosophy attempts to secularize, but in vain.

Rosenzweig consciously starts out with the idea that the formative unity of the Greek cosmos, together with the Greek myth, has been destroyed since the appearance of Christianity and Judaism in world history. The first volume of *The Star of Re-*

42. *Ibid.,* p. 65; concerning the concept of life, §10, §49, pp. 240f.; *Wesen des Grundes,* p. 95 n.

demption contains a pagan philosophy which attempts to show that the truth of the pagan world is of course an enduring truth, but unrevealing. It is "everlasting" only as an "element." [43] The place of the ancient cosmical order is taken over by the new order of creation in which man and the world belong together only as a creation of God. What keeps both together is no more and no less than an "and," but not in the sense of an idealistic synthesis that claims to be productive. [44] No matter how deeply it goes, again and again experience discovers in man only what is human, in the world only what is worldly, and in God only what is godly, but only in God what is godly, only in the world what is worldly, and only in man what is human. Experience refutes the continuity of man with the natural world, of the world with the spiritual life of man, and of God with both the world and man.

It is on the basis of the above that the first volume of *The Star of Redemption* attempts to show nothing other than the impossibility of tracing these three basic concepts back to one another. God, man, and the world are absolutely autonomous—the one from eternity to eternity and the others since their creation. They have a connection only because the one and eternal God created heaven and earth for the sake of man, revealed His own likeness to man, and will redeem both at the end of time. [45] God, man, and the world then are not "actually" different from what they appear to be in the immediacy of experience. [46] On the contrary, they are as experience shows them to be and not otherwise: God and man and the world are distinct and yet connected to one another, but not forced into a unity by means of such hyphens as we find in the phrase "being-in-the-world," and not without a beginning in a creation.

Correspondingly, all the remaining concepts are different from these fundamental concepts of God, man, and the world. The existence existing by mere contingency and potentiality of *Being and Time* corresponds to the *creation and redemption* of *The Star of Redemption;* the *freedom towards death* to the *certainty of eternal life;* the *being-momentarily for its time* to the *always being prepared for the coming of the kingdom at the end of time.* The thesis, "I myself am time" parallels the proposition that God's time is from eternity to eternity and therefore timeless. And the *temporal truth* of finite existence corresponds to the *eternal truth*

43. *Kl. Schriften,* pp. 381ff.
44. *Stern,* I. p. 183.
45. *Kl. Schriften,* p. 379.
46. *Ibid.,* pp. 377f., 395.

of *The Star of Redemption*.[47] Finally, as a decisive mark of distinction, there is the contrast between Heidegger's concept of "freedom towards death" and Rosenzweig's notion of "eternal life." Both point to the truth of existence and are thus expected to "manifest" and "prove themselves." [48]

Since Heidegger presupposes death as the "highest instance" of man's potential being, the relation to it becomes the most significant point of his entire ontology.[49] The "projection of an authentic being towards death" [50] leaves no doubt that being towards death as the "most intimate" and therefore also the "most authentic" possibility of our being must be the key to the discovery of the finite truth about *Dasein*. In contradistinction to the anonymous "one" which only occasionally fears death and does not possess the "courage to be anxious" in the face of death, the self that is always mine is freed from those illusions by means of which one usually conceals the uncertain but nevertheless definite impendence of death. Death is uncertain in its "when" but definite in its "that." Death as a *possibility* must be endured because the reality of the after-life or dying cannot be a question about existence, i.e., my *potential* being. Man should not wait until someday he has to die but he should *live ahead of time*, permanently and independently, in the face of this "extreme" possibility in the finite potentiality of his being. *Dasein* is opened up to its most extreme possibility because it is projected with resolution into death and in this way anticipates the end that is always there. Death as the extreme end is an "insurpassable" possibility, for its anticipation implies, by virtue of the definiteness of the anticipated death, the dropping of all preliminary and provisional matters. Only when facing death is the being of existence clearly at stake. The most genuine, extreme, and insurpassable possibility is, thus, also an "absolute" one, because the "being toward death" rids us of all kinds of solicitude and concern which otherwise would have been our support. The being toward death, or even more concretely, the fear of death, insulates man completely. But it is this very withdrawal into and anticipation of oneself by which the "potentiality in its entireness" [*Ganz-sein-können*] is proved.

At the end, however, Heidegger asks himself whether this ontological possibility of existing "entirely" by projecting ahead to the end does not remain a fantastic demand—unless there cor-

47. *Sein und Zeit*, §44; *Stern*, II, pp. 212ff.; III, pp. 155ff.
48. *Sein und Zeit*, §54ff.; *Stern*, III, p. 172; *Kl. Schriften*, pp. 395ff.
49. *Sein und Zeit*, p. 313.
50. *Ibid.*, §53. For criticism see A. Sternberger, *l.c.*

responds to it an ontic, actual capability manifested by the existence itself. But where and how does it manifest itself? The naive reader will involuntarily expect the actual manifestation of the "freedom toward death," displayed by Heidegger in italics, to be nothing but voluntary death or suicide, which in fact is established as the most extreme possibility of human existence. This expectation seems to be justified by Heidegger's characterizing the extreme possibility also as self-abandonment [51] and by his quoting a sentence of Nietzsche's *Zarathustra*, the chapter "On Free Death," which demands that one be able to die voluntarily "at the proper time." "Free to die and free in death, a holy denier when there is no longer the time for a Yea, thus being at home in life and death." To die in this way, that is to say, by ending freely the term of one's life on the climax of one's victories, is the best thing, while the second best is to die in battle and to waste generously a great soul.[52]

The expectation that Heidegger, too, may justify the freedom to real self-immolation by the freedom toward death is, however, bound to be thoroughly disappointed. The announced manifestation of the being-toward-death by no means changes the "possibility" as to how existential death must be construed [53] in reality: everything remains as it was—in the stage of possibility and thus of being-in-the-world. The existential manifestation is to be brought about through the formal structure of consciousness.[54] This, in turn, is made subject to an ontological interpretation, although the claim is made that the question of the totality of potential Being is one of actual existence and, therefore, is answered by a resoluteness which is surely actual. However, this inconsistency is delusive, for the anticipatory resoluteness lacks a definite aim! Upon what existence actually resolves remains an open question and undecided; for only when a decision is in the making is the necessary vagueness of its "for what" replaced by a definite aim.[55] To make up one's mind depends on the actual possibilities of the historical situations.[56] Hence, Heidegger refuses to be positive or even authoritative as to existential liabilities.[57] The resolve shall constantly be kept open to the whole being *"in posse"* which in-

51. *Ibid.*, p. 264. Cf. Sternberger, *l.c.*, pp. 111, 117.
52. Cf. Heidegger's lecture on "What Is Metaphysics?" (1929), p. 23, where it is similarly said that existence attains to its "ultimate greatness" by wasting itself heroically.
53. *Sein und Zeit*, p. 261.
54. *Ibid.*, §54.
55. *Ibid.*, p. 298.
56. *Ibid.*
57. *Ibid.*, pp. 248f., 312.

cludes the potential taking back of a certain decision.[58] The resolve thus does not come to any conclusion; it is a constant attitude, formal, like the categorical imperative, and through its formality open to any material determination, provided that it is radical. Suicide, however, does not even remain an open possibility: it is explicitly dismissed,[59] for it would terminate once and for all the possibility of a constant anticipation of a final reality.

But because *Dasein* possesses the inherent possibility to take its own life, it can only live authentically insofar as it consciously "takes over" its own facticity. The *Dasein* that has decided takes over the "hollow ground of its nothingness," along with the thrown freedom of the projection, i.e., its guilt, of which the call of conscience makes it aware.[60] The resolute *Dasein* takes over the "nothing," i.e., the fact that it has *not* brought itself into existence and has *not* established the foundation of its own being. It takes over and is "responsible to" its own *Dasein*. This self-appropriation, self-responsibility, and self-perpetuation brings out the irreligious import of Heidegger's concept of *Dasein* that acknowledges neither creation nor redemption.[61] But facticity remains as the stumbling-block to this will to self-determination, or to use the words of Nietzsche, it is the "it was," the *factum brutum* that I am always *already* in existence and am not the cause [*Schuld*] of my own existence.[62]

But why must *Dasein* be at all? How can Heidegger say that it exists and "has to be," [63] especially when he simultaneously establishes that essentially *Dasein* is a burden? [64] The question must be raised as to why *Dasein* should not be able freely to dispense with this burden, as all pagan philosophy allowed, and as the Stoics in particular not only taught but also practiced as the ultimate wisdom. Why does Heidegger not consider this possibility that is really attested to in *Dasein,* i.e., putting an end to its own existence? Is not the "anticipation" something that is provisional and something that can be overcome by a decision to take the life of which one is not the source?

Heidegger himself cannot give us any answer to this question, but an answer can be found in the hidden history of his concepts.

58. *Ibid.,* pp. 308, 391.
59. *Ibid.,* p. 261.
60. *Ibid.,* §§55 to 60. Heidegger uses the term guilt in the formalized sense of being the cause of some deficiency, or "nothing."
61. *Ibid.,* pp. 264, 305, 339; 42, 135; 383ff.
62. Cf. Nietzsche's *Zarathustra,* II, chapter "On Redemption."
63. *Sein und Zeit,* pp. 134, 276.
64. *Ibid.,* pp. 134, 284.

All of them originated in the *Christian* tradition, however much death, conscience, guilt, care, anxiety, and corruption are formalized ontologically and neutralized as concepts of *the Dasein*. The origin of these essential concepts of existence in Christian theology prevents Heidegger from freely acknowledging what is the real freedom towards death, i.e., the freedom towards death as it would have to be for a *Dasein* which makes itself independent and recognizes no higher court than its own death. Just as it is obvious to a believing Christian that as a creature of God he cannot take his own life,[65] it must be just as natural for a "thrown existence" that it can put an end to the burden of *Dasein*. If the author of *Being and Time* were not a godless theologian, whose ontology arose from theology in two senses, then it would be impossible to see what could prevent him from drawing stoical consequences out of the freedom to nothing as well as to being. Instead of doing the latter, he takes a fundamentally ambiguous position in regard to Christian theology.[66] He places upon it the burden of finding the existential analysis, for example, of "guilt," the "ontological condition" of the factical possibility of the state of corruption (*status corruptionis*).[67] R. Bultmann, the Protestant theologian, accepted in good faith this double-edged offer of a "philosophical pre-understanding." But Bultmann was able to do this only because Heidegger had already met theology halfway with a theological preunderstanding. Heidegger's entanglement of death, guilt, and conscience in a *Dasein* responsible to itself alone, uproots these concepts from their Christian source, but for that very reason they are dependent upon that origin.

In one passage only, the basically anti-Christian significance of this self-appropriation emerges clearly, i.e., where Heidegger speaks about the possibility of a "skeptic" who quite seriously makes the cognitive claim that it is not at all evident why there must be truth or even *Dasein*. Is any human *Dasein* ever asked whether it wants to exist at all? [68] Precisely because it is not asked, it can negate this basic presupposition of its *Dasein* in the "despair of suicide" that together with *Dasein* blots out both truth and untruth. "Just as little as it has been proven that there are 'eternal truths,' so little has it been proven that there never has been a 'real' skeptic. Those who attempt to refute skepticism basically

65. Thus Kant is his lecture on ethics (ed. Menzer 1924, pp. 185ff.), cf. *Grundlegung zur Metaphysik der Sitten* (*Reclam*), pp. 56, 65ff.

66. Cf. Löwith, essays in *Theologische Rundschau* (1930), No. 5; and *Zeitschrift fur theologie und Kirche* (1930), No. 5.

67. *Sein und Zeit*, pp. 306, 180.

68. *Ibid.*, pp. 228f., 284.

believe the latter despite their own arguments. This has been per-haps more often the case than the harmless attempts at a formal-istic-dialectical overthrow would care to suggest." [69] In principle, the "skeptic" is right because the necessity of a factical chance, such as there is in the case of *Dasein*, can never be proved. *Dasein* can of course catch up with its "there" through the return of anticipation, but it "must" only appropriate itself so long as and insofar as it assumes its own being. The assertion that it has "to be" does not at all mean, therefore, a *necessity* of being, but only a *potentiality* of being. It can just as well be as not be because it is always already there whether it wants to be or not. Hence, the having-to-be does not exclude but includes the fact that a real skeptic can actually "contradict himself." The Heidegger of *Being and Time*, however, is no skeptic but a godless "Christian theologian." Therefore, suicide for Heidegger is neither sin nor freedom, but an act of "despair." Suicide is not a case of dying at the proper time, as Nietzsche taught, in accordance with the classical model, but in the style of an anti-Christian sermon.

In contrast to this existential ambiguity in the concept of freedom towards death, which neither affirms nor denies suicide, Rosenzweig, in *The Star of Redemption*, clearly distinguishes be-tween anxiety in the face of actually dying and the act of suicide. In this way, he avoids the highly questionable separation of being-towards-death and natural death. For Rosenzweig, suicide is sim-ply unnatural because it is contrary to the nature of life to kill oneself, whereas death in the sense of dying is a part of life.

The awful ability to commit suicide distinguishes man from all other crea-tures, both those we know of and do not know of. Suicide characterizes precisely the departure from all that is natural. It is of course necessary that man separate himself in this way at least once in his lifetime. At least once he must have stood face to face with nothingness all night long. But the earth calls him back again. He cannot drink to the bottom the brown liquid of that night. There is another way out of the narrow pass of nothing-ness laid out for him. He does not have to plunge into the gaping abyss.[70]

The true way out of the narrow pass of nothingness is not, for Rosenzweig, a simple resolution to accept one's factical *Dasein*. Instead, the way out lies in the recognition that one is but a crea-ture and this can be accomplished by means of an openness to-wards revelation and the promise of eternity. This *way out* refers

69. *Ibid.*, p. 229.
70. Cf. Kierkegaard: "That God could create over against Himself free beings, is the cross which philosophy was unable to bear, but upon which having caught it hangs."

first of all, of course, to the Jewish people as the chosen race of God, whose name is "the Eternal." [71] The "wandering Jew" is not an invention of the Christian and anti-Semitic world, but a phenomenon of world history which contradicts all other experiences of the power of time. The authentic Jew can, in fact, say of himself "we" and continue with "are eternal" because the Jewish people, as God commanded and promised them, are made eternal through the natural procreation of the succession of generations.[72] In this way, the descendants attest to the faith of their ancestors. For the Jew, the belief in his own eternity is identical with belief in his God, because he knows that he is one of God's people. His faith, unlike that of the Christian, is not the content of a tradition based upon testimony, but the "product of a procreation."

Whoever is born a Jew bears witness to his faith because he continues the line of the eternal people. He does not believe in something but he *is* that belief itself in all its immediacy, something which no believing Christian can ever manage to be.[73]

Hence—in the community of peoples—one can only *be* or not be a Jew. The Christian, on the other hand, must *become* a Christian —as an individual.

Before they were even born, the being-a-Christian was taken away from them by the birth of Christ. The opposite is the case with the Jews. The Jew must possess the being of the Jew from birth on and carry it with him, because the possibility of *becoming* a Jew was taken away from him in past ages and the revealed history of his people.[74]

The Christian is originally, or at least by virtue of his birth, a pagan. The Jew, however, is only a Jew. Hence, the way of the Christian continually consists in freeing himself from his racial ties, whereas the life of the Jew leads him deeper and deeper into the line of his descent. Christianity is essentially a missionary activity [75] and must spread in order to maintain its existence in the world. Judaism, in contrast, lives always and only upon its own "remains" and maintains itself through its isolation from other peoples.[76] Through this believing community of blood, the Jew has at every moment of his historical miseries the guarantee that he is already "eternal" in the present.

71. *Stern*, I, p. 8.
72. Cf. Rosenzweig's essay on this in *Kl. Schriften*, pp. 182ff.
73. *Stern*, II, pp. 212f.; III, pp. 48f.; *Kl. Schriften*, p. 348; *Briefe*, p. 682.
74. *Stern*, III, p. 105.
75. *Ibid.*, p. 176.
76. *Ibid.*, p. 104.

Every other community, every one that cannot propagate itself by means of a blood relationship must, if it wants to perpetuate its "we" for all eternity, do it in such a way that it is assured a place in the future. Every bloodless eternity, so to speak, is founded upon will and hope. Only the community of blood already feels the guarantee of its eternity flow through its veins in the present. For this sort of community alone time is not an enemy that has to be subdued, that the community may conquer but also perhaps may not . . . it is instead a child and the offspring of a child. What is the future for other communities . . . is . . . for it alone already the present. The future is not something strange for the community of blood but a possession, something it carries in its own womb and can bring forth at any time. Whereas every other community which makes a claim upon eternity must make arrangements to pass the torch of the present on into the future, the community of blood alone has no need for such traditional arrangements. It does not have to trouble itself about the spirit. It has the guarantee of eternity in the natural perpetuation of the body.[77]

The blood, to which Rosenzweig refers above, is not that of a national ideology, but that of the "seed of Abraham" to whom God promised the future. It is a blood that from its very beginning is determined by a belief.

The peoples of the world cannot be satisfied through a community of blood. They must strike their roots in the night of . . . the earth and receive from its lastingness the guarantee of their own lastingness. Their will to be eternal is fastened upon the soil and its dominion, the region. The blood of their sons flows over the earth of the homeland. They place no trust in a living community of blood that would not be anchored in the firm foundation of earth. We alone put our trust in blood and left the land behind. Hence, the saga of the eternal people, in contrast to that of other peoples, does not begin with autocthony. He is earth-born and even *he* exists only in the body, being merely the father of mankind; but the ancestor of Israel emigrated because of the divine command that he should leave the land of his birth and go into a land that God would show to him. With this divine command the history of the Jew begins, as it is told in the sacred books. This people became a people through its Egyptian and afterwards its Babylonian exile, in the dawn of its primitive history as well as in the clear light of its later history. But the native land to which the life of a people becomes accustomed and into which it ploughs itself, so to speak, until it has almost forgotten that to be a people means more than to live in a certain country, is not the sense in which the eternal people will ever have a native land. . . . The eternal people only possesses a land as a land of its longing, the Holy Land. And it is for this very reason, again in sharp contrast with all the other peoples of the world, that the complete possession of a native land is disputed even when the people are at home. This people is only a stranger and a squatter in His land. God says to this people, "The land is mine." The holiness of

77. *Ibid.*, pp. 192f.; *Briefe*, p. 200.

the land kept it from being seized outright so long as the people could seize it. In turn, the holiness intensified the longing for what had been lost and at the same time prevented the people from feeling at home in any other land. This holiness then forced them to concentrate the full power of their will to be a people upon one aspect which for the other peoples of the world is but one among many others. This one aspect becomes for them the authentic and pure core of living: the community of blood. The will to be a people must not fasten upon a lifeless medium. It must be realized through the people alone. . . .[78]

The language of this one outstanding people preserved itself in the same way as its life; it remained eternally the same and did not undergo the living changes that the languages of other peoples did. All over the world the Jewish people speak the language of the people among whom they live like guests. For a long time, their own language has not been the language of their everyday life, but nonetheless it is not dead. It endures as the sacred language, but is only used in prayer and in worship. The Jew speaks one language with God and another one with his fellow men. Similarly, the sacred law (Torah) and the customs do not change. These, too, remain the same and have set the Jew apart from the time and history of all the other peoples of the world.

There are no lawgivers here who improve upon the law over the actual course of time. Even what is perhaps empirically an innovation must always appear as if it were already present in the eternal law and a part of revelation. Therefore, the chronology of the people cannot be the calculation of its own time, for the people is timeless, it has no time. Instead, it must count the years in accordance with the years of the world. And again . . . we see here in regard to their history the same relation that we previously saw in the case of its land and its language: how the people is denied a temporal existence on account of its eternal existence. It cannot live fully and creatively within the historical life of the other peoples of the world. It stands somewhere between the worldly and the holy, separated from both by one or the other from time to time. Finally, then, it is not alive like all other peoples. It is not situated in some visible place in the world with its own national way of life, with a national language that expresses its own spirit, in a definite national region of the world that is founded upon and delimited by the earth. It lives instead solely and simply in that which assures the perpetuation of the people in time, the immortality of its existence. It creates its own eternity out of the secret sources of the blood. But for this reason, namely, that it only puts its trust in its self-created eternity and in nothing else in the world, this people also really believes in its eternity. The other peoples of the world, however, are all basically similar as individual men

78. *Stern*, III, p. 49.

who must reckon with their own death at any time, no matter how far off that time may be. Even the love of its own people is heavily laden with this anticipation of death. Love is only thoroughly joyful towards mortal things. And the final secret of this joyfulness is disclosed only in the bitterness of death. Hence, the other peoples of the world can foresee a time when their land with its mountains and rivers will stand as it does today under the same sky but different people will live in the land. Their languages will be buried and their customs and laws will have lost their living power. We alone are unable to imagine such a time. Everything in which the other peoples of the world anchor their existence was stolen from us a long time ago. Land, language, custom and law are things that for a long time have been separated from the circle of the living and elevated for us from the earthly to the level of the holy. But we still live and live eternally. Our life is no longer intertwined with anything external. We struck roots in ourselves. Rootless upon the earth and therefore eternal wanderers, we became deeply rooted in ourselves, in our own body and blood. The guarantee of our eternity is that we have taken root in ourselves and in ourselves alone.[79]

The temporality of human existence does not mean for the Jewish people a life and death struggle with the historical fate of the world, but a wandering and a waiting which at every moment anticipates a completion. It does not know genuine growth and decay. The entire history of the world, of states, of wars, and of revolutions does not have the seriousness and importance for the Jew that it has for other peoples. Eternity is at all times present for the "people of God," whereas the other peoples require the state, its laws, and its power in order to preserve time for a period of time and assure itself of a relatively lasting permanence.[80] However, the people of Israel look unperturbed beyond the world and history to their own eternal purpose which is as present as it is distant.[81]

The eternal people sit undisturbed and untouched year in and year out around the root of their eternal life, despite the hours of eternity which the state with a sharp sword carves into the epochs of world history and into the bark of the growing tree of time. The force of world-history is broken by this calm life that does not even once glance sideways. Though it may always be asserted again and again that the newest eternity is the truest, we always oppose all such assertions with the peaceful, dumb image of our *Dasein* that forces both those who want to see, as well as those who do not want to see, to recognize that eternity is not whatever is newest. The arm of power may only force the newest into a unity with the last that is considered

79. *Ibid.*, pp. 49ff. Cf. *Briefe*, pp. 326, 335f., 686.
80. *Stern*, III, pp. 56f.; cf. *Briefe*, p. 270; Hegel, in *Theolog. Jugendschriften*, pp. 243ff., interprets the same peculiarities of Judaism, but from the viewpoint of Hellenism. He gave, therefore, a different evaluation.
81. *Stern*, III, pp. 91ff.

the most novel eternity. But that is still not the reconciliation of the latest grandson with the oldest ancestor. This true eternity of life, the turning of the hearts of fathers towards the children, is again and again displayed before the peoples of the world through our *Dasein*, at which they stare dumbly. Would that the worldly, all too worldly, apparent eternity of their world-historical moments that are made into states could prove them to be wrong. The course of world-history, so long as the kingdom of God is still to come, is reconciled always only with the creation in itself, the next moment is always only reconciled with the previous one. However, the creation itself as a totality is held together solely by means of the redemption in all time, so long as a redemption is still to come, through that eternal people which has been isolated from all the history of the world.[82]

Death as the unconditional end of our own potential being is a sort of substitute for eternity in Heidegger's *Being and Time*.[83] For Heidegger, death is the only thing that is certain ahead of time, absolutely permanent and eternal, a *nunc stans* against which temporality is shipwrecked and all care and provision ceases. However, at the same time, the prevision of death is the hidden motive of all *historicity* which belongs to the substance of existence. Through being-towards-death, existence receives the authentic energy and decisiveness that it uses to become engaged in something and become open to its fate. This grounding of historicality on the basis of finitude is in harmony with Rosenzweig's view that the genuinely historical peoples of the world reckon with death essentially and in anticipation of their own end become more firmly rooted in their earthly *Dasein*.

The boldness with which Heidegger has explained the fundamental connection of being-towards-death with the actual events of temporal *Dasein*, its fate and destiny in regard to the decisive "moment," [84] should at the same time illuminate in a concrete way, along with the temporality of the *Dasein* that is always mine, the world-moments of world-history and our age. Heidegger says in *Being and Time* that "historical" [*geschichtlich*] does not refer to the past as something that is no longer present; it refers instead to the past as the antiquity that is still present, the former world of a former *Dasein*. This past exists historically *a priori* insofar as it is basically a temporal being that exists towards its own final end. As an existence that is thrown into a temporal *Dasein*, it takes over at the same time its factical in-

82. Cf. *Briefe*, pp. 73, 123, and 209, where Rosenzweig tells why he did not deem 1914 an epochal year for himself.

83. *Stern*, III, p. 95.

84. Cf. A. Sternberger, *Der verstandene Tod, l.c.*

heritance along with its facticity. And the more openly man exists, the more decisively he would choose and would hand down the traditional possibilities of his historical inheritance. To the extent that *Dasein*, free towards death, takes over a traditional but nonetheless chosen possibility, it is brought into the simplicity of its own fate. Simultaneously, its fate is a general destiny because *Dasein* exists in the common world of the people as being-in-the-world and being-with-the-other among others. *Dasein* is world-historical because it first of all must be understood in terms of a public and social world. Its factical inheritance, as explicitly handed down, is *Dasein* when it repeats the possibilities of its existent past in the decisiveness that it is anticipating. The repetition does not bring the past back again unchanged, but responds to the possibilities of a past existence for the present moment, insofar as the repetition at the same time subjects to criticism the "today" that is merely consumed by the past in the light of a standard for what is possible in the future. But neither the critical view of the present nor the conservative glance backwards to the past, nor the vision of possibilities in the future, determines real historicity. Instead, these external references to the course of time first become *existential* and fateful when the self-assimilation of past possibilities towards the death that is anticipated leads to the *there of the moment* or the *historical situation* that crops up from time to time.[85] There is a historical situation, in contrast to an external situation, only for those who are decisive and encounter both the "accidental" and the necessary. The decisive person does not merely imagine a situation to himself but is engaged in the situation. The last word on the analysis of temporality or historicity [86] is "being present for its time," or "the decision within the world-historical situation." [87]

The finitude of temporality and together with it historicity cannot be affirmed more resolutely at the expense of eternity than it is by the author of *Being and Time*.[88] Even the inverted commas in which his "time" are set, in order to point out that it does not mean "today" in the "vulgar" sense of the word, do not imply any

85. It is an open question whether Rosenzweig's characterization of the eternal unhistoricalness of the Jewish people is not more or less applicable to all "oriental" peoples as far as they have not become Westernized.

86. *Sein und Zeit*, §§72–75.

87. *Ibid.*, pp. 299ff. As to the notion of "situation" see also K. Jaspers, *Die geistige Situation der Zeit* (1932).

88. *Sein und Zeit*, p. 385; cf. pp. 383f., 299f., 391.

limitation on a complete readiness towards temporal and historical existence as it is accidentally determined for Heidegger through Europe and Germany.

In 1933, when a decisive "moment" was present in Germany, Heidegger became decisively engaged in a world-historical situation. He took over the leadership of the University of Freiburg and equated the *Dasein* of *Being and Time* with the "German" *Dasein*. This political "engagement" in the factual events of the time, which of late is continually referred to as the "atomic age," was not a deviation from *Being and Time*, as the naive suppose. It was a consequence of Heidegger's concept of human *Dasein* as a temporal and historical existence that only recognizes temporal truths relative to its own *Dasein* and its potential being. Heidegger inadvertently deserves credit for the fact that his radical temporalization of truth and existence renewed and brought attention to the importance of a question that his Jewish contemporaries raised, the question concerning eternal being— the eternal God or the world that always exists without beginning and without end. Finally, it should be noted that in the scanty critical confrontations with Heidegger's work, this question about time is ignored as if his work were a discussion of the ontological difference between *entity* and *Being* rather than of *Being* and *time*.

[III] CONCLUSION

HEIDEGGER DESTROYED the Greek and Christian tradition that had been accepted up to the time of Hegel and for which true Being is always existent and everlasting. He destroyed it to the extent that he shows the "meaning" of Being to be finite time and eternity to be an illusion. In contrast to Heidegger, Rosenzweig was able to affirm the Star of David as the eternal truth within the limits of time, from what was a more fortunate position due to *his* factical inheritance, his Jewry and his conscious return to it. For Rosenzweig, the God who as Creator and Redeemer is present at both the beginning and end of his analysis of time is neither "dead" nor "alive" but "truth" and "light."

God is the truth. Truth is His seal by which He is recognized, even if at some time everything by means of which he made His eternity known in time, all eternal life and all of the eternal way, came to an end at that point where everything eternal also ends: in eternity. For it is not just the way that ends here, but life also. Eternal life lasts only so long as life in general lasts.

There is only eternal life in opposition to what is always only temporal life, the maker of the eternal way. The demand for eternity, whose longing can be heard from the caves of temporality, takes on the form of a longing for eternal life but only because it itself is temporal life. In fact, in the truth life also disappears. It does not become a delusion . . . , but it opens up to the light. It is transformed. If it were transformed, however, then the transformed would no longer exist. Life would ascend to the light. . . .[89]

At the end of his book on redemption, Rosenzweig speaks about this vision of the spiritual light.[90] The latter occurs at the conclusion of the book with a discussion about the books on creation as being "the everlasting foundation of things" and revelation as being the "eternally renewed birth of the soul" along with the "eternal future of the kingdom."

In 1931, in a lecture on the essence of truth, Heidegger transposed the biblical sentence that only the truth shall make us free [91] into the sentence that only freedom shall make us true. It is not possible to answer Heidegger with the sort of "eternal truth" that two plus two equals four, or that "values" are eternally valid. In the case of Heidegger, his challenge can only be answered when, for us as for Rosenzweig, it would be clearly established that once and for all there are only three possible answers to the question: who are you? These three possible answers are: pagan or Jew or Christian.[92] These alternatives, however, assume that man is essentially a historical existence. The pagan is only a "pagan" and therefore a pre-Christian possibility of historical existence when he is understood in terms of Judaism and Christianity. Jews and Christians, then, are that which they consider themselves to be only if the common nature of man is disregarded. There can only be eternal truths about the world and man if there is an always similar nature for all beings, e.g., an eternal coming and going. Rosenzweig's question about the "eternal," or that which always exists, continues to be *a question* for those who are not believing Jews, pious pagans, or Christians only in the way that one is German or French. However, where the attempt is seriously made within the limits of modernity to put eternity—be that in the sense of the physical universe or the God of the Bible—back into the life of man, it is condemned to failure. Both Kierkegaard's "eternal moment" and his religious

89. *Stern*, III, p. 155.
90. *Stern*, II, p. 213.
91. It was inscribed in large letters above the entrance of Freiburg University.
92. *Kl. Schriften*, p. 475; cf. E. Peterson, *Die Kirche aus Juden und Heiden* (1933).

discourse on the "immutability of God," [93] as well as Nietzsche's anti-Christian paradox of the "eternal recurrence" arose from the insight that we need eternity to be able to endure time.[94] But it is not directly the eternity at which they aimed that is convincing, but rather the critique of time with which they started. Something so old and yet always so new as eternity cannot easily be revived again, even with the most modern techniques.

Heidegger and Rosenzweig inclose both time and eternity because of the seriousness with which they give extreme answers to radical questions. But a seriousness that incloses is no longer either philosophical or free. For who is to tell us then that the questions about our own temporal and historical existence in general—be they religious or irreligious—must be answerable? Only those who are too weak to resist apodictic pronouncements will find the answer that Heidegger and Rosenzweig give about eternity and time an either-or about which a choice must be made in order to reach a decision. In fact, the views of both men result from the pressure of an age that advocates extremes which create conflict in the inquiring mind. But the mind is only inquiring insofar as and so long as it maintains a skeptical attitude towards the limits of the knowable. "Skepticism" is the philosophical position which, instead of proposing extreme questions that are necessarily aimed at dogmatic solutions, sets forth the *problems as problems* clearly and upholds their problematic character—without giving in to hasty solutions. The skeptic is the only intellectual, i.e., literally the judicious man and the precise investigator (*skeptomai*), who still believes that one may both know something and yet could not know it.

What man can know is not that there are timeless truths that refer to the world of which man is also a part, but that there is—in contradistinction to the different historical situations of a certain age—something everlasting which holds good for all time because it is the true. What *always* exists is not timeless; what always remains the *same* is not temporal.

93. *Works, V.,* pp. 78ff.; VII, p. 48; and "Über die Geduld und die Erwartung des Ewigen," *Religöse Reden,* translated by Th. Haecker (1938).

94. In the preface to the concept of the "unique individual," Kierkegaard worded this necessity both briefly and clearly; he begins by stating: "In these times [1848] everything is politics," and ends: "What the time demands," i.e., social reforms and a new political order, "is the contrary of what it needs, to wit something positively stable." The misfortune of the age is that it insists on the temporal and holds that it can dispense with eternity (*Angriff,* p. 458; cf. pp. 15f.). In like manner, Nietzsche bases his will to eternity on the inversion of that nihilism which says that everything is "in vain." Cf. K. Löwith, *Nietzsches Philosophie der ewigen Wiederkehr des Gleichen* (1935), and *Von Hegel bis Nietzsche* (1941).

5 / Man's Self-Alienation in the Early Writings of Marx

I

THE SPECIFIC CONCEPT that Marx uses in his analysis of the bourgeois-capitalist world is that of "human self-alienation," which expresses itself in the political economy as the "anatomy" of the bourgeoisie. "Political economy" includes, for Marx, man's economic existence as well as his human consciousness of it. Marx considers the material conditions of production to be the "skeleton" of society, and thus he transfers the emphasis from Hegel's "bourgeois society" to the "system of needs" as such. At the same time, Marx's idea implies the specifically "materialist" thesis that the material conditions of life are of fundamental significance for all other conditions. This eventually led to the vulgar Marxist thesis: that the so-called material "basis" is the foundation on which, as on an independent stratum, the super-structure is to rise; this superstructure must therefore be interpreted ideologically as derived from the "foundation." It was chiefly in this vulgarized form that Marxist doctrine became subject to criticism. However strongly Marx himself supported this interpretation—and Engels did so even more strongly—the fact remains that Marx had come to terms with philosophy before his criticism of political economy began to be dominant in his thinking.

In this respect, Marx's development can be summed up as follows: at first he criticized religion philosophically, then he criticized religion, philosophy, politics, and all other ideologies economically. According to Marx's own words, however, the economic interpretation of all manifestations of human life was but the "last result" into which his critical revision of Hegel's metaphysical and political philosophy developed—in Hegel's words, "a corpse which has left behind its living impulse." To rediscover this living impulse contained in Marx's analysis of man's self-alienation, we must turn from *Capital* to Marx's early philosophical writings; we can find, for example, the "living impulse" from which the first chapter of *Capital* resulted, in 1867, expressed as early as 1842 in a discussion of a theft of lumber, published in the *Rheinische Zeitung*.

The original form of Marx's critical analysis of the capitalist process of production is his analysis of the bourgeois world, which is characterized by the alienation of man from himself. To Marx, as a Hegelian, the bourgeois-capitalist world represents a specifically "irrational" reality and a world that for rational man is inhuman, perverted, and dehumanized. In the preface to his doctoral thesis and in a letter to Ruge in 1843, Marx called himself an "idealist" who had the "impertinence" to try "to make man a human being." Therefore we have first to show that man as such was Marx's primary concern and that this remained true even after his discovery of the "new" man in the proletarian. For what Marx ultimately aimed at was a "human" emancipation of man, not merely a legal one—that is, at "real humanism."

Among the German philosophers who were Marx's contemporaries, the tendency to consider man as such was basic with Feuerbach, in the latter's attempt to transform philosophy as metaphysics into philosophy as anthropology. To Feuerbach, Hegel's philosophy of the absolute spirit was the last realization of pure philosophy; and in opposition to Hegel's view, Feuerbach, like Marx, developed a critical study of man as man. Man as such does not play a principal role in Hegel's philosophy of the absolute, objective, and subjective spirit; he defines man's universal "essence" as "spirit" and as "self-consciousness" (*Encyclopedia of the Philosophical Sciences*, 377). In Hegel's social and political philosophy, man appears as "man" only under the title of a "subject of material needs," the "system" of which Hegel comprehends as bourgeois society. Therefore, when Hegel speaks of "man," he has in mind exclusively the "bourgeois" as the subject of material economic needs.

Neither Hegel nor Marx hold that in this determination man embodies his universal essence. He is a mere particularity—for Hegel, in relation to the universality of the ethical state; for Marx, in relation to the universality of a classless society. In his *Philosophy of Right* (§190) Hegel makes the following distinction:

In abstract right, what we had before us was the person; in the sphere of morality, the subject; in civil society as a whole, the burgher or bourgeois. Here on the level of needs what we have before us is the concrete idea which we call man. Thus, this is the first time, and indeed properly the only time, to speak of man in this sense.

It is true that Hegel did not completely dismiss the universal concept of man; but he acknowledged it only with regard to man as the subject of "civil rights and economy." This clearly shows Hegel's outstanding realism with regard to man's contemporary reality. He says that every man is first of all "man as such," regardless of his race, nationality, creed, social status, or profession (§209 and note to §270). He counts as man "by virtue of his manhood alone," and this—to be human—is by no means "a mere superficial abstract quality." Nevertheless, according to Hegel, the pith of this universal quality is the fact that only the recognition of civil rights creates self-respect in individuals who feel that they belong to bourgeois society and possess legal rights in it as persons. This specific kind of civic humanity, Hegel says, is "the root from which the desired equalization in the ways of thinking and disposition comes into being." He guards himself explicitly against absolutizing this determination of man as man. It is true that every man, in so far as he is valued as man at all (and not simply as an Italian or a German, a Catholic or a Protestant), is equal to every other man. But his self-consciousness—that is, his consciousness of being nothing but man—would become defective if it were crystallized in this way (as cosmopolitanism, for example) and thus were opposed to public life in the state as if it were something independent and fundamental, with a meaning of its own. Man's universal essence is not determined by his being "man" in any sense whatever, but by his being essentially "spirit."

When Hegel talks of self-alienation, therefore, he means something fundamentally different from what Feuerbach and Marx mean, although the formal structure of the idea is the same. The fact that being "man" means being a subject of material needs and civic rights is subordinated by Hegel to the ontological determination of man as *logos* or spirit. And only to man as the subject of rights and needs (of whom we can form only a "notion" but no proper philosophical "concept") does Hegel grant the name of "man." Obviously, he believed more in man's ontological essence, in his spirituality, than in his humanity.

It was Feuerbach's main endeavor to transform this philosophy of spirit into a human philosophy of man, and he characterized the task of his "new philosophy of the future" in this way: what is important at present [1843] is not to describe man but first to pull him out of the "idealistic mire" in which he is sunk; "to derive the necessity of a philosophy of man (that is, philosophical theology); and thus to lay the foundation of a human philosophy by criticizing the divine philosophy" (Preface to *Principles of a Philosophy of the Future*). The tendency to make man the subject of philosophy has its motive, says Feuerbach, in making philosophy the cause of humanity. In accordance with his anthropological principle, Feuerbach attacks Hegel's particularized determination of man. Referring to Hegel's definition, quoted above, Feuerbach continues polemically. The fact that man can be discussed in so many different ways—as a legal "person," as a moral "subject," and so on—implies that the whole human being is referred to, although each time in a different sense. It belongs to the very character of man that he can be defined as this one and as that one, as a private person, as a public person, as a citizen, by his social role, and by his economic relations. Feuerbach thus guards himself against Hegel's idea of particularity, though he does not show us how to reintegrate the particularized humanity of the modern bourgeois into the whole humanity of man. This indeed could not be achieved by the humanitarian communism of Feuerbach, or by the love of "I and thou," but only through social criticism of the division of labor in general and of its class-character in particular, as undertaken by Marx.

Marx also took Feuerbach's anthropological principle as his starting point for criticizing the man of bourgeois society and the whole modern world. In *The Holy Family*, he still identifies himself with Feuerbach's "realistic humanism." The first sentence reads: "Real humanism has in Germany no more dangerous enemy than spiritualism or speculative idealism, which puts 'self-consciousness' or 'spirit' in the place of real, individual man and teaches, like the Gospel: 'It is the Spirit that giveth life.'" And at the beginning of the *Critique of Hegel's Philosophy of Right*, Marx states that Feuerbach's reduction of theology to anthropology is the prerequisite to any criticism of man's mundane situation. His incidental polemics against Hegel's definition of man as a particularity show the same tendency. Marx compares the man of bourgeois society with a commodity—a product of simple labor. Like labor, man has a questionable double character in economic terms: a "value-form" and a "natural-form." As a commodity—that is, as embodied labor—a thing is worth this or that much money, and its natural quality remains irrelevant in comparison to its value; things having the same natural properties may have quite different values as commodities.

The same is true of the man of the world of commodities. In his bourgeois value-form, he may play an important role for others as well as for himself—as a general, as a banker, in short as a specialist of some kind, fixed and divided by his objectified activity. As a plain "man as such," however—in his natural form, as it were—he plays a "rather shabby" role. Here Marx refers, without further comment, to paragraph 190 of Hegel's *Philosophy of Right*. This reference has to be interpreted in the following way. If Hegel characterizes man as such as the subject of material needs and the rights of a citizen (besides other similarly particular determinations), this reflects nothing less than the factual dividedness of man's consciousness, the "spiritlessness" —or rather, the inhumanity—in the existential situation of modern humanity. To such a theoretical isolation, division, and fixation of man's existence corresponds the actually existing isolation, division, and fixation of particular modifications of human nature in abstract forms of existence. These do not concern man as such and as a whole, but as a specialist, objectified through his specific work and function. Examples of such living abstractions of human nature are the bourgeois and the proletarian class-man, the man who performs mental or bodily labor, and so on.

Most important, however, is the way in which the man of bourgeois society is divided into two contradictory modes of existence: that of the private man with his private morality and property, and that of the citizen with his public morality and dignity. It is true that in all of these partial expressions of human nature, man as a whole is co-present, but only in a self-contradictory way. Being essentially determined by this or that particularity, he is this particularity only with regard to some other particularity: he is a professional man over against an amateur or over against himself as a family man; he is a private person as distinct from himself in his public function. In all these particular and objectified expressions of human nature, he is man only in a restricted and conditioned way. At most and at best, he is man as private man—namely, within bourgeois society, which is a society of "isolated private individuals." Man as such does not play a fundamental role in our specialized, divided, and alienated society; what matters in this bourgeois society is not man as such, but particularized man. Furthermore, a man's economic existence and material needs depend on his special skills and accomplishments; "life" means "to make a living." Consequently, Marx says, Hegel's definition of man as a particularity determined by economic needs is not at all a contrived construction, but is the adequate theoretical expression of the actual inhumanity in the social situation of modern man. Hegel's distinctions indicate that in bourgeois society man as man is indeed alienated from himself.

To sum up the concept of man's self-alienation, as it developed from Hegel via Feuerbach to Marx: both Feuerbach and Marx emphasize that Hegel's philosophy of spirit reflects man only in a particular function and not as a complete human being, not as that which ought to be fundamental in any philosophical concept of man. In his analysis of bourgeois society, Hegel discovers the total and intrinsic particularity of modern man, but at the same time he conceals it by the illusory assumption that any partial alienation can be taken back into the whole existence of man, whose essence is spirit. Since Marx, however, is interested first of all in man as such and as a whole, his concern is to lay bare that particularity in its total consequences. He wants to show the shaky foundation of modern existence, which pretends to be human while it is only bourgeois. He is not satisfied with pointing out a single particularity, but shows the total particularity and consequently the alienation which man necessarily represents in such a society.

To free man from his total particularity and to abolish his self-alienation to a variety of specialized functions, the political and economic emancipation of man is not sufficient. Accordingly, Marx demands a "human" emancipation of man. By this term he does not refer, as Feuerbach does, to man as "ego and alter ego" or as "I and thou," but to the world of man; for man is his social world, since he is essentially a *zöon politikon*, a "common essence" [*Gattungswesen*]. For this reason, Marx's criticism develops as a criticism of modern society and economy—without losing, however, its basic anthropological, and thus its philosophical, meaning. "If man is social by nature, he develops his true nature only within society, and the power of his nature cannot be measured by the power of the single individual but only by the standard of society." Marx pursues the basic and universal alienation of man in all realms of reality, in its economic, political, and immediately social forms. The economic expression of this problem is the world of "commodities," its political expression is the contradiction between "state" and "society," and its immediate social expression is the existence of the "proletariat."

II

THE ECONOMIC EXPRESSION of man's self-alienation is the commodity. As Marx employs the term, "commodity" does not mean one special kind of object contrasted with other kinds, but the "commodity-form," a fundamental ontological character which, in the modern world, all kinds of objects have in common. It is the commodity-form or commodity-structure which characterizes the alienation or estrangement of man from himself as well as from things. Consequently, *Capital* begins with an analysis of the commodity. The fundamental meaning of this analysis lies in its criticism of a bourgeois society and bourgeois man. In *Capital*, this criticism of a bourgeois society finds direct expression only in casual notes and marginal remarks; it is, however, one main theme in an early debate concerning the law about the theft of lumber [*Holzdiebstahlgesetz*] of 1842. Here, Marx undertakes his first brilliant unmasking of the perversion of "means" and "ends," of "thing" and "man"—the perversion that implies the self-estrangement of man, his externalization, his transformation from himself into a thing: lumber. This highest degree of externalization, to behave toward oneself in terms of something different and alien, is labeled by Marx, in his doctoral thesis, "materialism" or "positivism," and he calls himself, as one who aims to abolish this estrangement, an "idealist." The externalization of man into an object is alienation from himself because, in their proper sense, things are what they are for man, while man is man for himself.

What Marx wanted to make clear in this debate can be summed up as follows. Lumber which belongs to a private owner (that is, to a capitalist), and which can therefore be stolen by a man who does not own it privately, is not mere lumber, but something of economic and social relevance and human significance, even though its significance is concealed in the lumber itself. Endowed with this human-social quality, lumber is not the same for its owner as it is for the man who owns nothing and steals the lumber. As long as one man is aware of himself solely or primarily as the owner of lumber, having only this narrow-minded, partial consciousness of himself, while the other man is accordingly regarded merely as a lumber thief, but not as a human being—as long as these unphilosophical ideas prevail, no equitable punishment (equitable from a human viewpoint, that is—not merely "correct" from the legal viewpoint) can be imposed. Both humanly and legally, a dead thing, an "objective power," something nonhuman, mere wood, determines man and "subsumes" him, unless he is capable of directing and controlling his material and objective relationships in a human-social way. The determination of man through mere lumber is possible, however, because lumber, like any other commodity, is itself an objectified expression of sociopolitical relationships. Like any other commodity, it has the character of a fetish. For this reason, "wooden idols rise while human sacrifices fall." In the words of Marx's concluding passage:

If, therefore, lumber and owners of lumber as such make laws, these laws will differ in nothing but the place where they are made and the language in which they are written. This depraved materialism, this mortal sin against the Holy Spirit of peoples and of mankind, is a direct consequence of the doctrine that the Preussische Staatszeitung preaches to the lawgivers: that when making a law about lumber, they are to think of nothing but wood and lumber, and are not to try to solve each material problem in a political way—that is, in connection with undivided civic reasoning and civic morality.[1]

When something like lumber, this seeming "thing in itself," becomes the standard for the being and behavior of man, man will necessarily be reified and alienated from himself. Interhuman relations also become reified, or materialized, inasmuch as the material relations of things become humanized to quasi-personal powers of man. This perversion is a "depraved materialism." Thus Marx insists on the fundamentally human character of his economic analysis. In *The Holy Family*, he emphasizes, in opposition to the views expressed by Proudhon, that a merely economic interpretation of such facts—as expressed in claims for equality of property or wages—is still an "estranged form" of the universal self-alienation of man. Elsewhere Marx says:

The fact that Proudhon wishes to abolish not-owning [*Nichthaben*], as well as the traditional way of owning, is identical with his desire to abolish the actually alienated relationship between man and his own human essence; that is, he wants to abolish the economic expression of man's self-alienation. But since his criticism of social economy is still trapped in the presuppositions of social economy, his concept of the reappropriation of the world

1. D. Rjazanov, ed., *Marx-Engels Gesamtausgabe*, Part I, Vol. 1, I (Frankfurt, 1927), p. 304. Page references in the text are to this volume.

of objects is still seen under the economic form of property. Proudhon contrasts . . . the old way of owning—that is, private property—with "possession." Possession, he declares, is a "social function." The significant point about a function, however, is not that it "excludes" another person but that it actualizes and realizes a man's own essential powers. . . . Proudhon has not succeeded in giving this thought adequate elaboration. His notion of "equal property" is the economic one—that is, the still alienated expression of the fact that the object, which exists for man, which is his objectified being, is at the same time his existence in relation to other men, the social behavior of man toward man. Proudhon abolishes economic alienation within economic alienation [*Proudhon hebt die nationalökonomische Entfremdung innerhalb der nationalökonomische Entfremdung auf*]. This means, Marx contends, that Proudhon does not really abolish economic alienation in any radical sense.[2]

In *German Ideology,* Marx raises the same question as in the debate on lumber, though he no longer treats it in the same way. He asks again: Whence comes the strangeness with which men behave toward the products of their own labor, so that they no longer have power and control over their reciprocal relationships? Why, instead, do these products become independent forces, so that "the power of their lives overpowers their own makers"? How does it happen that the personal behavior of the individual has to reify itself and thereby estrange itself, while it exists at the same time as an independent power outside the individual?

Marx replies that this perversion is caused by the division of labor. Accordingly, the way in which men have worked up to the present time must be abandoned; it must be transformed into "total self-activity." This transformation will include not only abolition of the division of labor, but also abolition of the separation between city and country—which is "the most striking expression of the subsumption of the individual under the division of labor." Abolition of the division of labor can be accomplished only on the basis of a universal communist order of society, which will not only make all property common property, but will also make man's very being, in all of its self-expressions, a common —that is, a communist—matter. Wherever there is a division of labor, the slavery of the social structure to objectified relations between things is inevitable, just as the division of any individual's life is inevitable because it is in part a personal life and in part subsumed under some branch of labor with its special conditions.

In 1856, ten years after *German Ideology* was written, Marx

2. Franz Mehring, ed., *Aus dem literarischen Nachlass von Karl Marx, Friedrich Engels und Ferdinand Lassalle,* 2nd ed. (Stuttgart, 1913), II, pp. 139–40.

looked back at the so-called "revolution" of 1848 and summed up his view of the perverted world as follows:

There is one great fact characterizing the nineteenth century which cannot be denied by any party: on the one side, industrial and scientific powers have developed which no former period of history could have fancied; on the other side, there are symptoms of disintegration surpassing even the well-known terrors of the late Roman Empire. In our time everything seems to be pregnant with its contrast. The machine is endowed with the marvelous power to shorten labor and to make it more profitable; and yet we see how it produces hunger and overwork. The newly emancipated powers of wealth become, through a strange play of destiny, sources of privation. . . . Mankind becomes master of nature, but man the slave of man or of his own baseness. The result of all our inventions and progress seems to be that material powers become invested with spiritual life, while human life deteriorates into a material force. This antagonism between modern industry and science, on the one side, modern misery and corruption, on the other side, this antagonism between the forces of production and the social conditions of our epoch, is a tangible, overwhelming and undeniable fact. Some parties may complain about it, others may wish to get rid of the modern capacities in order to get rid also of the modern conflicts. Or they may fancy that such evident progress in the realm of production cannot be achieved but by a corresponding regress in the social political life. But as for us, we recognize in this antagonism the clever spirit (Hegel's "cunning of reason") which keenly proceeds in working out all these contradictions. We know that the new form of social production, to achieve the good life, needs only new men.[3]

As shown by the introduction to the *Critique of Hegel's Philosophy of Right,* Marx had already decided who those new men were who were qualified to abolish the universal self-alienation. "They are the workers." Thus Feuerbach's philosophy of "real humanism" found in Marx's "scientific socialism" its adequate "social praxis," the possibility of realization. In *German Ideology,* Marx rejected Feuerbach's "real humanism," however, on the ground that it was a mere sentimental community of individual love.

Capital, too, is not simply a critique of political economy but a critique of the man of bourgeois society in terms of that society's economy. The "economic cell" of this economy is the commodity-form of the labor products; and the commodity, like the lumber in the lumber-theft debate, is an economic expression of self-alienation. Self-alienation consists of this: that a thing whose

3. "Die Revolution von 1848 und das Proletariat," in *K. Marx als Denker, Mensch und Revolutionär* (Berlin, 1928), p. 41.

original purpose is to be useful is not manufactured and exchanged for anyone's actual needs, but appears on the commodity market as an object with an autonomous commodity-value,
independent of its utility. This is true whether economic or intellectual products are traded, whether the commodities are
cattle or books. Only through the salesman, for whom the commodity has merely exchange value, can the commodity reach its
consumer, the buyer. The fact that an object intended for use
becomes autonomous as a commodity offers another illustration
of the general situation in modern bourgeois society, namely, that
products govern men, and not vice versa.

To uncover this hidden perversion, Marx analyzes the "ob-
jectlike appearance" [the German word *Schein* means both "appearance" and "disguise"] of modern conditions of labor as
expressed in the "fetish-character" of the commodity. As a commodity, a table or a chair is a "sensuous-supersensuous" thing—
that is, an object whose qualities are at the same time perceptible
and imperceptible to the senses. We perceive without difficulty
exactly what a table means as an object for use; but what it
means as a commodity—as an object that costs money because
of the invested labor (that is, the invested working time) that it
represents—is at first a hidden social phenomenon. As Marx
expresses it in *Capital* (Vol. 1, Book 1, Chap. I, 4), "The table no
longer stands with its feet firmly on the ground, but stands on
its head in front of all the other commodities, spinning whims
from its wooden skull, far more wonderful than if it were to
begin dancing of its own free will."

The commodity-form is mysterious because in it the social
character of man's labor appears disguised as an objective character stamped upon the product of that labor; therefore, the
relation of the producers to the sum total of their own labor is
presented to them as a social relation which exists not among
themselves but among the products of their labor. Later in the
same passage of *Capital*, Marx continues:

By means of this quid pro quo the products of labor become commodities,
sensuous-supersensuous or social things. . . . It is exactly that definite social
relation between men that assumes, in their eyes that fantastic form of a
relation between things. In order to find an analogy, we must have recourse
to the misty regions of the religious world. Here the productions of the
human brain appear as independent beings endowed with life and entering
into relations both with one another and with the human race. So it is,
in the world of commodities, with the products of men's hands. This I call

the fetishism which attaches itself to the products of labor as soon as they are produced as commodities, and which is therefore inseparable from the production of commodities.

At first the producers of commodities—that is, of any kind of objects in the ontological form of commodity—make their social contacts only by exchanging their products. As these contacts take place only through things, the social conditions that underlie the commodities do not appear to the producers as labor-conditions of men. On the one side, these social conditions appear as purely objective and material relations among the various producers of commodities. On the other side, because of the objective character of modern commodities, these social conditions acquire a quasi-personal character on the modern commodity market, which follows its own economic laws. At first, men are not aware of this perversion, their self-consciousness being reified at the same rate. Marx says that although this perversion had to come about, he does not consider it irrevocable. Like other social structures, it can be transformed through revolutionary action and theoretical criticism. At first, this revolutionary possibility is hidden behind the fixed and ready-made value-form of the commodity, which is money.

Thus it seems that only the price of a commodity can be changed, not its form as such. If we compare the economic order of our society with other social and economic epochs in history, however, we see at once the historical character of the present perversion of the economic order, by which the products of labor as commodities have acquired authority over their producers. Whatever else we may think about the so-called Dark Ages and Middle Ages, with their conditions of personal dependence, at least the social conditions of labor appear in these centuries as the personal conditions of the people and not disguised as the social conditions of things. For the very reason that personal relations of dependence constituted the social foundations of society, there was no necessity for labor nor its products to assume a fantastic form, different from their reality. . . . In those days, the particular and natural form of labor, and not its general abstract form—as is the case in a society based on capitalist production of commodities—was the immediate form of labor.

In the light of this historical perspective, Marx develops the possibility of a future communist order of society, in order to contrast the "opaque" perversion of the modern world of commodities—its inhumanity—with the "transparency" in a communist society of men's social relations to the products of their own labor. The world of commodities cannot be abolished except through a fundamental revolution in all the concrete conditions under which men now live. Not only "de-capitalization" is needed to change the commodity-form to the utility-form; it will also be necessary to reintegrate the particularity of a reified man into "natural man," whose human nature is, according to Marx, fundamentally social. Man is a *zöon politikon,* though not in an ancient Aristotelian *polis,* but rather in a modern industrial *cosmopolis.*

It is characteristic of the nineteenth century that Hegel could still justify as a productive externalization what Marx rejected as self-alienation or estrangement. In his *Philosophy of Right,* Hegel explains that man, in view of his particular bodily and mental faculties and activities, may very well externalize single products and their use for a limited time, because if they are thus limited they have but an "external" relation to human "totality" and "universality." Hegel explicitly likens this personal externalization to man's relation to the object. Concerning this relationship he argues that an object reaches its proper determination through the use which man makes of it and for which it is intended by its nature. Only the full use of the object—which appears at first as "external" with regard to the object "itself" or per se—allows it to gain validity in the whole range of what it is. Thus the substance of the thing is its "externality," which man appropriates, through use, to himself. In using a thing, one makes its one's own, one appropriates it properly; this is the original meaning of "property," and property is therefore constitutive for man. In the same way, the totality of human life and the total use of human powers are identical with the whole of substantial life itself. On the basis of this identity of the substance of personal life with the totality of its activities, or externalization, Hegel argues that a special single activity, directed toward a single product for a limited time—in other words, a "limited" external relationship of man toward himself cannot swallow up the totality of man, or determine man in the whole as a particularity, or alienate him from himself.

Hegel's philosophy, which holds that the "spirit," and therefore freedom to abstract and appropriate, is the "universal" character of man, was not greatly concerned about such particular externalization. This accounts for the following addition to the ideas previously expressed: "The distinction here explained is that between a slave and a modern domestic servant or day laborer. The Athenian slave perhaps had an easier occupation and more leisurely work than is usually the case with our servants, but he was still a slave, because he had alienated to his master the whole range of his activity." Marx concludes precisely the contrary from this. To him, the modern wage earner is less free than the ancient slave. Though he is legally the free owner of his working power and legally equal to the owner of the means of production, and though he does not sell himself in totality but "only" his working power for a limited time, he is nevertheless completely a "commodity" on the modern labor market because his working power is his only true property, which he is forced to alienate in order to live by it. To Marx, the "free" slave-laborer incorporates the whole problem of modern society; the Greek slave, by contrast, stood outside the society of his free fellow men, and his personal fate had no bearing on it.

III

In considering man's political self-alienation in terms of bourgeois society, Marx says: "The abstraction of the state as such belongs to modern times only, because the abstraction of private life belongs to modern times. . . . The true man (of modern times) is the private man of the present political constitution."

The political expression of man's self-alienation is found in the inner contradiction between the modern state and bourgeois society; in the contradiction, that is, that exists in a man of the bourgeois state and society because he is partly a private person and partly a public citizen, but in no way a whole man—what Marx would call "a man without contradictions." Indirectly, Marx's critique of the principle of economy as "political" economy criticizes at the same time the social and political conditions of this particular society with its particular kind of economy. While his criticism of the commodity as the essential character, the ontological structure, of all our objects, is directed against the perversion of man into a thing, he now directs his criticism of the bourgeois state and society against the bourgeois way of life—its bourgeois humanity, which is essentially "privacy," a privation. This criticism is a main topic in his *Critique of Hegel's Philosophy of Right* and also in his discussion of Bauer's essay on the Jewish problem. Both of these works give a systematic presentation of Marx's views about man's self-alienation in its social and political forms; his remarks on the same subject in *The Holy Family* are more or less incidental and can be omitted from consideration here.

In his critique of Hegel, Marx does not attack man as the owner of money and producer of commodities, but rather modern man's particularity as such, distinguished from his public life and opposed to it. The particularity of the bourgeois, the thing that distinguishes him and isolates him from the universality of public life—that is, political life—is that he is first of all a private person; he is "bourgeois" in this particular sense. Referring to Hegel's implicit criticism of bourgeois society—which Hegel had defined as a society of isolated, "atomized individuals"—Marx says, "Hegel should not be blamed for depicting the modern state as it is, but for presenting it as the essential structure of the state" (p. 476). Marx holds that Hegel beclouds the empirical world of the nineteenth century in such a way that his arguments are "crass materialism" (p. 526). Hegel is a materialist in so far as he acknowledges what happens to exist as if it existed by reason of some essential necessity and thus posits it philosophically. But according to Marx's interpretation, what Hegel really depicts is nothing else but the conflict between bourgeois society and the state. "Hegel is profound in this: that he perceives the separation of the bourgeois and political society as a contradiction. But he is wrong in this: that he is satisfied with the appearance of his dialectical solution" (p. 492). What Hegel had recognized as creating the "extremes" of bourgeois society, Marx placed at the center of his analysis: the fundamentally private character of the man of bourgeois society. His social status is "private"—he is deprived of his political status. Marx develops this idea further in the following passage:

As a real bourgeois he finds himself in a twofold organization: in the bureaucratic one, which is an external, formal feature of the political organization which does not touch him and his autonomous reality; and in the social organization, which is bourgeois society. In the latter, however, he stands as a private man outside the state; the social organization does not touch the political state. . . . Therefore, in order to become a real citizen, in order to acquire political importance and effectiveness, he has to step out of his bourgeois reality, to abstract from it, to withdraw from the whole organization into his individuality. For the only existence that he finds for his citizenship is his empty individuality; the state as government is complete without him, and his existence within the bourgeois society is complete without the state. He can be a citizen only as an individual—only in contradiction to these communities, which are the only ones that exist. His existence as a citizen is an existence which lies outside a common essence and is therefore purely individual (p. 494).

The division between particular and universal interests, which also divides man, living within them, into a person having a private existence and an inferior public existence, is conceived by Marx as a self-alienation of man. For the bourgeois—who is a private man in relation to himself—feels that his real self is as different, external, and foreign to himself as a citizen as his private life is foreign to the state. His state is an "abstracting" one, because it is merely administrative and thus abstracts or separates itself from the real or private lives of its citizens, just as individuals, in turn, abstract or separate themselves from the state. Therefore bourgeois society as a whole represents the full application of the principle of individualism or egotism. Its ultimate purpose is the existence of the individual, and everything else is but a means to this end. Man's condition as a member of the state, to live in it as his own, remains necessarily an "abstract" determination as long as modern life presupposes such a great separation of real life from life in the community of the state. As a private person, separated from the public life of the state, modern man represents only a privation of man. In a communist commonwealth, the contrary is true: every individual is supposed to take part in the *respublica* individually and in a most personal way.

Marx's purpose was to build a new world through theoretical criticism and practical destruction of the one that had grown old. Out of existing reality, with its specific forms of society and state (a state that is basically unpolitical because it is political in an abstract way), he wanted to develop the "true reality" in which essence and existence, or reason and reality, are one and the same. In 1852, ten years after he wrote *The Holy Family*, Marx gave a historical account of this world grown old in *The Eighteenth Brumaire* of Louis Bonaparte. He described that era of the bourgeois revolution as a caricature of the greater revolution of 1789. He contended that the passions of the later period were without truth, for its truth had no passion; that its reality was completely watered down and living on loans; that its development was merely a constant repetition of the same tensions and relaxations; and that its conflicts inflamed each other only to end in dullness and collapse. Its history was a history without events, its heroes performed no heroic deeds, its supreme law was irresolution. His criticism may be compared with the contemporary analysis by Kierkegaard, in *The Present Age;* both men turned against Hegel's philosophy of reconciliation, though in opposite directions.

According to Marx, the contradiction between private and public life must be resolved. The deficient private humanity of the man of bourgeois society is to be sublated in a commonwealth which embraces the whole existence of man—including his "theoretical" existence—shaping him from head to foot into a communistic, universally human being. Marx therefore explicitly distinguished his philosophical communism from the "real" communism of Cabet, Weitling, and others, which he calls a "particular and dogmatic abstraction" because it is a "phenomenon of the old humanistic principle, infected by its opposite, privacy" (p. 573). The whole socialistic principle, if taken as a single phenomenon, is but one side of the full reality of the true human essence.

To this radical destruction of all the isolated modes of existence that have become independent, corresponds the change of all particularities into man as such and as a whole. The real basis of any positive reform must be the recognition that human existence is now limited to private man, a limitation unknown to antiquity or to the Middle Ages. The private man of antiquity was the slave, for he had no part in the *respublica* and therefore was not "man" in the full sense of the word. Likewise, in the Middle Ages, to each private sphere of life there corresponded a public sphere. "In the Middle Ages the life of the people and that of the state were identical. The real principle of the state was man, but man *enslaved*" (p. 437). Only the French Revolution emancipated man politically as the bourgeois, thus changing man's private status to a specific status, notwithstanding the fact that it was the French Revolution that wanted to make every man a *citoyen*.

The destruction of the religious particularity of man is considered by Marx with reference to Bauer's essay on the Jewish problem. The concrete question of how to accomplish the political emancipation of the Jews in Germany is bypassed by Marx in his first sentence. He says that a political emancipation cannot mean anything unless the Jews are emancipated "as men." But in this sense they are no more emancipated than the Germans who are to free them. "Why do the Jews complain about their special yoke while they accept the general one?" As long as the state is Christian and the Jew Jewish, the first is as unfit to grant emancipation as the second is to receive it.

Thus far Marx agrees with Bauer; both consider that a change to purely "human" conditions is the only "critical" and "scientific" solution. But Marx blames Bauer for ending his criticism at the point where the problem ceases to be theological and begins to become real. What must be investigated is the relationship between political and human emancipation. The limitations of a merely political emancipation are found in the fact that "the state can be free even though man in it is not free." In order truly to emancipate the Jew as well as the Christian, freedom from all religion is needed, not merely a state that grants religious freedom. The problem is a universal and basic one, since it concerns emancipation from every particularity in the way of being man, including religious man as well as private man and modern professional man, in their respective abstractions from the universal interests of human society. Marx goes on to say:

> The difference between the religious man and the citizen is the difference between merchant and citizen, between wage-earner and citizen, between landowner and citizen, between the living individual and the citizen. The contradiction in which religious man finds himself in relation to political man is the same one in which the bourgeois finds himself in relation to the *citoyen;* the same in which the member of bourgeois society, with his political lion's skin, finds himself (p. 585).

Bauer, says Marx, passes over the cleavage between the political state and bourgeois society, directing his polemics only against the religious aspect of these types of social organization. The disintegration of man into Jew and citizen, or into Protestant and citizen, is not really a contradiction of citizenship, but rather a defective political way of emancipating oneself from religion. The particularity of religion is merely another expression of the thorough disintegration of modern man in bourgeois society; it is one more example of the universal "estrangement of man from man," of man's alienation from himself, of the inner-human diremption between his individual life and his group life. Consequently, according to Marx:

> We do not say to the Jews, as Bauer does, it is not possible for you to become politically emancipated unless you emancipate yourselves radically from Judaism. We tell them, because your political emancipation is possible without your complete renunciation of Judaism, therefore political emancipation is not yet identical with human emancipation. If you Jews want to be emancipated politically without being emancipated humanly at the same time, the contradiction lies not in you but in the nature of a merely political emancipation. If your thinking is trapped in this concept, you partake of a general prejudice. Just as the state acts as an evangelist when it behaves, though it is a state, in a Christian manner toward the Jews, in the same way the Jew acts as a politician when he asks for the rights of a citizen though he is a Jew (p. 591).

In Marx's view, the same defective approach to emancipation characterizes the French and the American concept of the "Rights of Man." It is clear to him that the *"Droits de l'homme"* were not rights of man at all, but bourgeois privileges, because that historical *homme* was, as a *citoyen*, divided from himself as a bourgeois. *The Declaration of the Rights of Man* presupposed that *de facto* the bourgeois man was the actual, true, and essential man. This assumption Marx contests as follows:

None of the so-called Rights of Man eliminates man the egoist, man as a member of bourgeois society—that is, an individual withdrawn into his private interests and arbitrariness, separated from the community. Far from comprehending man as an essentially common existence [*Gattungswesen*], the common life, society itself, appears in these Rights as an external frame for individuals, as a limitation of their original independence. The only ties, by which individuals are held together are natural necessity, material needs, private interests, and the conservation of their property and their egoistic persons . . . (p. 595).

Thus a declaration of the rights of man is insufficient: the truly human emancipation is still to be achieved. Marx describes it in these words:

Political emancipation is the reduction of man to a member of bourgeois society, to an egoistic, independent individual on the one hand, and to a citizen on the other hand. . . . Only when the real, individual man reintegrates into himself the abstract citizen and becomes, as individual man—in his empirical everyday life, in his individual work, in his individual relations—a common existence; only when man has acknowledged and organized his *forces propres* as social forces, and therefore no longer separates these social forces from himself in the disguise of political forces —only then is his human emancipation accomplished (p. 599).

The freedom to which man is to be emancipated is thus, in its formal structure, freedom as understood by Hegel: a "freedom of supreme community" [*Freiheit der höchsten Gemeinschaft*], contrasted with the negative freedom of the isolated individual, which is only a freedom from external coercion. In this respect, the man of the Greek *polis* was freer than the man of bourgeois society, and even the Christian idea of freedom is more democratic because it respects each individual as equally sovereign in his relationship with God. Thus Marx can say:

Self reliance [*Selbstgefühl*] of man, his freedom, has still to be awakened in the hearts of modern men. Only this feeling, which disappeared from this world with the Greeks, and into the blue haze of the sky with the Christians, can once more create from society a community of men dedicated to their highest aims, a democratic state (p. 561).

True personal freedom becomes possible only in a community that is related to man as such. It comes about through a social change in the way of being man, but it cannot be achieved either by an internal or an external approach exclusively. The freedom of private man in bourgeois society exists only in his own imagination. It is dependent and subsumed under the "objective power of things."

IV

IN DISCUSSING THE social expression of man's self-alienation in terms of the proletariat, Marx says: "If socialist writers attribute a world-historic role to the proletariat, their reason for doing so is not . . . that they consider the proletarians gods—but rather the opposite." And in the introduction to the *Critique of Hegel's Philosophy of Right,* we find the following statement: "The dissolution of the whole of modern society is represented in the particular class of the proletariat." In this group lies the positive possibility of a human emancipation, not because it is a class within bourgeois society, but because it is itself a society outside of the established one. It is a society

which can no longer lay claim to any historical title but only to the human title, which does not stand in one-sided opposition to the actions of the German state but in absolute opposition to its fundamental principles. Finally, the proletariat is a sphere which cannot become emancipated without emancipating itself from all the remaining spheres of society, thereby in turn emancipating them; it is, in a word, the complete loss of man and therefore can regain itself only by completely regaining man (pp. 619–20).

Marx's philosophy, in which man is a "common essence," has found its weapon in the proletariat, just as the proletariat found its weapon in his philosophy. "The head of this emancipation is philosophy, its heart is the proletariat." The possessing class and the proletariat represent, fundamentally, the same kind of estrangement of man from himself; the difference is that one class feels itself healthy and fixed in this state of alienation—though without any critical consciousness of it—while the other class is a dehumanization that is conscious of being dehumanized and therefore strives to overcome it. The proletariat is, so to speak, the self-consciousness of the commodity. It is forced to alienate itself, to externalize itself like a commodity; but for this very reason, it develops a critical and revolutionary consciousness, a class-consciousness. In the one way, however, the proletarian is less

dehumanized than the bourgeois.[4] Because the proletariat embraces in its own conditions of life the conditions of all contemporary society in "its inhuman extreme," it cannot liberate itself
without emancipating all of society as well. This universal function of the proletariat is elucidated as follows by Marx, in connection with the universality of the modern international world
economy, in *German Ideology* (Moscow ed., p. 296):

Only the proletarians of our time who are completely excluded from any self-
activity are in a position to enforce their complete and no longer limited
self-activity, which consists in appropriating the totality of productive powers
together with the corresponding development of a totality of faculties. All
seizures and appropriations by former revolutionary movements were limited
ones. Individuals whose self-activity was limited through the limitation of
the instruments of production and traffic took hold of these limited instruments of production, producing thereby just another limitation. Their production instruments became their property, but they remained subsumed
under the division of labor and under their own productional instrument.
In all such appropriations a mass of individuals remained subsumed under
one single instrument of production; in the proletarian appropriation a mass
of production instruments must be subsumed under each single individual,
and property under all. There is no way of subsuming the modern global
economy under individuals except by subsuming it under all.

Thus we find that Marx does not attribute fundamental and
universal importance to the proletariat because he considers that
its members are "gods," but rather because to him the proletariat
embodies potentially universal humanity—man's common existence though he is now in the extremity of self-alienation. The
fundamental importance of the proletariat corresponds exactly
to the commodity-form of modern objects. The class of the wage
earner has a universal function because the wage earner is completely externalized through "the earthly question in life size"—
because he is merely a salesman of his own labor, a personified
commodity and not a human being. In him, the economic phase
of life shows itself most clearly as human destiny and thus,
with the proletariat as the nucleus of all social problems, the
economy necessarily becomes the "anatomy" of bourgeois society
—as was pointed out at the beginning of this paper. With the
self-liberation of the proletariat as the universal class with no
particular interests, private capitalist economy, the foundation
of bourgeois privacy—dissolves. Private humanity is sublated in
universal humanity, based on a commonwealth which is indeed

4. See G. Lukacs, *Geschichte und Klassenbewusstsein* (Berlin, 1923), pp. 188ff.

common to all, with common property and a common economy. The negative independence of the bourgeois individual is replaced by the positive freedom of a supreme community, which is a community of public life and of direct mutual relationships among all single individuals.

Marx's investigations, unlike those of empirical sociology, are not concerned with mutual relations between single empirical fields, or with "factors" which are considered to be of equal significance and to represent, when added up, the whole of reality. He was no abstract empiricist, just as he was no abstract philosophical "materialist" who would deduce his theory from economic principles. Marx analyzes our entire self-contradictory human world in terms of man's self-alienation, of which the existence of the proletariat is the climax and the key to the whole. This self-alienation is investigated in terms of its possible abolition, and not—as in Hegel's work—in terms of its dialectical sublation. Marx intends no more and no less than the abolition of the contradiction of particularity and universality, of privacy and public life. This contradiction, which had been previously formulated by Hegel, must disappear in a classless society, because such a society rests on the universal essence of man as a social creature.

It is true that man's self-alienation is conditioned by the type and degree of development of the material conditions of production, by the division of labor, and by the sum of the concrete conditions of his life. But these conditions are structurally united in the social nature of man, who is his own world and whose self-consciousness is a world-consciousness. The sum of conditions cannot be derived from abstract economic factors; the latter must be integrated into the concrete system of historic human conditions. "Real" man is not man "in the irrationality of his existence . . . as he walks and stands . . . as he is externalized . . . through the whole organization of our society, a semblance of himself" (p. 590). In his true reality, man is an essence which has to be brought into existence through action. Marx was convinced that the reality that accounts for the problematic condition of our society drives with historic necessity toward the fulfillment of his views, just as his philosophy moves toward its historic realization.

In *German Ideology*, Marx had "settled his accounts" with his former "philosophical conscience." Nevertheless he still—in contrast to the scientism of so many Marxists—possessed a philosophical conscience, derived from his study of Hegel. His endeavor was to realize Hegel's principle of the dialectical identity of reason and reality, or of essence and existence, thus transforming Hegel's philosophy to Marxism. A full discussion of Marx's analysis of self-alienation would have to take into account his philosophy of history, which underlies not only Hegelianism and Marxism, but all post-Hegelian modern historical thinking.[5]

5. See Karl Löwith, "The Dynamics of History and Historicism," in *Eranos Jahrbuch* (Zurich, 1952).

6 / Man Between Infinites

THE GREAT ASTRONOMICAL DISCOVERIES of the six-
teenth century initiated a turning point in the intellectual history
of the West. At the beginning of the seventeenth century, the
concept of man's existence within an orderly universe appears to
have been losing ground. Writers and preachers were indulging in
what may be called a cosmology of corruption.[1] The universe
seemed to have lost all harmony and stability. Mutability extended
from the earth to the heavens and man was lost in an incoherent
world.

It was Pascal who drew the philosophical consequences from
the impact of the "new philosophy" of nature upon the condition of man. He reset, as it were, the compass of Christian faith
in accordance with a changed universe. His existential pathos
and his insight into the human condition can, therefore, neither
be reduced to the non-Christian perspective of contemporary
existentialism, nor can they be separated from the conception of
the universe. To understand existentialism historically as well as
systematically, we have to refer to the new concept of an infinite
universe which seems at first to be the farthest removed from any
immediate existential concern of a self with itself. It is my thesis
here that we "exist" (in the sense of existentialism) because we
are lost in the universe of modern natural science. This was
clearly realized by Pascal, but not by Kierkegaard and his followers.

For Kierkegaard, existence is the only "interest" of relevant
thinking; it is the inter-esse between theoretical thought and
reality, that on which theoretical metaphysics necessarily is

1. See V. Harris, *All Coherence Gone* (Chicago: University of Chicago Press,
1949).

stranded. Existence as such is, to use Schelling's term, "unfore-thinkable," and yet the only serious interest of an existing thinker. Irritated by this inexplicable fact of the contingency of our exist-ence, Kierkegaard advances the questions: "Who am I? How came I here? What is this thing called the world? ... Why was I not consulted? ... How did I obtain an interest in this big enterprise they call reality? ... And if I am compelled to take part in it, where is the director? I should like to make a remark to him."

Almost the same question was raised two centuries earlier by Pascal.

When I consider the short duration of my life, swallowed up in the eternity before and after, the little space which I fill . . . , cast into the infinite im-mensity of spaces of which I am ignorant and which know me not, I am frightened, and shocked at being here rather than there; for there is no reason why here rather than there, why now rather than then. Who has put me here? By whose order and direction have this place and time been al-lotted to me?

In spite of the resemblance of Pascal's last sentence to Kierke-gaard's sarcastic exclamations, there is a distinct difference of tone and intention. With Pascal, the frightful contingency of man's existence is apprehended within a definite frame of refer-ence: the spatial and temporal infinites of the physical universe. For Pascal, the world is not a "big enterprise," but the majestic and overwhelming reality of the physical universe. With Kierke-gaard and the existentialists, this physical universe, as conceived by modern natural science, is absent, or more precisely, it is pres-ent only as the insignificant background of man's forlorn exist-ence. Insignificant as this background seems to be existentially, it is the reverse of existence as understood by existentialism.

The "world" which Sartre, Heidegger, and Kierkegaard de-scribe and analyze concretely is neither a living cosmos nor a creation, nor is it the universe of mathematical physics. It is *our* world of selfhood and interhuman relations within an anonymous mass-society—it is a world without nature. With Sartre, nature is an opaque *en-soi*, over against the *pour-soi* of human existence, and accessible only in the natural appetites of the human body. In Heidegger, nature is subsumed under the lowest category of the merely "extant" [*Vorhandensein*], in distinction to the human *Dasein* which alone can exist and have a world. Neither the social world nor the natural world can relieve us of the necessity of taking over the sheer "factuality" of our contingent existence, of "being cast" into the world.

Kierkegaard is exclusively concerned with man's inner life. He resumes Augustine's quest for the soul and its relation to God as the only two things worth knowing. He thereby implicitly dismisses the classical concern with the logos of the cosmos as a pagan curiosity. A sentence like that of Anaxagoras, that the end for which man is born is the contemplation of the sun, the moon, and the sky, is utterly strange to Kierkegaard and his followers. It is equally strange to those of us who, unencumbered by a god or a soul, but clothed in psychology and psychoanalysis, are living on the capital of the Christian concern for man's soul. Confronted with the task of recapturing a Christian existence according to the law of the Gospel, Kierkegaard felt that he had to ignore the laws of the cosmos and the modern discoveries of the telescope. If Christ appeared today, he said, the Christian task of appropriating His message would still be the same as it was for the first generation of Christians. But the natural scientist, and all those who believe in the truth of science rather than of the Gospel, would demand an examination of Christ's brain under a microscope to determine whether He is the Son of God or a schizophrenic. Unfortunately for the sciences, all the modern discoveries by telescope and microscope are irrelevant for an understanding of the human condition in its inwardness. A thoughtful person, according to Kierkegaard, who wants to understand what it means to exist as a self before God cannot be interested in natural science; for it does not make any difference for man's moral choices and religious decisions whether the moon is made of blue cheese or something else. What is the use of explaining the whole physical universe or world history if one does not understand oneself, one's own single self? As an existing self, man is singled out from the physical cosmos and world history and their deceptive greatness. To Kierkegaard the concern with six thousand years of world history, or with some billion years of cosmic history, is an escape from one's self into an illusory importance.

Thus, if anything unites these philosophies of existence by a common pattern it is the negative experience that man has no definite place and nature within the natural universe. This metaphysical displacement is, however, not a novelty of the twentieth century, but rather the modern destiny. "Since Copernicus," Nietzsche said, "man is falling from a center toward an x." This universal destiny is aggravated by man's social solitariness amid a modern mass-society.

Neither classical philosophy nor Christian theology saw man's position in the universe in this way. For Aristotle, existence as such was an unquestioned element within the essential structure, order, and beauty of an imperishable and clearly delimited cosmos, a cosmos which included the existence of rational animals called men. As an animal, man shared in the properties of living things; as a rational animal he had the privilege of contemplating this perfect hierarchy of beings. For St. Thomas, man and the universe were contingent existences, but contingent to God and bound together by the act of creation. Though man alone was created in the likeness of God, and thus set apart from and above the animal world, the unified Christian concept worked for man and world alike. Only with the dissolution of these ancient convictions, classic and Christian, did existentialism come into its own. For if the universe is neither eternal and divine (as it was for Aristotle), nor contingent but created (as it was for St. Thomas), and if man has no definite place and status in the hierarchy of an eternal or created cosmos, then he begins to "exist" in it like an outcast in an "ecstatic" condition. And since none of us is exempt from the impact of the dissolution of these ancient beliefs and certainties, since we cannot restore the universe of Aristotle or St. Thomas, even less the post-Cartesian synthesis of Hegel, we are all "existentialists" whether we like it or not. It is not a "failure of nerve" (as has been suggested) which brought existentialism into existence. What failed us was not our nerve, but rather our belief in a divinely ordered universe in which man could feel himself at home, or *chez soi*, as it were. No social order of whatever kind, not even order plus freedom, can possibly make up for that lack of fundamental order in the universe. Hence, we have indeed "to be," or exist, in all those descriptive terms of sheer factuality, contingency, and absurdity which existentialism has brought to light. For how can one feel at home in an "exploding" universe, the chance result of statistical probabilities? Such a universe cannot inspire confidence and sympathy, nor can it give orientation and meaning to man's existence in it. We are indeed cast into this world and therefore must postulate ourselves, having postulated such a universe with such unexpected success. It is the character of our world and world concept which makes us exist existentially.

What makes us uncomfortable and throws us back upon ourselves is that our modern universe has no center and no limits. As an infinite universe of indefinite limits, it has no definite place for a finite man. If infinity has to be included in the image of the world, the point is reached where every image ends—the point of the nebulae of astrophysics, those scattered fragments of an initial explosion a hundred million light-years distant from us. We can disregard the important changes which, since Newton, have occurred in mathematical physics, for the world has not become again an encompassable world-order. Einstein's conception of "finite" space, and the assumption that beyond certain limits the concepts of space and time cease to be applicable, by no means restore the universe as an imaginable home for man. Such a universe can perhaps still be described, or rather calculated, but it can no longer be imagined; and the scientist who calculates it does not live in it as a human person.[2]

"Infinity" is a term which was at first applied not to the physical universe but was reserved for its creator.[3] The natural scientist of early modern times considered infinity to be an attribute of God. Thus, when Copernicus and Kepler studied the structure of the planetary system, they believed that they were finding the spirit of God in the mathematical laws of nature. When Newton explained Kepler's laws in terms of mechanics, it was held that the world could be explained in purely physical terms. What still defied mechanical explanation was the origin of the planetary system. But when Laplace rendered its mechanical origin probable, thus confirming the cosmological theory of Kant, he declined to speak of God and to involve practical moral reason, while theoretical reason, the understanding of nature, needed, as he said, only some matter to construct the physical world on a few principles invested in man's reason.

But Kant's "Copernican revolution" was already initiated by Descartes' distinction of man and world as *res cogitans* and *res extensa*. Consequently the modern consciousness is a profoundly divided one. It lives in two different worlds of extreme subjectivity and objectivity, worlds which are as opposed to each other as they are interdependent. In a famous passage at the end of his *Critique of Practical Reason*, Kant formulates it this way:

Two things fill the mind with ever new and increasing admiration and awe, the oftener and the more steadily we reflect on them: the starry heavens above us and the moral law within us. . . . I see them before me and connect them directly with the consciousness of my existence. The former begins from the place I occupy in the external world of sense, and enlarges my connection therein to an unbounded extent with worlds upon worlds and systems of systems, and moreover into limitless times of their periodic

2. See M. Buber, *Between Man and Man* (London: Kegan Paul, 1947), Chap. 5.
3. See C. F. von Weizsäcker, *The History of Nature* (Chicago: University of Chicago Press, 1949), pp. 6off.

motion its beginning and continuance. The second begins from my invisible self, my personality, and exhibits me in a world which has true infinity but which is traceable only by the inner understanding, and with which I discern that I am not in a merely contingent . . . connection.

Objectively, the two worlds are strictly separate: in the face of the universe natural man is nothing; in relation to his moral consciousness, as a person, he is all-important. In the *Critique of Pure Reason*, Kant goes even further. He realizes, like a radical existentialist, the impossibility of establishing the inner necessity of the whole creation, for to establish it, we would have to know that there is an ultimate principle of existence which exists necessarily or essentially. But we cannot conceive of *any* existence, not even of God, as necessarily existing, as the ultimate cause of contingent existences.

That unconditioned necessity, which we require as the last support of all things, is the true abyss of human reason. . . . We cannot put off the thought, nor can we support it, that a Being, which we represent to ourselves as the highest among all possible beings, should say to himself: *I am from eternity to eternity, there is nothing beside me, except that which is something through my will—but whence am I?* Here all sinks away from under us, and the highest perfection, like the smallest, passes without support before the eyes of speculative reason, which finds no difficulty in making the one as well as the other to disappear without the slightest impediment.

What remains is radical, universal contingency of existence, or existence "without support." Such a thought is, however, "intolerable" for human reason; while its opposite, inner necessity, is "undemonstrable" for it. The difference between Kant and contemporary existentialists is that the latter apparently have managed to find radical contingency tolerable and even liberating, and the demonstrability of an inherent necessity of existence to be unnecessary.

It is not difficult to imagine where Kant's admiration of the starry heavens above us and the moral law within us might lead. It needs only a slight shift in temper, from awe and admiration to a neutral recognition, and from there to a positivistic acceptance of the "findings" of the telescope on the one hand, and of the Freudian "superego" on the other, to circumscribe what is now commonly held to be man's position in the universe. For some people, the only link which still connects the firmament with humanity is the horoscope. If this disproportion between man and the universe is not always clearly felt, it is due to our obsession with the immediate problems of our social world and to the confusion of the natural universe with our scientific construction of it, which is indeed ours and not contrived by the universe itself.

To understand this disproportion correctly—that is, as an essential disorder—I refer now to Pascal as the first existentialist of the modern age.

Pascal and his older contemporary, Descartes, both realized that the order of the scholastic system had become untenable. Their common starting point was a radical doubt with respect to traditional certainties, in order to reach a new kind of assurance. Descartes believed himself to have attained the new certainty, beyond any doubt, by radical reasoning. Pascal felt, as Kierkegaard and Nietzsche felt after him, that Descartes' doubt was still superficial and also, consequently, the certainty which he had extracted from it. According to Pascal, only the certainty of faith can counterbalance the fundamental doubtfulness of our human being and knowing, including the knowledge of the abstract sciences. For the ultimate axioms of mathematics are as evident as they are undemonstrable. "It may be that there are true demonstrations; but this is not certain. Thus, this proves only that it is not certain that all is uncertain"—which testifies once more to the "glory of skepticism." The master of both Descartes and Pascal, who stimulated in them the sense of skepticism, was Montaigne; but he was satisfied with undermining all kinds of dogmatic certainties, while enjoying the superior refinement of skeptical suspense.

In our doctrinaire age, where people long for guidance, security, and constructive results, skepticism has fallen into disrepute. The deprecator of skepticism has forgotten, however, that genuine skepticism (which means, literally, keen observation and investigation) is the result of a radical search for truth. Only by the highest standard of truth, whether attainable or not, can one realize the doubtfulness and the illusions of our human judgments. The degree to which Descartes' and Pascal's doubt is radical, therefore, is in direct proportion to the rigor of their quest for certain truth. Descartes is striving for absolute certainty by means of his doubt; Pascal erects religious faith on the "truth of skepticism."

The never-failing spring from which Pascal drew his skepticism was the study of man on the pattern of Montaigne; but he probed much deeper than his master into the ultimate ground of man's uncertainties, illusions, and contradictions. The two opposite and extreme standards by which his skepticism has to be judged are the lawful certainty of mathematical demonstration on the one hand, and the fleeting certainty of faith on the other.

Thus, the wealth and acuteness of Pascal's moralistic observations and reflections, the range of his study of man, have to be interpreted within the context of Pascal, the scientist and the believer.

Pascal combined in his person the genius of a creative mathematician with the insight of a profound moralist and Christian believer, or to use his own terms, the "spirit of geometry" with the "spirit of subtle intuition" (*esprit de finesse*), and both with the "reason of the heart." As a natural scientist, he had the intellectual superiority of knowing the kind of world into which we are cast. As a keen moralist, familiar with the habits and passions of the men of the world in the grand style, he had the social superiority of the *honnête homme*. As a Christian believer who had suffered the joy of a mystical experience, he had the spiritual superiority of radical submission and renunciation over all those whose experience is confined to that of a mastering scientist and a skeptical moralist. But even as a moralist and believer, Pascal was informed by the sobering "spirit of geometry." The piece of paper on which he had jotted down his mystical experience relates it with the precision of a scientific observer; and in the *Pensées*, the rationality of faith is demonstrated in the famous fragment on the theory of probabilities.

Pascal defines man by outlining his definite limits. Since man is not merely a corporeal being with definite and definable properties, but exists consciously and thus surpasses himself, human nature has to be defined in terms of the "human condition." Pascal's basic definition of it at first seems purely formal and external. He defines it in terms of mathematical limits. Man is a "seeming mean" between the two mathematical infinities, the infinitely great and the infinitely small, the Infinite and the Nothing of spatial and temporal extension. Or, to use an arithmetical analogy, man exists like a zero between an ever increasing and an ever decreasing series of numbers. The zero itself is not a number like other numbers, but qualitatively different. The infinitely great and the infinitely small (in number, space, and time) are similar to each other, but are dissimilar to the finite standpoint from which they are judged as infinite. This position between two horizons of infinity is to Pascal analogous to the condition of man within the universe. Man exists between two fathomless infinites or "abysses." Between two such precipices, however, man has no definable standpoint, but rather his position is "floating." His position is the condition of a "seeming mean" between the All and the Nothing. It is man's condition to be "Nothing in comparison with the infinite, an All in comparison with the Nothing."

The word "condition," therefore, does not have the same meaning as in the popular phrase of "being conditioned," scientifically, socially, psychologically, and so forth. What Pascal has in mind is not particular conditions which determine man's range of freedom, but the total and unique situation of man within the whole of being, something which is quite independent of the question of determinism and free will. Pascal's definition is an attempt to locate man, to assign him his correct place within the universe. But this place turns out to be nowhere and everywhere. This condition in the universe outside us is at the same time analogous to man's inner condition. Man is suspended, not only between the two mathematical infinities of the infinitely great and the infinitely small, but he is also extended and suspended between greatness and misery.

In bare outline, this is the human condition sketched in fragment No. 72 of the *Pensées*, which opens a section on "Man." Though editors have improved the context of Pascal's thought by rearranging the 924 fragments of the *Pensées*, this work remains, like Nietzsche's last work, a disorderly mass of notes which Pascal had jotted down during the last years of his short life with the intention of defending the Christian faith against the sophisticated gentlemen of his time. It is a modern apology because it applies the infinite horizon of modern science to the elucidation of the condition of man. The arguments lead up to the crucial point where man has to find for himself the answer to those questions which are involved in his essential displacement, his being *égaré*, bewildered, and gone astray.

In a note which can be considered as a preface to the section on "Man," Pascal states that he had spent much time in the study of the abstract sciences but had been disheartened by the small number of fellow students with whom he could converse about these difficult matters. Thus he turned, like Descartes, to the study of man. But he found that still fewer studied man than studied geometry, for a serious study of man is even more exacting and solitary than that of the abstract sciences. To study the human condition correctly, one has to relate it to the condition of the universe, because it is the very disproportion between man and universe which reveals the true condition of man. Under the title "Disproportion," Pascal elaborates on the human condition thus:

Let man then contemplate the whole of nature in her full and grand majesty, and turn his vision from the low objects which surround him.

Let him gaze on that brilliant light, set like an eternal lamp to illumine the universe; let the earth appear to him a point in comparison with the vast circle described by the sun; and let him wonder at the fact that this vast circle is itself but a very fine point in comparison with that described by the stars in their revolution round the firmament. But if our view be arrested there, let our imagination pass beyond; it will sooner exhaust the power of conception than nature that of supplying material for conception. The whole visible world is only an imperceptible atom in the ample bosom of nature. No idea approaches it. We may enlarge our conceptions beyond all imaginable space; we only produce atoms in comparison with the reality of things. It is an infinite sphere, the center of which is everywhere, the circumference nowhere. . . .

Returning to himself, let man consider what he is in comparison with all existence; let him regard himself as lost in this remote corner of nature; and from the little cell in which he finds himself lodged, I mean the universe, let him estimate at their true value the earth, kingdoms, cities, and himself. What is a man in the Infinite?

But to show him another prodigy equally astonishing, let him examine the most delicate things he knows. Let a mite be given him, with its minute body and parts incomparably more minute, limbs with their joints, veins in the limbs, blood in the veins, humours in the blood, drops in the humours, vapours in the drops. Dividing these last things again, let him exhaust his powers of conception, and let the last object at which he can arrive be now that of our discourse. Perhaps he will think that here is the smallest point in nature. I will let him see therein a new abyss. I will paint for him not only the visible universe, but all that he can conceive of nature's immensity in the womb of this abridged atom. Let him see therein an infinity of universes, each of which has its firmament, its planets, its earth, in the same proportion as in the visible world; . . . Let him lose himself in wonders as amazing in their littleness as the others in their vastness. For who will not be astounded by the fact that our body, which a little while ago was imperceptible in the universe, itself imperceptible in the bosom of the whole, is now a colossus, a world, or rather a whole, in respect of the nothingness which we cannot reach? He who regards himself in this light will be afraid of himself, and observing himself sustained . . . will tremble at the sight of these marvels. . . .

For in fact what is man in nature? A Nothing in comparison with the Infinite, an All in comparison with the Nothing, a mean between nothing and everything. Since he is infinitely removed from comprehending the extremes, the end of things and their beginning are hopelessly hidden from him in an impenetrable secret. . . . Through failure to contemplate these Infinities men have rashly rushed into the examination of nature, as though they bore some proportion to her. It is strange that they have wished to understand the beginnings (principles) of things, and thence to arrive at the knowledge of the whole, with a presumption as infinite as their object. For surely this design cannot be formed without presumption or without a capacity infinite like nature. . . .

Our intellect holds the same position in the world of thought as our body occupies in the expanse of nature.

Limited as we are in every way, this state which holds the mean between two extremes is present in all our impotence. Our senses perceive no extreme. Too much sound deafens us; too much light dazzles us; too great distance or proximity hinders our view. Too great length and too great brevity of discourse tend to obscurity; too much truth is paralyzing. . . . First principles are too self-evident for us; too much pleasure disagrees with us. Too many concords are annoying in music; too many benefits irritate us. . . . Extreme qualities are prejudicial to us and not perceptible by the senses. . . . Extreme youth and extreme age hinder the mind, as also too much and too little education. In short, extremes are for us as though they were not, and we are not within their notice. They escape us, or we them.

Pascal concludes that if this constitutional incapacity of man to comprehend the infinites and to reach an ultimate ground and end is well understood, "we shall remain at rest, each in the state wherein nature has placed him." For in comparison with these unattainable infinities, all finites are equal, i.e., equally far removed from the first and the last things of philosophical and theological presumptions. The final result of Pascal's considerations thus seems to lead us back to the skeptical wisdom of Montaigne, who concludes his "Defense of Raymond Sebonde" with an explicit rejection of the idea that man should surpass the natural limits of his nature. It seems to be in the spirit of Montaigne when Pascal says that since we cannot grasp the extremes, and thereby the whole, "nothing is good but mediocrity. The majority has settled that and finds fault with him who escapes it at whichever end. . . . To leave the mean is to abandon humanity."

Yet, Pascal is far from identifying himself with the settled skepticism of Montaigne. He acknowledges the human condition of mediocrity—this analogy of the "seeming mean" between the two infinites—only with the qualification that it is most contrary to our deepest aspiration: to surpass mere humanity by the search for an ultimate foundation from whence to reach the Absolute.

What completes our incapacity to know something perfectly, in the whole and to the end, is that we are composed of mind and body. If we were simply matter, we would not know anything. Being body and mind, we know that we are mind and body and that each reacts upon the other; but we do not understand how a mind can be at all united to a body, since mind and body are not different modes of a single substance, but separated in principle by an infinite distance. The infinite distance between mind and body is, however, not the last riddle. It is only a weak analogy to an "infinitely more infinite distance," namely that between mind and charity, in the Christian sense, "From all bodies together we cannot draw forth one little thought; this is impossible and of another order. From all bodies and minds, we cannot produce a feeling of true charity; this is impossible and of another, supernatural order."

The distinctions between matter, that which does not know itself, body and mind, that which knows itself and something else, and charity, that which lives by the knowledge of faith, have their analogy in three different orders of the human condition: the men of material or worldly power, the men of spirit, and the men of holiness. In all three kinds of order, greatness and power are possible and deserve respect and admiration. The saints have their power, glory, and victory, but they have no need of the wordly greatness of kings and the rich, or of the intellectual excellence of men and of genius. The power of kings over subjects and the power of great minds over inferior ones neither add to nor take from the superior rank of saintliness, of which the other kinds of greatness are but an analogy. Jesus Christ, the perfect model of holiness, was without any worldly power and riches and without any exhibition of knowledge. "He did not invent, he did not reign." He was humble, patient, and holy to God, without sin, and his greatness was manifested in lowliness. "But there are some who can only admire worldly greatness, as though there were no intellectual greatness, and others who only admire intellectual greatness, as though there were not infinitely higher things in wisdom." These three orders of greatness constitute a discontinuous hierarchy, as discontinuous as the geometrical hierarchy between a point and a line, a line and a plane, a plane and a body. For a point cannot be extended into a line, nor can a line be divided down to a point. To sum up with Pascal's words:

All bodies, the firmament, the stars, the earth, and its kingdoms, are not equal to the lowest mind, for mind knows all these and itself, and those bodies nothing. All bodies together, and all minds together, and all their products, are not equal to the least feeling of charity. This is of an order infinitely more exalted.

Thus man's "disproportion" in the universe does not imply the absence of any order, but rather indicates a kind of discontinuous order evidenced by the three different and yet analogical kinds of greatness.

Man's aspiration toward greatness is, however, inseparable from man's essential misery, deficiency, and want. It is the mark of man's excellence that, whatever possessions and gifts he may have, he is never satisfied with his condition. The greatness of man is proved by his wretchedness. That we *know* our misery is, however, essential for misery itself. If we did not know how to be miserable, we would not be so. A crippled tree or a ruined house is not miserable because it is not aware of its state. Thus the greatness of man lies in the fact that he knows himself to be miserable. On the other hand, one cannot feel miserable without some knowledge of a better state. Nobody is unhappy because he does not have three eyes or two mouths, but anyone is miserable if he is deprived of what he once had. Thus the present misery of man proves his greatness—it is the misery of a "deposed king." But how to explain this fallen state of man if not by the doctrine of original sin—though the latter itself may be inexplicable? The arguments in Pascal's search for an answer to the problem of man thus lead up to the mystery of man's original sin and the corresponding mystery of God's revelation in redeeming man. Both mysteries ultimately explain, for Pascal, man as the "seeming mean" between the All and the Nothing, between greatness and misery, power and impotence. It is the Christian faith alone which can elucidate the combination of greatness and misery in the human condition; for the philosophical schools which stress either man's misery or his greatness are each unable to comprehend the contradicting truth of both states. Nor can the half-truths of both schools be combined to make a whole truth; rather, on their own level they annihilate each other, to make way for the truth of the Gospel. The Christian faith teaches us to attribute man's misery to his fallen nature and his greatness to grace. This union of nature and grace, of misery and greatness, is but an image of the two natures in the single person of Jesus Christ, the man-God. The crucified Christ unites perfectly both infinite greatness and infinite misery. On the human level alone, the contradiction remains unresolved; man as such is a monstrous confusion. "We have an idea of happiness, and cannot reach it. We perceive an image of truth and possess only a lie. Incapable of absolute ignorance and of certain knowledge we have thus been manifestly in a degree of perfection from which we have unhappily fallen." Seen in the light of the Christian revelation, nature is such that she testifies everywhere, within man and without, to a lost God and a corrupt, unredeemed nature. Now the two mathematical Infinities, the All and the Nothing, can be understood in their true significance: the infinity of space and time is the greatest mark of the almighty power of God, who created the All out of Nothing. The extremes between which man is placed "meet and reunite by force of distance, and find each other in God, and in God alone."

If we depart from the Christian coordinates, the greatness and misery of man are liable to be leveled down to the trivial experience that all things human are ambiguous and that everybody enjoys and suffers equally his ups and downs. Pascal knew, of course, the average condition of man, between *ennui* and *divertissement*, between idleness and busyness, pride and despondency; but he saw it from a vantage point which surpasses it. He became more and more firmly convinced that only the Christian doctrine and the Gospel can answer the quest which is Man. Accordingly, in his last years Pascal retired to a monastery where he wrote the *Pensées* during the intervals of his meditations, after having given away his worldly possessions and renounced his pride in the pursuit of science, particularly geometry, "the most beautiful trade in all the world," but after all only a trade, like that of any "skillful artisan." "Philosophers," he once remarked, "they astonish ordinary men who are less educated; Christians, they astonish philosophers." Pascal was both, a philosopher trained in mathematics and physics and also a modern apologist in the succession of Augustine. As a Christian thinker, he wrote against Descartes, blaming him for having extended the certainty of reason too far. As a modern Christian thinker, he realized the condition of modern man as no one else before or since.

7 / Skepticism and Faith

In Memory of Erich Frank

I think, Socrates, and I daresay you think so too, that it is very difficult and perhaps impossible to obtain clear knowledge about these matters in this life. Yet I should hold him to be a very poor creature who did not test what he said about them in every way, and persevere until he had examined the question from every side and could do no more. It is our duty to do one of two things; we must learn or we must discover for ourselves the truth of these matters; or, if that be impossible we must take the best and most irrefragable of human doctrines, and embarking on that, as on a raft, risk the voyage of life, unless a stronger vessel, some divine word, could be found, on which we might take our journey more safely and more securely.

(Plato, *Phaedo*)

FOLLOWING A CHAPTER in Kant's *Critique of Pure Reason*, we can distinguish three degrees of holding a thing to be true: *Meinen, Glauben,* and *Wissen,* to have opinions, to believe, and to know. To have mere opinions is to hold something to be true, with the consciousness that it is insufficient, both subjectively and objectively. If the holding true is sufficient subjectively, but insufficient objectively, it can be called believing. If it has sufficient reasons, both subjectively and objectively, it is knowing. It would be absurd to hold mere opinions or beliefs in pure mathematics. In contradistinction to these three degrees of theoretical certainty, one may have a pragmatic belief on which to act. A physician, for example, may feel that he has to do something for a patient, even though he does not know the nature of the illness. He will act on pragmatic belief which also admits of degrees. The surest test of the firmness of such a pragmatic belief is betting. But the higher the bet, the more easily do we become aware that the certainty of our beliefs has shaky foundations. And if we have to stake the truth and happiness of our whole lives, the certainty of our judgment drops considerably and we discover by the test of betting that our belief does not reach so far.

Now, what is characteristic of our time is that people are longing for guidance, security—economic, moral, and intellectual—and constructive results, that there is a need for firm convictions and a strong faith, for the very reason that people are so terribly insecure and skeptical, if not cynical. But faith, religious faith, particularly Biblical faith, is neither the possession of a credit nor a pragmatic belief, nor is it a provisional substitute for a knowledge not yet attained.

Faith, as we may learn from Job, Augustine, Luther, Pascal, and Kierkegaard, is a costly achievement, not simply to be willed. It is an unconditional trust and as such it is rarely found in inter-human relations and is unwarranted with regard to the human world as it is. At the same time, neither ordinary suspicion nor sitting on the fence is identical with philosophical doubt. It would be foolish to have unconditional trust in a businessman who wants to sell us something. It would be unwise to have unconditional trust in a teacher who has not absolute knowledge. It would be generous to have unconditional trust in a friend, though he may deceive us, which is, then, to his own discredit, but not to ours. Unconditional trust is not a rationally assured belief. It is only possible and reasonable when referring to an absolutely trustworthy being. As such a being is the God of the Old and New Testaments conceived. Faith is as rare and unpopular as its seeming counterpart.

People are naturally neither radical skeptics nor radical believers. Ordinarily we are and we do everything only to a "certain," that is, very uncertain, degree. We are ordinarily common sense and common faith dogmatists, living by "animal faith," never questioning whether a single one of our intellectual, social, and moral habits can be reasonably maintained.

As radical attitudes, both skepticism and faith challenge our average scientific knowledge whereby we know more and more about less and less. And since most people today do not believe in anything except science—among which there are many artificially construed pseudosciences—it will do no harm to question with the skeptics the certainty of our knowledge and to support with the believers, though on the philosophical basis of skepticism, the possibility of faith in undemonstrable things.

I

ORIGINALLY, the word skepticism did not mean a passion for doubt. Neither did it mean, as with Descartes, a method for attaining certain truth by way of excluding everything doubtful. This Cartesian doubt is an answer to the refined skepticism of Montaigne, which consists in considering in a well-tempered way the divergent aspects of things, their pros and cons, without taking sides. Kant called the skeptics "nomads" of the spirit, because they frustrate any permanent cultivation of the soil. But Montaigne's skepticism should by no means be scorned. It paralyzes only the weak minds; others will be stimulated by it. This kind of *skepsis* opens unexpected perspectives in what seemed commonplace; it questions the traditional distinctions between the rational and the irrational, between truth and error. It knows that there is nothing so improbable that human thinking and acting would not be capable of it. It is Montaigne's unprejudiced but inconclusive doubt, which leaves the truth in suspense, to which Descartes and Pascal responded: the one with philosophy as a science, the other with the certainty of faith. Their response to Montaigne puts them both in indirect relation to the classical skeptics whom Montaigne often followed literally. The main source of classical skepticism is a work by Sextus Empiricus, physician and philosopher at the end of the second century and contemporary of Tertullian, a passionate adversary of philosophical skepticism and apologist of the Christian faith. To Tertullian, skeptics and philosophers were one and the same, for he saw the whole difference between philosophers and Christians in the fact that the former were still engaged in skeptical search while the latter had found the truth by faith.

In classical philosophy, skepticism means keen observation and investigation, seeking, searching. That which skepticism seeks is, however, not doubt but truth. Skepticism is, therefore, search for truth, and the one who searches has to continue his search until he has found what removes his doubt. Thus skepticism is a highly respectable philosophical school or, rather, discipline of the mind.

Sextus Empiricus begins his *Outlines of Pyrrhonism* by classifying the philosophers according to the relation between searching and finding. All of them seek truth but with different results: the seeker finds what he has been looking for and then he knows the truth; or he gives up his search for truth because he is unable to find it; or he persists in seeking. The first are the traditional philosophers or dogmatists among whom Sextus Empiricus counts Aristotle, the Stoics, and the Epicureans, but not Plato whom he suspects of having been a skeptic. The second are the so-called Academicians. The third are the true skeptics, those who persist in seeking and searching and abstain from premature judgments. Their skepticism is so radical that the common reproof that a skeptical statement contradicts itself simply by being a statement, as dogmatic as any other, is not pertinent. For the true skeptic puts his own statements, too, in a skeptical way: he does not contend that something is or is not so; he only says how a thing appears to him, now and for the time being. He is intentionally irresolute and undecided, the opposite of a "decisionist" who insists on a resolute decision, whether right or wrong, because he lacks objective wisdom.

The skeptic knows that all things exist only in relation to other things and to man as the perceiving, apprehending, and knowing subject. The world is our world and it appears to man differently from the way it does to animals, and again is different for different men and animals. Everything is how it is "in-relation-to." Greatness—for example, physical, moral, historical greatness—is relative to what appears small to us. There is no way to decide what historical greatness is per se, in relation to itself, according to its own nature. Health is relative to disease, hope to despondency, and so on. This skeptical relativism is applied to the relativity of theological concepts as well. Sextus Empiricus discusses the doctrines of God's essence and existence. Both are matters of argument because God is obviously not "wholly revealed" and therefore needs to be demonstrated. To try to prove God by means of something else which is wholly revealed would be illogical. To try to prove Him by means of something which is not wholly revealed would be impossible. Furthermore, the concept of God includes that of divine providence; providence provides either for everything or for some things only. Among the things of this world, however, there are evils. Since it would be impious either to make divine providence responsible for the existence of evil or to assume that God was incapable of creating a world without evil, the dogmatic assertion that God is all-providing puts one in danger of blaspheming. In the face of such contradictory viewpoints and statements, the skeptic remains in suspense while, in pursuing his practical life, he holds no decided opinions. He is religious in the traditional sense, for such a radical suspense of judgment can only be practiced in the realm of theoretical wisdom. The searching skeptic honors the gods, but he cannot decide which religion is the true one, whether the world has been created by God, or whether it is eternal without beginning and end or has merely a contingent existence. And supposing that philosophy begins with amazement, this, too, would be relative, namely, to the customary. A first experience of an earthquake, a first view of the ocean, a first crossing of the Andes by plane, a first blitz—all these amazing experiences necessarily lose this character as soon as we become used to them—and there is hardly anything to which man does not become used.

Because of this relativity of all things to inner and outer situations, to different customs, laws, doctrines, philosophies, and creeds, the skeptic does not venture to decide what a thing is per se, but confronts each one-sided viewpoint and statement with an equally one-sided counterpoint, and goes on searching, instead of judging prematurely through affirmation or negation. Such abstinence produces an intellectual standstill which is joined by a tranquillity of the soul, resulting in ataraxy, that is, a moral imperturbability which corresponds to the theoretical one. The ultimate aim of skeptical wisdom is, therefore, a willed suspension of judgment in all that which is a matter of theoretical uncertainty, and a calmness of mind with regard to the things life imposes upon us. The dogmatists, who do not understand the existential relativity of all our experiences, react foolishly because they believe that things are in themselves good or bad. These relativities were examined so completely by the classical skeptics that there was little left to desire. It is a prejudice to think that only modern historical relativism has brought about the destruction of all dogmatic positions.

Of course, in a given situation, everybody will have to decide in this or that way, without theoretical certainty. But such a practical resolution always falls short of the theoretical insight into the unresolved pros and cons. Practical decisions do not settle the matter philosophically but spring up from the very uncertainty of a purely rational solution. So little do decisions rest on certain insight into what is true and right that they try, rather, to eliminate all skeptical considerations.

If these arguments of classical skepticism seem to be somewhat superficial, Sextus Empiricus has an answer for that. He concludes his essay by saying that the skeptic, for reasons of benevolence, tries to cure the dogmatists by way of persuasion. However, just as physicians administer medicines of different strengths, according to the seriousness of the ailment, the skeptic's arguments, too, have to be lighter or stronger depending on how superficial or deep-rooted the dogmatist's folly is. For this reason the skeptic, intentionally, does not refrain from using weak arguments occasionally—which is, by all means, a compliment.

At this point, one cannot abstain from asking about our own state of wisdom when even within philosophy we are told, by pragmatists and existentialists, to substitute "decision" for insight. It seems that in spite of all our practical skepticism we have become thorough doctrinarians. We have lost the sense of *skepsis* so completely that there is not even as much left as is still alive in Kant's criticism. It is true that Kant believed that by his critical method he had left behind skepticism as well as dogmatism, and that he had found a way out between the two (see the last paragraph of the *Critique of Pure Reason*). And Hegel thought that he had overcome Kant's criticism with his dialectics wherein skepticism is only a vanishing element in the knowledge of the absolute. In absolute wisdom, the skeptical insight into the relativity and uncertainty of all that at first appears certain is, positively, sublated and, at the same time, abolished. The course of the phenomenology of mind is, according to Hegel, "skepticism fulfilling itself," a process in which absolute wisdom gets the better of the incomplete skepticism of searching and researching. With Hegel, skepticism is, therefore, only the "negative side of the knowledge and of the absolute." Hence, Hegel can argue that skepticism is not directed against reason but, like true reason itself, against the dogmatism of abstract human understanding. Skepticism dissolves legitimately all finite determinations without, however, grasping absolute truth. Skepticism shows the contradictions between one-sided determinations without advancing, like Hegel's logic, to the dissolution of the law of contradiction itself.

The doubtful presupposition of Hegel's seeming superiority to the old conflict between skepticism and dogmatism is his concept of reason [*Vernunft*] and its identification with faith. To him both are a comprehension [*Vernehmen*] which comprehends the absolute. In his essay, "Faith and Knowledge," Hegel says that the progressive culture of our time has risen so much above the old antagonism of reason and faith, of philosophy and religion, that this distinction now has its place within philosophy itself, while, on the other hand, critical reason has gained so much influence upon positive religion that the polemics of philosophers against miracles and the like are no longer of avail. In this, however, Hegel deceived himself. It is not by chance that his attempt to reconcile skeptical reason with faith in a philosophy of religion has called forth, with Marx and Kierkegaard, the counterpositions of a materialistic atheism and of a paradoxical faith, both disrupting Hegel's reconciliation all over again.

The simple and genuine difference between searching and finding is too fundamental to be obliterated by either critical or dialectical thinking. It is bound to reappear whatever its guise. And who of us can pretend to possess the whole truth and to be free of doubt? If anything characterizes our intellectual situation, it is that we have become conscious of not being in possession of the truth, whereas former ages honestly believed that they possessed it.

And yet there is no great skeptic who, like Socrates, is able to charm the youth or, as his enemies said, to corrupt them. We look in vain for philosophers who go on with their skeptical search without settling down on so-called findings and who do not pose their questions in such a way as to predetermine the answers. If we were to follow Socrates on his many ways and byways of searching and researching, of questioning and inquiring, we would have to resign ourselves to the fact that there is not a single Socratic dialogue which settles the problem in a more than provisional way. This inconclusiveness corresponds to the literary form of the Platonic dialogue with its divergent perspectives of different partners. Thus all questions retain an open horizon, ending inconclusively, which is also true of every genuine conversation where no one is supposed to have "the last word."

Ironical Socrates did indeed not know what he himself was, what man and what death are, and even less what Being is. He also was not sure whether in all circumstances life is worth living. In his *Gorgias*, he raised the question of whether a man who has been carried safely through many perils with his wife and child and all his goods into port has to be grateful to his captain. The philosophical captain has a modest opinion of his service. He asks only a few drachmas for it because—as Socrates points out—he is doubtful whether he has done his passengers any good by saving their lives. He is aware that none of them is, after the landing, better off as to his soul and body than before his departure. And if, for example, a man was suffering from an incurable disease of body or of soul, it was rather unfortunate for him to have been saved. Only an ironical genius like Socrates could afford such a serious jest. Even the skeptics lost his sense of irony and therefore became skeptical dogmatists.

Kierkegaard, who flattered himself that he was a "Christian

Socrates," was most critical of Hegel's dogmatic system on the ground that existential truth cannot be taught directly and systematically. Yet, his own method of "indirect communication" resulted, and not by accident, in a fanatical and direct testimony to the Christian truth as he understood it, entirely different from the testimony of Socrates who, ironically enough, accepted his death sentence for the sake of a truth unknown to him. The daimonion which gave him his ultimate security and ease was not explicable in terms of knowledge. On the other hand, Kierkegaard's "irony" ends in the sarcasm of his final attack upon present-day Christendom. He is unironical from the very outset. Even in his doctoral thesis on Socratic and romantic irony, he radicalizes the Socratic irony to an "absolute negativity." A total and radical skepticism is, however, no longer ironical and skeptical —and a "Christian Socrates" is therefore a contradiction in terms.

The strange fact that Socrates remained inimitable, that his skeptical irony died out with him, may have its cause in the passionate seriousness of the Christian faith, which in its intellectual elaboration can well be paradoxical but never ironical. The Christian search for redemptive truth and certainty of faith is incompatible with classical irony, skeptical suspense, and ataraxy. Doubt, too, has become more total and intense through Christianity than it ever was in antiquity. Augustine, Pascal, Luther, Kierkegaard—they all seek and search and doubt in a new, passionate way. Classical skepticism discussed rational contradictions with regard to their truth or falsity; Christian and modern doubt refers to the question whether man, who sins and errs, can be "in the truth" at all.

To sum up: to be a skeptical philosopher means to search by relentless questioning: it does not mean to feel sure of a revealed or eternal truth. Christian thinking means to think on the basis of faith. But he who really believes is no longer searching; he has found the truth in the revealed word of God which liberates and saves, though it may be necessary time and again to renew the act of faith. Philosophy, in a Socratic and skeptical way, ceases where faith begins, because the search of researching skepticism ceases when seeking is fulfilled through finding.

On the basis of this simple and fundamental distinction, which seems to be more essential than the traditional contradistinction of reason and revelation, or of knowledge and faith, Tertullian discussed the relation of philosophical skepticism and faith. Granted that this is a radical distinction, there still remains the question whether it would be possible to cross over from the *skepsis* of knowledge to the certainty of faith, or whether they can coexist. These three questions—the radical difference between philosophical skepticism and faith, the possibility of crossing over from the one to the other, and their possible coexistence—can best be made clear by drawing on Tertullian, Kierkegaard, and Pascal.

II

IT IS NOT by chance that the relation between skepticism and faith can be elucidated only through such Christian thinkers, or, in other words, that the problem lies in the relation of faith to skepticism and not vice versa, because philosophical skepticism as such has no proper affinity to faith. The skeptical and critical knowledge of the limits of our knowledge and the awareness of the uncertainty of our traditional certainties do not by themselves lead beyond these limits to faith. On the other hand, faith cannot avoid taking into account the possibilities of knowledge and doubt because the Christian faith itself is the result of a conversion, liable to relapse into doubt. The more interesting unbelievers are those who once believed.

Tertullian's fight against philosophical skepticism is directed against philosophy as such. He also explains all Christian heresies by their dependence on respective philosophical schools. He knows of only one alternative: either "Athens" or "Jerusalem," to be either a philosopher or a Christian. "I don't care if they invent in God's name a Stoic, Platonic, or dialectic Christianity. Since Jesus Christ we need not trouble ourselves with any more researching. If we believe we do not wish for anything beyond our belief. For this is the first thing: that we believe that there is nothing left, beyond faith, to see, to find or to believe. . . ." Tertullian interprets the parables from the Gospel of St. Matthew: Seek and you shall find; knock and the door will be opened unto you; for everyone who asks receives. . . . He wants to show that, at that time and for the Jews, seeking was still necessary but that this is no longer true for us who are already in possession of the message of Christ. Christ taught us what we believe and we have only still to seek to make us fit for believing it. Christian search is no endless research. "We have to seek until we find and to believe when we have found. Then there is nothing else to do but to hold fast what we have seized in faith." The right faith sets bounds to all seeking and searching with ever new findings. Only he who never had faith, or abandoned it, will look for something new. Nobody seeks but he who never had or has lost what he had. If, however, somebody goes on seeking because he does not find, then he seeks where there is nothing to be found and knocks where there is nobody to open. Furthermore, it is against the meaning of honest seeking and asking to do so without trust—that is, faith —or to ask those who are not trustworthy. This means that Christian seeking and finding necessarily takes place within the presupposition of faith. "Let us search in that which is ours, with those who are ours." For a Christian, there is no sense in holding counsel with people who have to admit that they themselves are still seeking in uncertainty. In taking counsel from them, one would fall into the same pit of doubt with them.

In spite of this radical difference between philosophical *skepsis* and faith, as Tertullian stated it, there is, however, a way of crossing over from doubt to faith, though not by a comfortable bridge. Only he who seeks with passion so that his doubt grows into despair may come to believe. But seeking and doubting in such a passionate way is no longer in line with classical skepticism and its ideal of unshakable equanimity, of passionless ataraxy.

Kierkegaard, in his thesis on Lessing, is at first in seeming agreement with him, taking the side of skepticism and doubting that we can ever be sure of the truth. He quotes approvingly Lessing's well-known statement: If God held in his right hand all perfect truth and in his left the vital striving for it and if he, Lessing, had to choose, he would ask for the imperfect and possibly erroneous striving, for pure truth is for God alone. Kierkegaard stresses this preference for the experimental search for truth by praising Lessing for his "skeptical ataraxy" and "religious sensibility," as against the philosophical dogmatists whose childish earnestness lacks the suspense of irony. Concerning Lessing himself, Kierkegaard realized that one could never be sure whether he has attacked Christianity or defended it, for he was at home in the dialectical duplicity of jest and earnestness which prevented him from being in deadly earnest and thereby superficial. Like Socrates, Lessing kept the "wound of the negative" open, which is sometimes the condition for a cure; the all-too-positive ones allow it to heal prematurely. Lessing also knew that there is no direct crossing over from an evident historic truth (for example, the historical person of Jesus) to faith (in Jesus as Christ), except by means of a bold "leap," that is, a risky decision which Lessing (in his famous controversy with Jacobi) refused to undertake, with the ironical excuse that his heavy head and old legs would not permit of such a *"salto mortale."*

Kierkegaard insisted on the "leap of faith" as the "category of decision." Lessing, he says, experimented with doubt, while he himself experimented with faith. Kierkegaard was of the questionable opinion that nobody can embrace the Christian faith, or had ever embraced it, except by such a desperate leap into faith. But to venture it makes sense only if, in the process of skeptical search, one has got into a dead end and if rational doubt has turned into passionate doubt or despair. Kierkegaard's despair of finding the truth through philosophy was not the least reason for his leap into faith. But even so, the encounter with God remains a certainty of faith "on the boundless ocean of uncertainty," for the "Archimedean point of the religious life" is a mere point on which there is no comfortable dwelling.

The simile of the Archimedean point reminds us of Descartes who, too, by his methodical doubt, wanted to find such an unconditional point and he thought he had found it in the self-consciousness of the doubting Ego. Kierkegaard radicalized Descartes' theoretical doubt about the sensual appearance of the corporeal world to a passionate despair about man's being-in-the-world. The doubting Ego is, for him, not a rational self-consciousness but an existing human self. Doubt does not enable him to attain a rational concept of the world but to become his own self in the passion of despair—and despair becomes a springboard from which to dive into faith, which is itself a "passion." One has to doubt "in earnest," says Kierkegaard in opposition to Descartes, and to try to "exist" as a skeptic. It is possible to doubt theoretically, without committing oneself to it, but it is impossible to despair without being fully engaged in it. Despair is totally what theoretical doubt is only partially. Doubt moves with the difference between a theoretical and a practical attitude; despair is comprehensive.

Kierkegaard's radicalization of the Cartesian doubt to an existential despair rests on the fact that he no longer took seriously philosophical theory or contemplation; only the practical, the existential, mattered to him. He no longer approved of the classical and the Cartesian distinction between what can be sensibly doubted in theory though not in practice. The skeptic, says Kierkegaard, must be caught in the practical, ethical realm, because it is much worse to act when we are uncertain than to state our doubt theoretically. According to Kierkegaard, the contradiction between radical theoretical skepticism and practical compromise cannot be maintained. The fact that the ancient skeptics and Descartes tolerated this contradiction seemed to Kierkegaard explicable only on the assumption that they felt sure of their practical conduct at least and thus had some certainty apart from their theoretical doubt. It is the refusal to accept the separation of practical conduct from skeptical search which motivated Kierkegaard to radicalize doubt to despair. Only when doubt has become desperate can it be related to faith, and Kierkegaard interprets this despair as a "sickness unto death," that is, within the perspective of faith.

Quite different from Kierkegaard's is Pascal's position with regard to the relation between skepticism and faith. Pascal combined three qualities in his person: he was a man of science, the exacting science of mathematical physics; he was a profound skeptic; and, last but not least, a Christian believer. As a scientist, he ranks with the great mathematicians and physicists of his time; as a skeptic, he was a disciple of Montaigne and, through him, of classical skepticism; as a believer, he took his place in the tradition of Paul and Augustine. No one of these elements that constituted Pascal's mind disturbed the others; rather, they supplemented each other. "We must know where to doubt, where to feel certain, where to submit." Doubt, scientific certainty, and religious submission unite in Pascal as skeptic, mathematician, and believer. All three ways of conduct are reasonable in their respective fields. One has to understand that there are many things which reason cannot grasp and that there is nothing so conformable to reason as to disavow itself. One has to reach the point where one understands that nowhere in life can a whole and certain truth be attained, either intellectually or morally, that all our principles are partly true and partly false and that such half-truths combined together do not make a whole truth but destroy each other.

In a special fragment (No. 434) Pascal speaks of that which constitutes the main strength of skepticism: the uncertainty of our presuppositions and fundamental decisions. Compared with them, all the uncertainties which classical skeptics have demonstrated are of minor importance, though most people dogmatize on such shaky foundations as the relativity of our historical, social, and psychological conditions. What is more essential is that, without a revealed truth, there is no absolute certainty available for the truth of our principles. Of course, we may feel that certain principles are true and certain. But this kind of natural feeling is not convincing proof and cannot efficiently refute the excesses of skeptical reasoning. Setting aside the certainty of faith, there is no certainty of any kind to prove whether man has come into being through a good creator or through a wicked demon or just by chance. This fundamental uncertainty of our origin also includes the uncertainty of our nature and no dogmatist of natural certainty will be able to give an answer that stands the test. A faint breeze of skepticism compels the dogmatist of natural certainty to let his booty go. In this war of dogmatists and skeptics, everyone has to take sides, for those who intend to remain neutral are already on the skeptics' side, the advantage of which is that all those who are not against them are for them.

"What is man going to do in this situation?" asks Pascal. Shall he doubt everything, whether he wakes or dreams, whether he really doubts, whether he exists at all? He seems to be a strange monstrosity, the only creature that knows something about himself and the whole of being, "a depositor of truth," and at the same time "a sink of error," "the pride and refuse of the universe." Human reason and skepticism must humble themselves and comprehend "that man transcends man infinitely," namely, as a being from God and toward Him. Man has to learn his true condition not from himself, but by listening to the word of his creator. He has to understand particularly two Christian teachings in order to comprehend his human condition: the corruption of human nature by the fall of man, and man's redemption through Jesus Christ. Both are mysteries superseding our natural reason and they alone can explain our condition. Without the mystery of sin and the forgiveness of it, man is to himself less comprehensible than these mysteries. Pascal resolves the perplexity of the human condition through faith, but with the aid of skepticism, which prepares man for the seeking of the truth of religion by shaking up all alleged certainties of his philosophical wisdom. Radical skepticism may open the way to faith, and the certainty of faith in one single thing can afford skepticism with regard to all other things. A man who sets his hope exclusively on the will of God can be thoroughly skeptical with regard to the will and the world of men. The higher our standard of truth, the more can we realize the depth of our illusions.

Thus, skepticism does not simply lead to faith by hitting against the limitation of knowledge. It leads us merely to the threshold of faith and this threshold can be crossed only if God's revelation and grace come to meet man's "will to believe." Hence

Pascal can say, with regard to classical skepticism, that it was downright "true" because before Christ man did not yet know his real condition. But even after God's revelation in Christ, skepticism remains the last wisdom of true searching as long as philosophical search does not surrender to faith in revelation. Of course, one can conceive of a new philosophy after Christ, that is, when a philosopher has become a Christian, but then his position toward the problem of faith is no longer that of a skeptic philosopher but that of a Christian apologist. Hence, there are only three spiritual alternatives: "either to believe in revealed truth, or to deny it, or to doubt well." These three ways of thinking, Pascal says, are to man what the race is to a horse! Accordingly, he distinguishes three classes of men: those who serve God having found Him (they are reasonable and happy); those who seek Him, not having found Him (they are reasonable and unhappy); those who pass their lives neither seeking nor finding (they are foolish and unhappy).

Pascal was little impressed by those who protested that they had eagerly been seeking the truth but could not find it. He suspected them of being busybodies who deceive themselves and whose lack of faith is due to negligence. On the other hand, there are many who think they have faith but are merely superstitious and believe by habit. Pascal realized also that the certainty of faith does not give security.

If we must not act save on a certainty, we ought not to act on religion, for it is not certain. But how many things we do on an uncertainty, sea voyages, battles! I say then we must do nothing at all, for nothing is certain, and that there is more certainty in religion than there is as to whether we may see tomorrow; for it is not certain that we may see tomorrow, and it is certainly possible that we may not see it. We cannot say as much about religion. It is not certain that it is [true]; but who will venture to say that it is certainly possible that it is not?

Behind and above Pascal's acceptance of the uncertainty of our knowledge *and* faith there stands, however, his passionate yearning for an ultimate assurance, and the power and range of his skepticism has to be measured by his will for truth as true certainty. Pascal's memorial begins with a strict distinction of the personal, Biblical God from the God of the philosophers, but immediately there follows twice the word "certitude" and only afterward "peace and joy," namely, on behalf of such a certainty. This insistence on truth as certainty has its motivation in the Christian presupposition that truth is redemptive truth and man's error sin. Apart from such a concern with sin and salvation, the certainty of truth could only be second-rate. It would be difficult to persuade a philosophical skeptic that he should attain absolute certain truth if everything in this world and in the human condition is so profoundly uncertain and all our thinking a constant experiment with truth.

Nietzsche once defined philosophy as the "art of distrust": You propose to teach distrust of truth? Pyrrhon: yes—distrust as it never was yet on earth, distrust of anything and everything. This is the only road to truth. . . . Do not imagine that it will lead you to fruit trees and fair pastures. You will find on this road little hard grains, these are the truths. For years and years you will have to swallow handfuls of lies so as not to die of hunger, although you know that they are lies. But those grains will be sown and planted and perhaps some day will come the harvest. No one may promise that day unless he be a fanatic.

But Nietzsche, "the most pious of the godless," had a religious passion for the absolute and therefore did not abide in his skeptical search and extreme distrust. And if we may trust the wisdom of language, we must indeed doubt whether the search for truth can ever rest on skepticism alone and be divorced from some sort of faith. Not only does the Hebrew word for truth imply nourishment, fidelity, and trust; the English word also derives from the Gothic "trow" [German: *trauen, treu, vertrauen*], that is, to trust, to believe, to have faith. If this is so, then even the most skeptical search for truth would require a faith in order to be true to itself. At this point, our presentation of the problem of skepticism and faith would have to be revised and reversed.

8 / The Quest for the Meaning of History

THE LIMITLESS QUESTION about the meaning of history in general is quite different from the more limited question about the sense of specific events. Both of these problems are distinct from the investigation of those events whose occurrence poses no problem, because they take place naturally, independent of the will of man whose activity brings about the suffering of history. All natural events, such as the history of the earth and the universe, are not historical in the human sense of history. These events occur beyond good and evil and beyond sense and nonsense. We can inquire into the meaning of historical revolutions because we interpret their significance, but we cannot inquire into the sense of re-volution, taken literally, i.e., as the orderly rotation of the heavenly bodies. The rise and fall of civilizations does not take place like the rising and setting of the sun. Thus, we look upon natural catastrophes differently than we do historical catastrophes, although the destruction of a city by an earthquake is no different in its final effects from technically planned destruction by bombs.

When we discuss the meaning of history in its totality, which we glibly call world-history [*Welt-geschichte*], we consider our human world and lightly ignore the rest of the world. Further, this sort of discussion also implies that there is meaning in history in the sense of a purpose or goal toward which the larger historical movements are aiming. If the history of humanity were, in the final analysis, an aimless movement which had no purpose, then —according to the sense of "meaning" assumed in such an inquiry —it would be meaningless. The term "meaninglessness," however, like the term "Godlessness," is ambiguous. It can mean that history has no meaning; more positively, it can also mean that

[131]

we have extricated ourselves from the question about meaning, that we are free of it because we do not believe that history can give a meaning to human existence which it would not have even outside of history or which it would lack without history.

It is hardly accidental that in everyday usage we do not distinguish "sense" from "purpose" and that we interchange "sense" and "aim." Usually, the purpose, the "wherefore," determines the interpretation we put on something's "meaning" or "sense." The meaning of all contingent things which are not what they are by nature, but are willed and created by God or man, is determined by their purpose. A table is what it is because, as a dining table or desk, there is a purpose for which it was made. Even historical events point toward a purpose beyond themselves in that the action which brings them about has an end which determines their sense and meaning. Because history is a temporal movement, the purpose which is its aim must be in the future. Particular events or a series of events, although they are important for man, are not yet meaningful and purposeful as such. The fullness of meaning is a matter of fulfillment that lies in the future. Any pronouncement about the final meaning of historical events is only possible if their future *telos* has been made known. When a historical movement has disclosed its direction and scope, then we reflect on its first appearance in order to determine the meaning of the entire event on the basis of its ending.[1] (Here, "entire" is used in the sense of having a definite beginning and a definite ending.) Therefore, the assumption that history in general has an ultimate meaning anticipates some ultimate purpose as its final aim. The temporal dimension of a *telos* is an eschatological future. But the future is there for us only because we can anticipate something which is not yet present. We "know" the future only through belief and expectation.

Hegel claimed in his philosophy of history that, by and large, one could not only await, hope for, and believe in a final aim of history, but also that this aim could be known, that it could be

1. See Schiller's Jena acceptance speech, *What Is Universal-History and Why Do We Study It?* "The actual sequence of events leads down from the origin of things to their present organization; the universal historian pushes up from the present world-situation toward the origin of things. When he makes an intellectual ascent from the current year or century to the recent past and notices events among events in the recent past which hold the key to the next adjacent period— when he has followed this path, step by step to the beginning of our recorded memory, then he can turn around and retrace his footsteps, using as a guide those events which he has already described and he can descend easily and unencumbered from the very beginning to the present age. This is the world history which we have and which will be presented to you."

grasped philosophically. This is also the thesis of historical materialism. In fact, for Marx, the science of history is the "only" true science because it encompasses everything of human concern, has a definite end and therefore a meaning—the future "kingdom of freedom" whose realization requires a classless society. And even Heidegger's construction of the entire history of metaphysics from Anaximander to Nietzsche in terms of the history of Being [*Seinsgeschichte*], which is nothing less than the entire history of Western thought, is inconceivable without Hegel's philosophy of world-history and history of philosophy. However, for Heidegger, the question about the meaning of history becomes pointless, since rapidly changing human destinies which man, historically, must take upon himself take the place of an ultimate historical purpose.[2]

In the introduction to his lectures on the philosophy of world-history, Hegel sharply distinguished philosophical world-history from "naive" or "factual" history which reports simply and unreflectively what happened in the past. The point behind the distinction was to make history philosophically and rationally understandable as a purposeful and meaningful progressive movement and to justify it for common sense, which sees in history only aimless meandering or else a monotonous repetition of the same old story. Hegel singles out as representatives of factual history the Greek and Roman historians, i.e., those who, unlike Hegel, did not think in terms of a Christian theology of history and its belief in a divine providence, but possessed instead an unbiased view of the changing struggle for power. There are numerous examples of factual history: Herodotus' account of the Persian wars; Thucydides' commentary on the Peloponnesian war; Polybius' recording of Rome's rise to world-dominion; Caesar's description of the Gallic wars; the *Storie Fiorentine* by Machiavelli; *Histoire de mon temps* by Frederick II; and, in our own century, Churchill's *Memoirs*. These histories constructed a unity out of events in past political history and preserved them for the memory of future generations without going into the problem of historical meaning and purpose. The unity which they present is concerned with a sharply limited area of experience. As a result of this limitation, their reports are clear, concrete, and instructive because they record only what they as explorers, statesmen, and generals have seen with their own eyes, actually experienced or made a

2. Heidegger's characteristic play on the word "history" [*Geschichte*] in the meanings of *Geschick, Schickung,* and *Schicksal* cannot be reproduced in other European languages. *Storia, histoire,* and history have nothing in common with *destino, destin,* and destiny. See M. Heidegger, *Denker in dürftiger Zeit,* by Karl Löwith (1960, pp. 44ff.).

part of their experience. However, to quote Hegel, what the experience of history teaches is "that nations and governments never learn anything from history and have never acted according to lessons which could have been drawn from it." [3] But this is exactly what is instructive in factual, straightforward history in contrast to the philosophy of history.

If one wants to study what is essential in history—the spirit of nations—or when one wants to live and to have lived in and with them, then one must become engrossed in these factual historians and pass some time with them. In fact, one cannot spend too much time with them. Here, one has the first-hand history of a people or a regime that is fresh and full of life.[4]

Hegel adds that one could almost rest content with such authors if he had no express desire to become a scholarly historian—not to mention a philosopher of history.

But why was Hegel not content to rest with the factual standpoint and remain within its point of view? Why did he not only go further but so far beyond them? Hegel was not able to find in this factual history the "eye of reason," which discloses the course and development of world-history as a "rational progress in the consciousness of freedom," by whose means all the evil of world-history—"that slaughtering block upon which the happiness of peoples and individuals is sacrificed"—is finally redeemed. The pragmatic reflection of the ordinary historical approach, of course, cannot see in history any such redeeming purpose. Although it is generally acknowledged that laws, and therefore reason, rule in the natural world, no one has yet attempted to point out the precise place of reason in the development of the spiritual world of history and to prove that there is an inner necessity and lawfulness behind what is apparently accidental and chaotic. This reason in history is brought about by those individuals in world-history who know what they want and act accordingly. "The philosophical approach has no other purpose than to eliminate the accidental," [5] and to recognize in the historically important phenomena of *change* the *development* towards increasingly richer and higher stages of spirit [*Geist*] and its freedom.[6] For Hegel, the *logos* of the universe is a "world-spirit" which does not reveal itself in its higher stages in nature but in the historical world of man, because only man is a reflective and active spirit. This absolute

3. *Die Vernunft in der Geschichte.*
4. *Ibid.*, p. 8.
5. *Ibid.*, p. 29.
6. *Ibid.*, pp. 150ff.

world-spirit which first realizes itself in man is at the same time a *will* and, therefore, a spirit of freedom.

We must confront history with the confidence and conviction that the world of *will* cannot be handed over to the accidental. We must assume that a final purpose rules the happenings in nations, that reason prevails in world-history—not the reason of some particular Subject, but a divine, absolute reason. The proof of this truth is our treatment of world-history itself.[7]

We cannot discuss here to what extent Hegel's philosophy of world-history, with its progressive direction toward a meaning which realizes its final purpose, is influenced by the *procursus* toward the kingdom of God in the Christian theology of history, which it secularized.[8] It must suffice to point out that Christianity completely transformed the meaning of history, but this raises the question as to why the Greek philosophers left history to the historians and never made it a subject of philosophical knowledge. Even Aristotle—the teacher and friend of Alexander the Great, who had conquered the Far East and founded an empire—did not devote a single work to history, even though he examined almost everything else: heaven and earth, plants and animals, politics and ethics, rhetoric and poetry. It would be absurd to believe that Aristotle could have seen in Alexander what Hegel saw in Napoleon—a personification of the "world-spirit"—for this would presuppose that the *logos* of the eternal cosmos could enter into the transitory *pragmata* of the history of mortal man. But despite this lack of reflection upon world-history, we cannot assume that the Greeks still did not know what history was and had not yet experienced it "authentically." The Greek historians investigated and reported histories which revolved about important political events, but the Fathers of the Church developed a theology of history from Judaic prophecies and Christian eschatology which extended from the Creation to the Last Judgment and Salvation. Modern post-Christian man invented a philosophy of history which secularized the theological principle of salvation into a promise of worldly fulfillment. When we consider that Deutero-Isaiah and Herodotus were almost contemporaries, we can gauge the distance between Greek wisdom and biblical faith. The "discovery" of the historical world and a historical existence whose meaning lies in the future is not the result of a philosophical insight but the prod-

7. *Ibid.*, p. 29.
8. On this question see, by the same author, *Weltgeschichte und Heilsgeschehen* (1953) [English translation: *Meaning in History*]. Also, E. Gilson, *Metamorphosen des Gottesreiches* (1960).

uct of a confident expectation which originally looked forward to the coming of the kindom of God and only later to a future of man.[9] Certainly, the Christian confidence in a future fulfillment has been lost for the modern historical consciousness, but the focus on the future as such is still predominant. This perspective permeates post-Christian European thought and is the cause of all our anxiety about the purpose and destiny of history. Not only the radically secular philosophies of progress of Condorçet, Saint-Simon, Comte, and Marx are oriented eschatologically toward the future; so are their more recent transformations which appear as negativistic theories of progressive decay. The fatalistic view of progress which is dominant today strikes a balance between these extremes.

F. Schlegel summed up the origin of our historical thought and action in the following way: "The revolutionary desire to realize the kingdom of God is the elastic point of departure for our whole progressive culture and the beginning of modern history." The desire is revolutionary because it reverses the original and natural sense of the *re-volutiones,* and all post-Christian culture is progressive because it continually secularizes the theology of history—from the Augustinian *procursus* towards the kingdom of God ("the pilgrim's progress"), to the Hegelian "progress in the consciousness of freedom" and the Marxian expectation of an earthly kingdom of freedom. But whoever regards all historical events *a priori* from the perspective of the future and of progress directed towards that future, or even as a progressive decay, must look upon all that has happened thus far as preliminary stages in a pre-history whose purpose has not yet been realized. Just as the Old Testament was a *praeparatio evangelica* for the Fathers of the Church and a promise for the future which was only fulfilled by the New Testament, so, in general, the interpretation of the past is now made into a retroactive prophecy. Thus, the past is understood as a meaningful preparation for the future even by the ordinary historian, whose job it is to determine what happened. The modern historian asks, as Tocqueville did, in his introduction to *La Démocratie en Amérique,* "Ou allons-nous donc?" while the classical historian asked how it all came about. Greek history was not oriented toward the future. When it did have occasion to consider the future, it did not do so in the opinion that everything which had happened so far would first realize its meaning in the future, but from the completely different conviction

9. See, by the same author, *Gesammelte Abhandlungen zur Kritik der geschichtlichen Existenz* (1960).

that even future events would submit to the same laws as past events. For the Greeks, human nature does not change fundamentally and it is "the nature of all things to mature and pass away," as Thucydides said. Polybius, who witnessed the collapse of Macedonian hegemony and the rise of Rome to world-dominion, thought it fitting to recall the prophetic words of Demetrius who, in his essay *On Fate*, had foretold what was actually to happen one hundred and fifty years after Alexander's conquest of the Persian empire:

For if you do not keep in mind a countless number of years or many generations but merely the last fifty years or so, you will see in them the cruelty of fate. I ask you if you consider it possible that fifty years ago . . . if a god had prophesied the future, whether the Persians . . . or the Macedonians . . . would ever have believed that during our lifetime the very name of the Persians would be completely wiped out—they who ruled over almost the whole world—and that the Macedonians, whose name was almost unknown, would now be masters? But this fate, which never comes to terms with life, which always upsets our calculations with fresh blows and proves its power in destroying our hopes—this same fate now makes it known to all men that, in furnishing the Macedonians with all the wealth of the Persians, it has only granted them these blessings until it decides to distribute them otherwise.

(Polybius, *History* XXIX, 21)

In the same way, Polybius himself, as a Greek emigrant and a friend of the Roman Scipio, recorded the latter's remarks after the destruction of Carthage. Scipio observed that the same fate which the power of the Romans had just visited upon their enemy would someday befall Rome, just as it had formerly befallen Troy. Polybius adds that it would be difficult to find a remark that was more statesmanlike and more profound. It is worthy of a great man that in the moment of his greatest triumph he reflects on the possible reversal of fate.

How can we fail to see that this supra-historical wisdom is superior to the illusions of the modern historical consciousness? We can hardly conceive of a modern statesman who, after the victorious outcome of the last world war, would reflect, as did Scipio after the destruction of Carthage, that the same fate which has just been meted out to Berlin will someday befall Washington and Moscow. The modern historical consciousness, whether it is based on Hegel, Marx, or Comte, does not know how to unite the remote future with the remote past because it does not want to admit that all things on earth come and go. In this respect however, Greek and Christian thought were completely in agreement and equally far removed from the modern belief in progress. It was as evident for Augustine as for Polybius that political empires are as mortal as individual men, though they may endure somewhat longer. But we need not limit ourselves to Greek and Christian examples alone. In Japan, it has always been customary and proper for leading statesmen and generals to withdraw into Buddhist monasteries after a war—not out of any subsequent surrender to history, but because of a mature insight into the frailty of all things human. Tacitus says the same thing as Polybius: "The more I reflect upon the events of past and present, the the more the illusion and unreliability of all things human are manifested in deliberations and occurrences" (*ludibria rerum mortalium cunctis in negotiis*). It would be foolish to suppose that this complete absence of a belief in the meaning of history makes factual history superficial because it does not discover the hidden design of a divine Providence.

The difference between the classical and the modern historical consciousness can even be shown through language. The Greeks and the Romans had no specific word for what we in the singular call *the* history; they knew about histories (*historiae*) only in the plural. In German, we distinguish between "*Geschichte*" and "*Historie.*" The word "*Geschichte*" has the sense of "occurrence" [*Geschehen*], while "*Historie,*" in contrast, is a foreign word from the Greek which refers to the investigation and reporting of investigated events. In regard to this distinction, Hegel stressed the essential continuity of *res gestae* and *historia rerum gestarum,* because actual *historical* acts and events are simultaneous with historical *consciousness* and historical *accounts.*[10] Nations which live without a historical consciousness have no real history, although many things may happen to them. For this reason too, the principle of Hegel's own interpretation of world-history with its theme of progress towards freedom, i.e., "being-with-oneself in otherness" [*Beisichsein im Anderssein*], is essentially a progress in the "consciousness" of freedom. Freedom can only transform its activity into an actual world of freedom if it is fully conscious of itself. The constitutive connection between historical consciousness and historical events, which Hegel raises to the level of a principle, was just as unknown to the Greeks as all ontology of consciousness. The latter originates with the Christian experience of the self and results in a devaluation of nature which does not know itself, in contrast to a "spirit" or "mind" [*Geist*] which does. History, in Greek, is a verbal concept and simply means investi-

10. *Ibid.,* pp. 164ff.

gating, knowing, being informed, and reporting; it does not refer to any particular and special area of investigation which separates the history of mind from nature and a historical "world" from the natural world. The classical historians record histories but they have no conception of a meaningful progressive world-history. They investigate and record *pragmata,* i.e., events which come about through the political actions of men and not simply through nature. History, in and of itself, can refer to anything that can be investigated and therefore includes natural events too, as in the "natural history" (*historia naturalis*) of Pliny.

The Greeks were deeply impressed by the eternal order and beauty of the visible world, but no Greek thinker would ever think of connecting this well-ordered eternal cosmos with the transitory *pragmata* of human histories in a "world-history." Herodotus, Thucydides, and Polybius investigated and recorded the great events and deeds of their time. But neither the war of the Greeks against the Persians, Athens against Sparta, nor the rise of Rome to a world empire inspired contemporary philosophers to construct a philosophy of history. The reason for the absence of philosophy of history is not apathy toward great events, but the clear recognition that while there can be reports or "histories" of changes which are unique and occur only once, there can be no reliable knowledge. The classical philosophers did not consider history thematically and did not reflect about the meaning of world-history, because as philosophers the object of their inquiry was the unity and totality of natural being and of that which always is. They left in the hands of the political historians the changing historical fates which might always have been other than they are.[11]

Taken literally, "world-history" is a misnomer, for only the natural world is really the all-inclusive or universal "world." Our historical human world is something transitory within the natural world and can disappear like Icarus in Breughel's painting, whose leg alone is still visible as he plunges from heaven into the sea. On the horizon the sun is shining, while on shore a fisherman squats and on the hill a shepherd tends his flock and a farmer ploughs his field as if between heaven and earth, nothing at all

11. See also P. Valéry, *Discours de l'histoire* (1932): "Observez ceci sur vous-mêmes: Toutes les fois que l'histoire vous saisit, que vous pensez historiquement, que vous vous laissez séduire à revivre l'aventure humaine de quelque époque révolue, l'intérêt que vous y prenez est tout soutenu du sentiment que les choses eussent pu être tout autres, tourner tout autrement. A chaque instant, vous supposez un autre *instant suivant* que celui suivet: à chaque présent imaginaire où vous vous placez, vous concevez un autre avenir que celui qui s'est réalisé."

has happened. World-*history* does not stand and fall with man, for the world itself can exist without us; it is supra-human and absolutely self-sufficient. However, since the beginning of the modern age, this unitary and total world has been split into two different worlds: a physical world-project, the world of modern science; and a historical human world, the world of the humanities. The world of nature was philosophically grounded anew by Descartes in the seventeenth century, and the world of history (*il mondo civile*) a century later by his opponent, Vico. At the end of this split between nature and history, there stands the assertion of Hegel's pupil, Marx, that "history is the true natural history of man," that is, that the world which is natural to man is not the world of nature but the world of history because man produces the latter by means of his own labor.[12] Similarly, in the context of the bourgeois philosophy of the nineteenth century, Dilthey remarked, "We do not carry over any meaning from the world (of nature) into the life (of man). We are open to the possibility that sense and meaning originate first with man and his history." [13] The question, then, is this: Who is Dilthey's "we"? Clearly, it is modern post-Christian man who believes that he can find his own meaning in the world of history while he ignores the world of nature, the only truly independent world, and thereby forgets that historically existing man is only in the world because the world of nature produced him.

Nature, for Marx, as for Hegel, is only a subordinate precondition of the historical activity of man, e.g., in producing geographical and climatic circumstances which condition human activity. According to a sarcastic comment of Marx, a superiority of nature over the history of man exists only "on some Australian coral islands of recent origin." What Marx finds interesting in, for example, an apple, is not that there are trees in nature which bear fruit, but that this apparently natural product was imported into Europe during a certain period due to certain economic and social conditions and was traded as merchandise for money. From this radically historical point of view, it is unimportant that man, who in cultivating nature is historically productive, is also a creature of nature and not a self-made *homunculus*. The principle of such historical standpoints is that the self-production of the historical world by means of human labor changes the world of nature. The only fundamental insight which Marx was consciously aware of having taken from *The Phenomenology of Mind* is that

12. See Marx, *Capital*, I, pp. 4, 13.
13. *Collected Works*, VII (1921).

man creates his own world and hence his own self by the activity of work which transforms everything. *Physis*, which at the beginning of Western thought was the "all" and originally the self-sufficient essence of all being, both *natura rerum* and *natura deorum*, is almost nonexistent for historical thought, while history, whose stories the classical philosophers left to the political historians, has, so it seems, become everything. Marx liked to quote Hegel's remark that the most criminal thought is more magnificent and sublime than all the wonders of the starry skies because the criminal, as mind, is conscious of his thoughts whereas nature does not know itself. Marx is no longer astonished by those things which are by nature what they are and cannot be otherwise. Instead, he is indignant because things are not different in the historical world. He therefore wants to "change" the world, a demand which can only be met if, and to whatever degree, the "world" is a world for man.

Thus, the "material" dimension of historical materialism is not nature but the appropriation of nature by man. Whenever Marx refers to the "material" conditions of life, he denies Hegel's starting point—the experiences of "consciousness"—and asserts that these conditions are the historical conditions of work and production. The simple and fundamental meaning of "historical materialism" can be found in this return to a mode of life understood "materialistically" as the historically determined conditions of work and production. Its critical peak was reached through Marx's conflict with the German idealism according to which the real history of humanity is a history of the "idea," the "spirit," and "consciousness." Marx formulated his materialistic thesis in opposition to that preoccupation with consciousness as a point of departure which originated with Descartes. According to Marx, consciousness does not determine "being," but just the reverse; the material, i.e., the social, economic, and historical *being* of man determines his consciousness. For Marx:

One can distinguish man from the other animals by means of consciousness, religion or whatever else one chooses. Men begin to distinguish themselves from animals as soon as they begin to *produce* their means of life. In producing the means of life they indirectly produce their own material existence itself.

This mode of production is not just a reproduction of physical existence, but rather a definite kind of human activity, a historically determined way of life. Individuals are what they express about their lives through the active production of something. "What they are coincides with what and how they produce." The moral, religious, political, and philosophical ideas which men consciously possess about themselves and their world are no original and independent foundation, no point of departure, but rather the ideological reflection of their actual activity in the real conditions of human existence. History does not begin with the so-called history of the spirit and of consciousness, but with the production of the most primitive means for the satisfaction of basic needs. This fundamental history is differentiated and extended through the increase and multiplication of our needs. Through the extension of various modes of production and trade, history becomes world-history which corresponds to a world-market. Marx distinguishes this socio-economic concept of world-history from the Hegelian notion of a "world-spirit" which, according to Marx, is only a fictitious subject.

The Communist Manifesto appeared two years after Marx had finished The German Ideology, his critical discussion of post-Hegelian philosophy. Like the earlier work, the Manifesto is based entirely upon a philosophical concept of history. Its major thesis is that the course of human history consists in a process of perpetual antagonism, in which the conflict between rulers and ruled, exploiters and exploited grows steadily and becomes so critical that it must finally be resolved through the clash of the capitalistic bourgeoisie and the propertyless proletariat. At the end of this conflict there is, for Marx, the ultimate historical expectation that communism will do away with the rule of man over man by abolishing private property. Communism "solves the riddle of history."

Marxist thought and its opponents seem to be worlds apart only so long as we overlook the profound unity between their exclusively historical points of view. Non-Marxist philosophy of history is helpless against Marxism because its thought is just as historical and ideological. It would also like to change the world which it has reduced to world-history—but not quite so radically and at less expense. A century after Marx, non-Marxist philosophy has also discovered that contemporary man is "alienated" and realizes, like Marx, that it stands between "a world that has grown old" and a new historical beginning. Like the young Marx, it is unhappy about the fact that the "old gods" are dead and a "new god" has not yet appeared. With Marx, but also with Nietzsche and Heidegger, it is convinced that man must become something other than he has been in the past and that the whole previous history and philosophy of Europe has reached its end. Thus, it no longer calls itself "philosophy" but the "thinking of being" or of that "which is," namely now and in the future—but not of what always is! In its own way, it shares the "materialistic" thesis that consciousness does not determine being, but that being determines consciousness. It shares Marx's skepticism about a Hegelian "world-spirit" and agrees further with Marx that the path which led to Hegel cannot be followed, that instead there must be a "descent from the summit of metaphysics" and a denial of the absolute and the unconditional. Finally, the non-Marxist view is as godless as Marxism, although it is not as self-satisfied in its unbelief as the professed atheism of the nineteenth century.

Nevertheless, contemporary philosophy, despite its posthumous relationship with Marx, has no dogma, i.e., it has nothing to teach about history that could be used as an answer to the challenge of Marxism. The historical mode of thinking of quasi-Marxists, of converts from Marxism, and of anti-Marxists, lacks the absolute character of historical materialism. These contemporary opponents of Marx stand upon the tottering foundation of an epochal, historical consciousness, but their thought is relative and relativistic, while Marx and Marxism are convinced that they know "what is," what everything depends upon, and at what history is aiming.

Nor, since non-Marxist philosophy has no doctrine, can it indoctrinate the masses. This is both an advantage and a disadvantage. Considered historically, the lack of doctrine is an obvious disadvantage, but from a philosophical and human point of view, it is a modest advantage. That the absence of dogma, or, positively put, skepticism, is an advantage, can only be claimed, however, when there exists a readiness to question the dogmatic presuppositions of non-Marxist thought. Historicism is an example of a thoroughly dogmatic presupposition of contemporary thought, i.e., the belief in the absolute relevance of what is most relative: history. The capitalist and bourgeois world of the West, whose self-criticism is the doctrine of Marx, believes in neither a live cosmos nor a kingdom of God. It has faith only in the "spirit of the age," the *Zeitgeist*, "the wave of the future" or "historical destiny," understood either vulgarly or in a more sophisticated manner. Thus, there are hidden links between idealistic and materialistic historicism and contemporary historico-ontological [*seinsgeschichtlich*] thought which seems to be equally far removed from Marx and from Hegel.

Hegel, the contemporary of Napoleon, conceived his completion of the European history of the spirit to be the fulfillment of an undeveloped beginning that was two thousand years old; Heidegger, the contemporary of Hitler, regards the same history as the completed development of nihilism. Like all radical criticism of the nineteenth century, Heidegger's thought stands at the extreme outer limit of a tradition which has barely lasted until now and it calls into question everything which is fundamental to this tradition—even the logical principles of thinking itself. At the same time, Heidegger's thought moves exclusively within this very same tradition. Even the "fate of being" is limited to the early and late history of the West, as if the universal Being of all beings had some particular preference for the Occident.

9 / The Fate of Progress

THE CONCEPT of progress is often confused with that
of development. We speak of "underdeveloped" nations and mean
countries which still have to develop by assimilating the progress
made by Western civilization. We speak of the progress of science
and in the same sense of its development. Hegel even asserts that
truth has the tendency "to develop," i.e., to unfold in the history
of the spirit. Since this process leads to increasingly complex
and higher stages, Hegel calls this principle of history, in which
reason develops in the world, "progress" in the consciousness of
freedom.

Both development and progress have the formal structure of
becoming rather than of static being. Development and progress,
as forms of becoming, are directed towards the future. Both concepts would be unnecessary in a time that had no future, in an
eternally recurring present. Hence, progress is a movement toward
something in the future, but for that reason alone not every
becoming and not every development is progress. The flowing
waters of a river's course move toward an end but the river does
not make progress. All organic life develops toward some end but
it makes no progress. The seed of a plant develops and becomes
a tree; a fertilized egg becomes a fully developed animal; a human
embryo becomes a mature human being; and the changes which
occur in these processes of growth are often so great that the
original form of the creature can scarcely be recognized in the
final stage.

This natural process of growth and change does not continue
endlessly with ever novel variations, but has its specific end in
every mature member of a species. A fully developed organism
has attained the natural end of its growth; it has become that

which it was in germ from the beginning. This end towards which a living creature naturally develops is the final cause of its first changes. The purpose behind its growth directs and regulates in advance its entire evolution and also awakens the energies that are required for its full development. If a certain seed were not predisposed to become a beech tree, then it would not follow one particular pattern of development rather than another.

Even the history of the evolution that led from single-celled creatures to man represents for the most part progress only if the increasing differentiation of biological organization and the formation of a central nervous system with a brain is taken as a standard. Furthermore, in this case the supposed continuity of biological evolution must be interpreted teleologically, as if all of nature had aimed from the very beginning toward man. This schema of historical development, however, ignores the fact that many highly differentiated species of animals have already become extinct and that even the human animal would disappear if the geological conditions of life were to change. At any rate, the emergence of man cannot be understood as the result of an uninterrupted descent without mutation from the animals any more than as the result of a unique and divine creation. Only man, in contrast to all non-human organisms, can relate himself to his own existence; he can accept it or reject it. He must, however, will his own life because he can also destroy himself. Therefore, he cannot simply "develop"; he must begin to do things on his own very early so that he can become a human being. The first achievements essential for human development involve learning to walk and talk. These must be accomplished first so that man can learn to work and to teach himself how to produce other things. Man and only man cultivates nature and in this way cultivates himself.

It is, of course, true that man is also a human animal that through becoming acquires his own particular being, like all other living things. He develops from a fertilized egg to birth, from infancy to puberty, which is the natural end of growth. Upon reaching puberty, he is considered an adult. However, the biologically mature individual is not *eo ipso* a fully developed and mature person. Most of us remain grown-up children throughout our entire lives, immature and infantile. It is obvious that natural development does not suffice for becoming human, that to become human we must make our own way through life, our own progress. Progress in the individual development of man and in the overall changes in the history of mankind, however, does not lead to any natural perfection. Progress never realizes its purpose. It must always go forward and its final end cannot be foreseen.

The whole of this imperfectible human history is based upon the fact that man does not leave nature as it is, but cultivates the earth by working on it, changing its natural character, domesticating wild animals. All progress, then, is originally a progress in the appropriation of nature, in which man takes control of nature. Culture does not take form from within (*hap' automaton*) like *physis;* it is a result of a human advance beyond nature and away from it. This sort of progress in the cultivation of nature is brought about by human art or skill. Artifice, however, is as natural to man as the automatic processes of organic life, because he cannot live a human existence without cultivating his environment and thus cultivating himself. No matter how great the difference between the most elementary cultivation of nature with primitive instruments and the most modern technical machine production, there is, in principle, no difference, for progress—the movement beyond nature and away from nature—belongs, fundamentally, to the nature of man.

The original history of man in which progress first occurs does not begin with recorded history, but in pre-history, in the remote past when man first came into existence as man. Lucretius' description of progress is no different from Herder's in his *Ideas on the History of Humanity.* Progress, along with its corresponding retrogression, belongs only to the history of human life. If this progress in the cultivation of nature and of himself, which is natural to man, attains its aim and reaches a relative stopping point, then it is referred to as completion or perfection. This completion or perfection, however, is not absolute but relative, for two reasons: first, because the standards of perfection vary according to the basic tendencies of a culture, and second, because only an imperfect creature like man is also perfectible. An absolutely perfect being, such as God, cannot perfect himself in a progressive way, for if he could then he would not already be perfect. And even a natural creature that simply is what it is and cannot become other than what it is, in its own way, is also perfect.

Man, because he is capable of so much, is imperfect and therefore so are his works. A suspension bridge, produced by human technical skill, can always be improved and perfected still further. The threads which spiders have spun with their own bodies for millions of years, always in the same way, from which to suspend themselves and their webs, are neither capable of improvement nor in need of it. The ultimate that a work of human skill can achieve, be it a building or poem or painting, is the appearance that it could not be otherwise, as if it were a work of inner natural necessity that could not be improved. However, as a product of human will and capacity, it could be other than it is; in fact, it could just as well not exist as exist. To this extent then, works of human skill fall short of nature because all human capacities are subject to further progress.

Possible advances toward a relative perfection, therefore, are an integral part of the history of human existence. They are relevant to all definite particular advances. Nor do these possible advances rest upon a belief in progress; they are no illusion, but an undeniable phenomenon of human history. However, they do not indicate that history as such and on the whole is a continual movement forward in the sense of a purposive progress.

Lucretius, in the fifth book of *On the Nature of Things,* tracing the natural history of the world, describes first the evolution of life and earth and finally human life. Man belongs in this natural history because he too is produced by the earth, and the earth, though still relatively young, together with the heavens, will not remain as it is forever, but, having originated in time, must also some day pass away. The cultural progress of the human race falls under this supreme law of growth and decay in nature. Man has gradually progressed in the course of time (*paulatim progrediens*)—in the arts of agriculture and navigation; in the construction of cities and the formulation of laws for society; in the refinement of the comforts of life; in the arts of painting and poetry, "until the highest point is reached in all the arts." But for Lucretius, this progress in the development of the human race does not prove that the condition of man becomes progressively better and better. For all new achievements also bring new dangers and evils. *Ergo hominum genus incassum frustraque laborat:* "So the race of man toils fruitlessly and wastes its life in idle cares." Man does not know how to control his greed or to observe the limits of genuine desire. "It is this inability that in time drove the life of man out upon the sea and aroused the powerful waves of war."

This classical view of progress is confirmed in its sober truth by the description of the Athenian plague in which all hope of further progress is destroyed and which closes the didactic poem.

Death is the absolute limit of all mortal being and Lucretius regards heaven and earth as mortal, too, for in their present form they will pass away.

A whole world, the world of the Christian tradition, separates the classical view of progress from all post-Christian philosophies of history which aim at fulfillment and perfection. F. Schlegel very strikingly expressed the Christian origin of our progressive thinking and acting: "The revolutionary desire to realize the kingdom of God is the elastic starting point of our whole progressive civilization and of the beginning of modern history." The desire is revolutionary because it reverses the originally natural sense of *re-volutiones*, that is, the orderly revolving of celestial bodies. All post-Christian civilization is progressive because it has continually secularized the theology of history; this movement can be traced from Augustine's *procursus* to the kingdom of God, through Hegel's progress towards the freedom of consciousness, to Marx's expectation of a kingdom of freedom on earth. Whoever sees the events of history from the perspective of a future which is directed toward progress, including even a progressive decay, will see in the past only the preparatory stages of a pre-history that has not yet been fulfilled. Just as the Old Testament was, for the Fathers of the Church, an evangelical preparation (*praeparatio evangelica*) and a promise for the future which had been fulfilled by the New Testament, so the interpretation of the past becomes a retrospective prophecy and the past comes to be understood as a meaningful preparation for the future.

The Christian faith in an ultimate fulfillment, it is true, has disappeared from the modern historical consciousness. However, faith in the future as such and in some indefinite consummation has remained dominant. A devotional book of the seventeenth century, John Bunyan's *The Pilgrim's Progress*, describes in allegorical form the progress of the pilgrim, namely, "from this world to that which is to come." But in the same century, the world to come began to be understood, not as a kingdom of God beyond this world and its history, but as a kingdom of man, a better world in the future. The other-worldly destiny of man gave way to a worldly purpose. Man no longer "transcended" to God as the *summum bonum* but to a human world capable of improvement. The radical philosophies of progress of Condorçet, Saint-Simon, Comte, and others, whose common idea is the progress of "science," i.e., of mathematical physics, are not alone in their orientation toward the future. The same orientation is found in the transformation of these philosophies into theories of decay which look upon progress as something negative and which interpret the entire history of Europe as a single, consistent development of a "nihilism" which will be consummated in an "age of complete absurdity."

Rousseau had already questioned in principle the idea of progress, which was to dominate the historical thinking of the eighteenth and nineteenth centuries. A century later, Leopardi, Flaubert, and Baudelaire were to ridicule it in a manner which has yet to be surpassed. However, for the ordinary unsophisticated person, the belief in progress has only been in disrepute since the First World War; until then, it had been the pride and hope of civilized mankind. A few years before the First World War, there appeared two books by Georges Sorel, the French sociologist and philosopher, entitled *The Illusion of Progress* (*Les Illusions du progrès*) and *Reflections on Violence* (*Réflexions sur la violence*). Both books oppose the widespread belief that civilization had now progressed to such a point that it would dispense with violence. Sorel, however, had advanced beyond this "bourgeois" belief in progress. But despite his unconventional disbelief in the peaceful progress of civilization, it is undeniable that Sorel too, impressed by the Russian revolution, wished to move beyond the *status quo*.

That derision of the idea of progress which has become customary among the educated is just as shortsighted as the moral expectations which in an earlier period were aroused by scientific progress. It would be just as futile to deny that in the last hundred years technology and medicine, both based upon physical science, have made enormous progress as it would be to argue about whether or not the great literary works of the ancients surpass those of the moderns—since we do not recognize either as a standard but "interpret" both from a historically conditioned point of view. Scientific progress has not only realized, but far exceeded, the expectations of Bacon and Descartes in the seventeenth century, and of Turgot, Condorçet, and Comte in the eighteenth and nineteenth centuries. Our technically developed mathematical physics is not just one science among other sciences, but *that* science which for the past century has stamped and, what is more, continues to determine the total public existence of civilized mankind. Even those who no longer have *faith* in progress and would never make a religion of it make continual use of its actual advances, for they can neither do without them nor escape from their influence. There are no longer any blessed isles that progress cannot reach. Nestroy made the famous remark that "in general, it can be said of progress that it appears to be much greater than it is in reality." But just the opposite seems to be true, i.e., that in general it can be said of progress that it is in reality much greater than it appears to be, but we scarcely notice progress any longer because we have become so accustomed to it.

The concept of progress referred at first to advances in science and art; the word *progrès* was used in its plural form. In Germany, the word *Fortschritt* came into use around 1750 alongside the older *Fortgang* as a translated term borrowed from another language. During the French Revolution, *progrès* became synonymous with *nouveauté*. The famous literary dispute, *querelle des Anciens et des Modernes*—the "quarrel of the ancients and the moderns"—in which Fontenelle in France, Swift in England, Vico in Italy, and Lessing in Germany took part, was decided in favor of the moderns because they had *progressed* beyond the ancients. For a long time France was the nation which marched in the forefront of progress.

In our own century, the idea of the West with its progressive civilization has been transplanted to America. Since America now has taken over the position of power which formerly belonged to Europe, it is quite simply considered to be *the West*. Russia has become the chief competitor of America since it has been progressively modernized through industrialization and scientific technology. In America, the idea of progress has always been dominated by the scientific positivism of August Comte; in Russia, by Marxism as "scientific socialism." However, both share a positivistic, scientific will-to-progress and a belief in the possibility of producing a better world even though, viewed historically, neither country is the source of this will-to-progress. Its origin can be traced to Europe and the European philosophies of history. And how decisive a belief in progress has been even for Marxist thought is shown in its criticism of the literary productions of the "bourgeois" world. The Marxist critic passes judgment on this literature from the simplistic standpoint of whether or not it is "progressive" or "reactionary." And in America, too, the word "progressive" is, in itself, a positive judgment of value.

This positive evaluation of progress became common from 1830 on, with the beginning of industrialization, for nothing was more in evidence than progress; for example, in social welfare and social security, in the struggle against epidemics, disease, and the high mortality rate, and in the spread of education and knowledge through compulsory schools and through newspapers and magazines. A country in which a large percentage of the population is still illiterate, and in which sanitary conditions as well as electricity, telephone, and similar conveniences are still rare, is everywhere looked upon as backward. The number of schools in which reading and writing is taught, the huge editions of the daily newspaper, the greatest possible distribution of radio and television sets, the large editions of pocketbooks, and the Everyman's Library—*Rowohlt-Taschenbücher* in Germany—are all evidence of progress in the pursuit of increased knowledge and education. The same is true of economic conditions. A continually increasing number of consumer goods, which a few generations ago were looked upon as luxuries for a small but wealthy minority, have become available to all and are now regarded as universal necessities. What was originally a luxury is now an ordinary necessity, because the standard of living is rising continually, i.e., our expectations and demands are forcing it up. Within the very broad range that includes both education and economic conditions, progress is by no means an outmoded ideology or an illusion, but a historical fact of supreme significance.

The penetration of a country by scientific technology and industry and the progress which accompanies it changes everything very rapidly. The nations of East Asia are no exception. It is not accidental that social change in this part of the world is pursued under the banner of Marxian communism, for it is Marxist ideology which has introduced the concept of scientific and technical progress into these countries. Communism in the Orient means something quite different than it does in the West. Its affinities are with the revolutionary origin of the European labor movement. In the East, communism is the incarnation of progress, a sort of secular religion of progress. For centuries, the people of India, China, and Africa knew nothing about the radical and revolutionary demand for progress. But once progress is experienced, something is set in motion that cannot be stopped.

The demand for progress itself becomes progressive. This happened in the West; and now it is happening in the East. Nehru recognized this clearly, when he declared that progressive social change must come about quickly enough to keep alive the hopes that are bound up with it; the quicker the pace of progress, the better the prospects for reform. In this way, a sort of competition arises between actual progress and the progressive demand for such progress. Progress, in itself, has no limits; it is insatiable. The more progress we achieve, the more we demand and pursue. If it took twenty-five hours to fly from Frankfurt to New York a few years ago and now it takes only six hours, then there is no reason why the flying time cannot be reduced still further in the near future. If the average life span can be extended from forty to sixty years, then why not from sixty to ninety years? And so it is with everything in which any sort of progress is possible.

Progress as a universal fact is not associated with just any science but with one particular one, with modern physical science as it arose in the seventeenth century and which, up to the nineteenth century, was regarded as the *only* science. Today, even more than then, it is regarded as the only science. Its methodological paradigm was Descartes' project for a universal science of mathematics that was intended to explain and to help us control the forces of nature. Similar to this, for Kant, was Newton's world-science [*Welt-wissenschaft*], as he called Newton's mathematical physics, which he considered to be the only genuine science. And for Comte, too, social science is thought of as *social physics* (*physique social*), while Pareto, in turn, followed Comte in his orientation towards natural science. If Hegel and Marx declared in the nineteenth century that the science of history is more inclusive and more fundamental than the physical sciences, then their inspiration—the inspiration of historical materialism, idealism, and of historicism in general—was the experience of the French Revolution. This is the experience that now man can "stand on his head," because he can change the world in accordance with his own will.

In regard to this modern revolutionary concept of the history of humanity, it has been said with some justice that history has become for us the most urgent, universal, and serious problem. However, this supremacy of history only apparently contradicts the actual predominance of physical science. History has only become a pressing concern because of the advances of physical science which brought about radical changes in our historical existence. History has become an urgent problem within the last century just because scientific technology, and military technology in particular, have altered human relations at an extremely rapid rate. Modern physical science is a power which changes and destroys tradition; since it never ceases to move forward, it cannot leave things as they are. For us, history is no longer the occurrence of change within a world that has a stable natural order, but everything which, for us, *is the world* is drawn into the historical process. And since history is the opposite of all that is constant, enduring, and eternal, and since, in its modern character, it transforms radically whatever exists, it is impossible to take a firm foothold in history from which to proclaim truths valid for all time.

What we scarcely still realize, because it has become so much a part of everyday life, is that the revolution of progress was originally a utopian program. Modern scientific technology had already been foreseen by some forward-looking thinkers of the late middle ages, in particular by Roger Bacon, a Franciscan monk of the thirteenth century. In his thought, alchemy and astrology were strangely blended with mathematics. Both magic and mathematics, he felt, should be used to manipulate nature in such a way that it could be controlled for the benefit of man. He himself had already projected a sort of experimental science, whose results could be used practically for the transformation of elemental natural forces. The word "experiment" at that time meant a magical action by means of which power might be gained over man and nature. For example, Bacon conceived of automatic ships, airplanes, and submarines that would strengthen the power of man and unleash the hidden powers of nature. His ultimate aim was the utility of science for mankind. Science, for him, was no longer the *theoria* of Aristotle, i.e., knowledge for the sake of knowledge; instead, science was to be cultivated because of its practical usefulness, just as the aim of the experiments of the alchemists was to produce gold for the use of man. Although the concept of progress which lay at the basis of this experimental science had its origin in alchemy, its tendency, nevertheless, was modern, for it sought to establish the superiority of the "secular" sciences over theology. Roger Bacon argued for this superiority on the grounds that only "secular" science could bring about practical improvements and progress. All this was done in the service of the church and under instructions from Pope Clement IV. It was hoped that the new experimental science would serve the Pope's desire for world-dominion at a critical time for the church, when the Mongolian hordes invaded the Christian world.

Roger Bacon was convinced that a universal Christian state could only be established by means of this new scientific and technical mastery of the world. He proposed to the Pope the substitution of the mission of science for the traditional foreign mission of preaching, because only an efficient science could make people accept the truth of the Christian faith. He conceived of means of destruction, such as gunpowder, which he already knew how to produce, and the invention of burning reflectors that could be used to destroy any hostile army at great distances. He also imagined other special materials that would do away with non-Christian enemies. At the same time, he took care in his projects that these means of annihilation and of "miraculous utility" (*mirabilis utilitas*) would spare the lives of righteous believers. In his opinion, Saint Louis might succeed in his Crusades if he would go into the Holy Land with the burning reflectors mentioned above and with some technical experts. He even based his experimental science on a passage from the first book of Moses where it is written that God created man in his own image that he might make the earth subject to him. But he also referred to the myth of Prometheus, whom he called a "great scholar" and a "philosopher."

Christopher Columbus, who lived during the fifteenth century, was a Prometheus of the Christian world. Like Roger Bacon, he still lived within the magic-hermetical sphere of the Middle Ages, fearfully waiting for the break of Doomsday and at the same time passionately seeking the gold of the new world which he supposed to be somewhere near Japan. His belief that he could reach India by sea, which resulted in his accidental discovery of the New World, was based upon certain arguments of Roger Bacon and also upon Josaiah's prophecy of a new Heaven and new earth. He also considered his daring enterprise to be a Christian mission. The seamier side of this missionary zeal was the promise made to the Spanish king that he would enslave the natives and deport them to Spain at the same time that he announced the discovery of gold. Two years later, Pope Alexander VI issued an edict drawing a line from the North Pole to the South Pole in order to separate the Spanish and Portuguese spheres of interest.

A century later, Francis Bacon, the philosopher and statesman, wrote his utopia, *Nova Atlantis*. This, along with his other famous work, *The Advancement of Learning*, set forth a program for scientific progress whose aim was "proficiency" in the betterment of human life. The motto of his utopia was *scientia et potentia in idem coincidunt:* knowledge and power are the same. The greater the extent of our knowledge, the greater our power over nature. With this motto Bacon provides the key to the development of the modern world up to the present time. Theoretical speculation is only one part of science; Bacon wanted to make science more practical and efficacious in its application for "the kingdom of man." Through science, man must subject nature to transformations whose purpose is to change the world by continually improving it. In this respect, Bacon compared himself to Columbus, as the title, *Nova Atlantis*, already reveals. The goal which he formulated for his program was to produce as much as possible, artificially, through the transmutation of elements, the production of artificial materials, and, finally, the discovery of the elixir of life. Bacon's project has become reality. Today, we accelerate the blossoming of plants, increase the size of fruits and animals, develop new species, and crossbreed old ones. We practice vivisection and experiment on animals with poisonous substances; through artificial means, we kill and bring to life again; we produce giants and dwarfs; we sterilize, desterilize, and breed artificial deformities. And in the scientific industrial plants of Bacon's utopia, there are already meteorological stations, cold-storage depots, weatherchambers for the treatment of the sick, hydraulic power plants, skyscrapers, heating apparatus, and even artificial remedies for obesity and malnutrition.

The practical science outlined by Bacon came to be an independent mathematical physical science in the seventeenth century through Descartes, Galileo, and finally Newton. The essential significance of this period is that mathematical physics was finally set free, that is, it was disengaged from everything that was not mechanically and quantitatively determinable. This separation led to the divorce of nature and natural science from the life of the universe and all questions of theology and morality. For the first time, the natural world was transformed from a partner into an object that can be manipulated through calculation and experiment for the purpose of *utilitas* and *potentia*.

Kant was the first philosopher to reflect clearly on the new situation which had been created by physical science. He acknowledged unconditionally that the world had been conquered by an objectifying science, but he recognized too that it explained neither biological phenomena nor the human being as a moral person. Thus, he drew a distinction between theoretical and practical reason and sought the ground of the genuinely human sphere in moral postulates, not in the theoretical knowledge of science.

Only Goethe revolted against the dichotomy between man and nature and against modern physics. The central theme of *Faust* is the problem of the Promethean will to technical mastery of the world. He, Goethe, foresaw that with the nineteenth century an era had begun whose dominant tendency was progress toward more power, greater wealth, and increasing speed—toward what he called *"das Veloziferische."* In 1825, in a letter to Zelter, he wrote:

Everything nowadays is *ultra*, everything is being transcended continually in thought as well as action. No one understands himself any longer; no one can grasp the element in which he lives and works or the materials that he handles. . . . Young people are stirred up much too early in life and then swept along in the confusion of the times. Wealth and speed amaze the world and it is these that all are striving for. Railroads, steamers, all the possible means of communication are the sort of things that the civilized world seeks but it only becomes over-civilized and thus persists in its mediocrity. This is also the effect of dispersion, of the fact that an average culture has spread out and become a common culture. It is the century of clever practical men who have a certain limited talent and feel superior to the masses, although they themselves have no higher gifts.

At the end of the last edition of his works, Goethe affixed his poem "Pandora" in which Prometheus and Epimetheus symbolize the discord of the time to come. Epimetheus is the prototype of the visionary, the reflective and ascetic man who still experiences the world as a "cosmos." Opposed to him stands Prometheus, the prototype of Faust, the man who is constantly planning and acting, the man for whom everything is useful, the *homo faber*.

The *fatefulness* of this progressive development lies precisely in what seemingly justifies it in its colossal *success*. The path of the revolution that now covers the earth with a technical superworld of industries and traffic centers, which multiplies continually the size of the population, and now makes it possible to hear, speak, see, and speed around the world in a matter of seconds, has led from the kinetic theory of gases to the steam engine, and from quantum theory to the splitting of the atom. Because of the incredible advances made possible by scientific progress, the physicist has taken the place of the theologian; planned progress has taken over the function of Providence. The vision of the Franciscan, Roger Bacon, of the Christian mission of natural science, has been realized in an unchristian manner and the original optimism about progress has given way to a fatalism.

Within one generation, two world wars have shaken the self-confidence of the eighteenth- and nineteenth-century belief in progress, and have awakened us to a consciousness of the total forces that are at work in the midst of all this rational planning and foresight. Otto Hahn, the discoverer of nuclear fission, sees an analogy between atomic physics and primitive magic, which he described in a work significantly entitled *Modern Alchemy*. "If we still understand alchemy today as the artificial transmutation of one element into another, then perhaps we can justly characterize the natural scientists of the present century as the true alchemists." In fact, modern physics is not only concerned with the artificial transformation of elements into other elements, but also with the synthetic production of elements that cannot be found in nature at all. To this, which a generation ago would have been considered inconceivable, must be added the breakthroughs in the areas of the immeasurably small and immeasurably large which go far beyond the old program of progress, because they not only render usable a nature that is given to man, but also create a new world of artificial forces. This acceleration of scientific progress is paralleled by the progressive alteration and dissolution of the old European traditions in religion, morals, politics, and social life. The two world wars stimulated new inventions which, in turn, have had political repercussions. What was once "utopian" has now been realized, and the only "problem" which still remains is how to transform man so that he can come to terms with his own inventions. Thus, Nietzsche's lament that man has become "homeless" is already obsolete, for we are at home nowhere precisely because we can be anywhere and everywhere. Man is now able to put himself in a metal capsule that can go around the earth and return within a short time.

Promethean man now knows that unusual and radical efforts are needed if he is not to be destroyed by the forces that his own productivity has unleashed. Over a century ago, Marx had already grasped this problem under the notion of "self-alienation," which became the central concern of his thought. In sharp contrast to Marx's clear understanding of the anti-religious character of modern scientific progress, Catholic and Protestant theologians have attempted to convince themselves and their flocks that these progressive developments are God's will, as if the Vatican radio transmitter were something like the miracle of Whitsuntide. The stage in the utilization of natural forces through technological science which is now beginning is the atomic age. When the first atomic bomb was dropped, the dilemma of progress became inescapable.

Within the area of nuclear weapons, the effect of scientific progress has been that each nuclear power fears the other as a potential enemy that may be advancing too quickly and this fear then stimulates a mutual competition for further nuclear "progress." The history of the production of nuclear weapons, which Robert Jungk describes in his book, *Brighter Than a Thousand Suns,* gives a telling description of a sort of schizophrenia on the part of responsible scientists and politicians. After having invented this miraculous weapon and after the first atomic bomb was dropped on Japan, the physicists placed the responsibility for it on the politicians, while the technicians and military men who carried out the mission held the physicists responsible for having invented it. However, after these temporary pangs of conscience passed, most of America's nuclear physicists returned to their national institutes for research and continued experimenting, thereby making use of the millions of dollars they received in grants from the armed forces and federal government.

But even this situation is not as novel as it appears. Alfred Nobel, the inventor of the most disastrous, destructive material of his time, was the prototype, so to speak, of this kind of schizophrenia. Nobel hoped that through the production of dynamite, no one would make war in the future. After his hope came to nought, he went into self-imposed exile. Shortly before his death, he established the Nobel Prize, which is granted both for endeavors in the advancement of world peace and for scientific discoveries which make possible the most radical sort of destruction.

Caught up in the race between progress and annihilation in 1955, eighteen Nobel Prize winners from all parts of the world professed their *allegiance to science* on one hand, but confessed on the other to their helplessness in the face of the possible consequences of unlimited scientific progress. Just as in Aeschylus' drama, *Prometheus Bound*, the Promethides exchanged the vision of the future that was denied them for the most deceptive of all the gifts of Prometheus—blind hope—so the appeal of these atomic physicists was inspired by the same blind hope that all nations would voluntarily decide in favor of a renunciation of force. However, fear of the final outcome is concealed by the vision of enormous peaceful advances and benefits. An uncanny coincidence of fatalism and a will to progress presently characterizes all contemporary thinking about the future course of history. Progress now threatens us; it has become our fate.

The question which now confronts us is this: is there any way to moderate this progress, which in itself is so lacking in moderation, or is it inevitable that *man will do everything and anything that he is able to do*? Are there any bounds to the freedom for everything and nothing? At this crucial point, modern post-Christian thought—which no longer accepts biblical religion, but still maintains, in the Christian tradition, that the world has been created for man—diverges sharply from Greek thinking as expressed in the myth of Prometheus. A reflection on the myth of Prometheus can be very revealing. Man received the *gifts* of Prometheus—and these are the gifts of man as such which set

him apart from gods and beasts—*together with their dangers*.
A naked worship of technology was unknown to the Greeks. Prometheus, to be sure, frees mankind with fire stolen from the gods,
but he does not redeem man; in fact, he is himself punished and
put in chains by Zeus. And we who now stand at the end of this
original rebellion, an end which we call the beginning of the
atomic age, are also *set free* and yet *imprisoned* by our own power.
The optimism that surrounded the idea of progress in the eighteenth and nineteenth centuries did not foresee that freedom can
also enslave. And if a century ago Comte prophesied that the
progress of science and industry would make vast destructive
wars in the future impossible, so it is just the reverse for us, for
from being optimists about progress, we have become fatalists.
Progress itself goes on progressing; we can no longer stop it or
turn it around—a state of affairs which sheds a remarkable light
on Hegel's thesis that history is the history of a progressive realization of freedom.

In the cult of Prometheus, the Greeks atoned for the theft of
the heavenly fire in the myth of the chained Prometheus, because
they felt deeply that this theft had provided man with a power
which must be kept within the strictest limits if it were not to
destroy him. The myth reveals a holy awe in the face of every
assault upon the powers of nature, upon the physical cosmos
which the Greeks regarded, in sharp contrast to human powers, as
something divine. All such awe seems now to have vanished.

In the present age, we live in a mixture of amazement at
the technical progress which we are making and anxiety in the
face of its success. We experiment freely; we calculate everything
that can be calculated, and we do everything that can be done.
From mythical prehistoric times to the end of the Middle Ages,
every such inventive assault was accompanied by religious cere-
monies and sacrifices which dispelled the powers which had
been conjured up. The same sort of thing took place with the
founding of every Greek city-state—a violation of the sacred
earth—and with every ship that was put to sea. One relic of
these sacrificial customs which is misunderstood, for the most
part, is the smashing of a bottle on the bow of a ship ready to
sail; and another, the ribbons put on the top of a newly built house.
But, it cannot even be said that the attitude of modern physical
science toward nature is sacrilegious, because it is without awe.
Sacrilege would presuppose that the world of nature, the physical
cosmos, is something higher than man, something sacred and
divine, and not just a relational system of quanta of energy that

can be represented in mathematical equations. And as long as we do not fundamentally revise our entire relation to the world, but still assume, in the tradition of the biblical story of creation and the Christian roots of modern physical science, that the world of nature is there *for man,* then it is hard to envisage any possible change in the dilemma of progress.

As we noted above, progress is only possible in a time that is essentially oriented toward the future. There is neither development nor progress in an everlasting present. In contrast to the classical and literal sense of the word "history," however, it is characteristic of the modern historical consciousness that it is thoroughly drenched by the sense of the future and in consequence lives both in fear and hope. The will to progress is kept alive by expectations for the future. The decisive question, therefore, in regard to our being as it exists in the future, is whether the time of the world is a perpetual and everlasting time, in contrast to the finite and mortal time of man. It is difficult to see how we could conceive of finite time, if we exclude the possibility of an eternal time. Nevertheless, the idea of progress would lose the significance it has for us if there were something like an everlasting universal time in which new things are continuously created and old things pass away. The gravity and immense significance of the problem of progress today springs precisely from the fact that we know of nothing which lasts forever.

10 / Hegel and the Christian Religion

Philosophy is required to justify its starting point, its mode of cognition; in this way it became opposed to religion. Conversely, the church and religion have shown hostility towards philosophizing and condemned it. Even the Greek folk-religion banished several philosophers; this hostility is present even more in the Christian church. Hence, it is not only a question of whether one must take religion into consideration in the history of philosophy, for, in fact, philosophy has taken religion into consideration and religion has done the same with philosophy. Since neither of these fields has disregarded the other throughout history, we must not do so either. Thus, we must speak openly and honorably about their relations: *aborder la question*, as the French put it. We must not wrangle about whether such a discussion is too delicate, whether we can extricate ourselves by talking around the subject, or look for other excuses and evasions; otherwise, in the end, the discussion will no longer be understandable. We must not pretend that religion ought to be left alone. This pretence is due to nothing other than our desire to conceal the fact that philosophy has turned against religion.[1]

Hegel received his first scientific education in the theological seminary at Tübingen, where Schelling and Hölderlin were his fellow students. At the age of 20 he became a tutor in philosophy in order to devote three additional years to the study of theology. In 1793 he passed the examination in theology and became a candidate for the doctorate. In a *curriculum vitae*, written by Hegel himself, he says: "I took up the profession of holy orders because of the desires of my parents and remained true to my intention to study theology because of its relation to classical literature and philosophy." Hegel, then, from the start was a *theologian—for the sake of philosophy*. Accordingly, he first of

1. Hegel, *Works*, XIII, p. 80. We cite the works according to the edition published by a society of friends of the deceased. (Berlin, 1832ff.), 2nd edition.

all chose a profession which "was independent of the business of the minister's office." This profession afforded him the leisure to devote himself "to classical literature and philosophy," that is to say, as a tutor first in Bern and later in Frankfurt (1793–1799). Finally, he decided solely in favor of philosophy and attempted to acquire a teaching position at the University of Jena.

At the beginning of this period (1802) there appeared his important work, *Belief and Knowledge*, in which he took issue with Kant, Jacobi, and Fichte. Extensive outlines for essays on Greek folk-religion, the spirit of Judaism and Christianity, and the life of Jesus had preceded this work. These early studies also contained topical essays on the economic and political constitution of the contemporary world, whose foundations had been shaken by the French Revolution. Ever since Christianity had burst upon the ancient world, religion and politics had been divided from each other by the separation of the supernatural kingdom of God from the natural human world. Hegel's thoughtful and penetrating examination of these fields formed the basis on which he painstakingly, but steadily and systematically, worked out the fundamental concepts of his philosophy of subjective, objective, and absolute spirit. It is both the greatness and the peculiarity of Hegel's philosophy that even though it is saturated with reality, at the same time it views reality with the power of thought which can abstract the structure from content and thereby characterize the real in abstraction from matter, hence, according to its "concept" [*Begriff*]. Even the formal categories of logic refer to content: they determine the essential forms of all that exists. Hegel's logic is *onto-logy* just as ontology is, for Hegel, at the same time *theology: onto-theo-logic*, or more popularly expressed, philosophy of religion. In this respect it is noteworthy that at Berlin in 1829, Hegel recommended as complementary to his lectures on the proofs for God's existence his lectures on logic, which were given during the semester, and that his last lecture in 1831 had the ontological proof as its theme, the relation of "being" and "concept." Hegel's lectures on the philosophy of religion, held four times during the years 1829–1831, are the mature result of his youthful desire to understand about what it means "to come close to God" [2] and to ground intellectually "the kingdom of God." Thus, Hegel moved along the path, although with increasing critical distance, that had been marked out for him in the religious writings of Kant, Fichte, Mendelssohn, and Lessing.

2. Letter to Schelling of August 30, 1795. Cf. *Letters by and to Hegel*, ed. J. Hoffmeister. I (Hamburg, 1952), p. 29.

From the beginning, Hegel's relation to the Christian religion and theology was essentially ambiguous because it consisted in a philosophical *justification* of this religion by means of a *critique* of religious modes of thought. Or, to use the fundamental concept of Hegel's philosophy whose meaning is twofold: it consists in the "sublation" [*Aufhebung*] of religion into philosophy.* Philosophy "sublates" religion in the sense of both preserving and destroying it, because it raises through reflection the figurative ideas [*Vorstellungen*] of religion to the level of concepts [*Begriff*]. For example, at the very beginning of his lectures, Hegel remarks that the expression "philosophy of religion" is somewhat misleading, because it gives the impression that religion exists for philosophy like an object among other objects. But in fact, philosophy is, in itself and regarded as a whole, already religion and "only explicates itself in explicating religion." [3] The need and interest of philosophy is the same as that of the Christian religion and its theology: "God, nothing but God, and the explication of God," [4] who as absolute spirit or mind [*Geist*] is the absolute truth which makes us free.[5] This determination of God as mind or *Logos*, which is basic to everything else, is taken from the philosophical gospel according to John. However, it is based just as much on the *nous* which thinks itself of Aristotle's *Metaphysics* (XII, 7), quoted at the end of the *Encyclopedia of the Philosophical Sciences*, that last *Summa* of knowledge—as if the Aristotelian *nous* and the *Logos* of John were one and the same *mind*.

Even though Hegel distinguishes himself from his predecessors through his compromise between Christian and Greek tradition by a sort of gnostic Christology [6] and through the twofold meaning of his "sublation" of the Christian religion, he nonetheless operates out of that critical tradition which is common to all of modern philosophy. This tradition extends from Descartes' rational proof of God's existence (designed to convince atheists since it does not require faith) through Spinoza's critique of the

---

* Since there is no adequate English translation of the complex sense which Hegel bestows upon the German *Aufhebung*, we have chosen to render it by the somewhat artificial English term "sublation." "Sublation" has the double sense of "cancel" and "elevate," where the meaning of whatever is taken up into a higher synthesis is "canceled," to emerge transformed in a new content.—Trans.

3. *Phil. of Religion*, Part 1, pp. 28f. We cite according to *Hegel: Lectures on the Philosophy of Religion*, ed. G. Lasson. Parts 1–3 (Leipzig, 1925–30). (Parts 2 and 3 are divided into half-volumes, cited thus: Part 2/1, etc.)

4. *Ibid.*, p. 29.

5. See *Encyclopedia of the Philosophical Sciences in Outline*, §1 and §382; *Phil. of Religion*, Part 3/1, p. 35.

6. Inspired by Hegel, F. Chr. Baur described *The Christian Gnosis or the Christian Philosophy of Religion* (1835) in its historical development.

Bible and Kant's *Religion Within the Limits of Reason Alone* to Fichte's *Critique of All Revelation* and Schelling's *Philosophy of Revelation,* which outlines a third gospel of the Holy Spirit whereby the Catholic and Protestant Christianity of Father and Son, which had prevailed up to that time, shall develop from a partial "gnosis" into universal philosophical truth. These transformations of the Christian religion into philosophy are far removed from the harmlessness of what is called, in American universities and theological seminaries, "the philosophy of religion." The aim of Hegel's philosophy of religion is not to provide a supplementary philosophical foundation for religion and theology but to "translate" the figurative ideas [*Vorstellungen*] of religion into philosophical "concepts" [*Begriff*], thereby to render them superfluous as *religious* notions and thus "sublated." The absolute knowledge of the Absolute no longer requires an unexamined "positive" religion, that is, belief which presupposes and accepts its content as something already established and given. "Philosophy as the conceptual understanding of this content has in contrast to the ideas of religion the advantage that it understands both religion and itself. The same claim, however, cannot be made by religion." [7]

The true philosophy is already a "divine service," that is, it needs no biblical stories, religious practices, and church dogmas in order to raise itself to the infinite and the divine. It needs no external authority at all. If theologians reply that it is presumptuous to attempt to know God through human intelligence and to perceive His providential plan in the course of the world, then the despair of theology must be left behind for the reliability of philosophy, knowing the One, or else that pursuit of knowledge of the One which matters and upon whom everything else depends will have to be abandoned. "If God cannot be known, the only realm which remains for the spirit is the realm of the human, the limited, finite." But a philosophy which knows only what is finite is no philosophy; it is, at best, knowledge of the world and man, run aground on "the sandbar of the temporal" with all its inconstant cares and miseries.

The essential ambiguity of Hegel's relation to the Christian religion and theology, which consists in the fact that the relationship is critical but has the form of a justification, is unambiguously expressed in letters to Schelling during this period of the early theological writings. Hegel writes with unabashed *Schadenfreude* about the perplexities of Protestant theology which be-

7. *Works,* XIII, p. 96. Cf. I, p. 80, on the analogous relation of speculative philosophy and common sense.

lieves that with the help of the Kantian or Fichtean philosophy it can avoid the "conflagration of dogmatism."

What you tell me about the Kantian (*si diis placet*) theological course of philosophy at Tübingen is not surprising. Orthodoxy cannot be shaken as long as its profession is bound up with worldly advantages and is woven into the total fabric of the state. Put up with all that is offered to them and be satisfied with whatever they can get from these old humdrum systems. However, I believe it would be interesting to disturb as much as possible the ant-like industriousness of these theologians who furnish critical construction materials for the foundation of their divine temples. Everything should be made difficult for them. They should be driven out of every place of refuge until they can no longer find any and their nakedness is exposed completely to the light of day. . . . In his *Critique of All Revelation* Fichte indisputably laid bare every nook and cranny of the nonsense which you write about and whose mode of reasoning I can, accordingly, imagine for myself. He himself made moderate use of his own *Critique*. But if his principles are accepted one day as established, then there will no longer be any means for setting limits to the logic of theology. He argues on the basis of the holiness of God, what He must do by virtue of His purely moral nature, and so on. But in that way he reintroduced the old mode of proof in dogmatics.

Hegel concludes with an enquiry about a mutual acquaintance:

Can you, on the basis of your friendship with him, ask him to become active and to write polemics against contemporary theology? The very existence of this theology makes clear the necessity for such polemics and shows that they are not superfluous. . . .

The kingdom of God is coming and our hands should not rest idly in our laps! . . . Reason and freedom are our slogans, and our rallying point the invisible church.[8]

If the reference to the coming kingdom of God and the invisible church were merely a manner of speaking, lacking weight or sig-

8. Letter to Schelling, end of January, 1795. *Letters by and to Hegel*, I, pp. 16ff. Cf. Hölderlin's letter to Hegel of October 7, 1794. Schelling answered Hegel on April 2, 1795: "What you have in mind to do is just splendid! I beg you to get to work as fast as possible. If you have made up your mind not to waste time, then here is a field ready for harvesting, a great service to perform. You still have to nail shut the last doors of superstition. You wrote yourself that as long as the sort of thinking represented by Fichte's *Kritik aller Offenbarung*—motivated perhaps by a desire for accommodation or else to make fun of superstition and, laughingly, to receive the thanks of the theologians—can still appear and be regarded as valid, then philosophical stupidity has not yet disappeared. How often, irritated by this theological mischief, have I wanted to take refuge in satire and demand of the whole dogmatic theology, together with its appendages from the dark ages, that it return to practical grounds for belief! But I don't have time and if such a satire were actually written, God knows whether the majority might not take it seriously and whether in my young years—silently, at least—I might not have the pleasure of sparkling as a philosophical light of the church. The matter must be taken up seriously and from your hand, friend, I look forward to a beginning."

nificance, it could be disregarded and the issue of "reason and freedom" stressed instead. What is extraordinary about these and similar utterances is that Hegel holds forth against contemporary theologians because he believes that he has a better knowledge of God. As a more rational and a freer thinker, what he desires, in fact, is no less than to prepare, through reflection, what is called "the kingdom of God" in the language of the New Testament, i.e., a kingdom in which man is truly "with himself," can feel at home, and can enter into his true essence, which is "mind" or "spirit" [*Geist*]. Because the God of the New Testament, particularly in the Gospel according to John, is essentially *Logos* or mind and can only be known by the mind, Hegel is able to transform the theological kingdom of God into that "kingdom of spirits" [*Geisterreich*] which forms the conclusion of his great work, *The Phenomenology of Mind*. Knowledge of God is acquired through the absolute knowledge of the Absolute, whose development begins "with the direct knowledge of the immediate," that is, with the certainty of sense-experience.[9] This transformation, however, presupposed the annihilation of the "positive form" [*Positivität*] of the Jewish and Christian religions. This is the constant theme and major point of dispute in the early theological writings, so much so, in fact, that the critique of religion takes precedence over its justification. If B. Bauer [10] had been acquainted with these early writings, he would have found more support here for his thesis that Hegel's position is "anti-Christian" than in Hegel's later philosophy of religion, where the dogmas of the Incarnation and the Trinity are "translated" into speculative philosophy. Hegel's "kingdom of spirits" prepared the way for Marx's godless "kingdom of freedom," in which there is no longer any alienation and the individual spirit is completely with itself in its otherness.

[I]   HEGEL'S CRITIQUE OF CHRISTIANITY IN HIS EARLY WRITINGS (1795–1800)

"THE REASONS for belief in Christ are based upon history," upon historical tradition. However, to believe in something which is based upon the reports of others is infinitely easier

9. For the history of the idea of the "Kingdom of God," see C. L. Becker: *The Heavenly City of the 18th century Philosophers* (1932), and E. Gilson: *The Metamorphoses of the Kingdom of God* (1959), which does not include Hegel and Marx, but concludes with A. Comte.

10. See especially *Die Posaune des jüngsten Gerichts über Hegel den Atheisten und Antichristen* (Leipzig, 1841). Available again in *Die Hegelsche Linke*, ed. K. Löwith (Stuttgart, 1962).

than to reflect upon it ourselves. Such a belief, which is based upon historical evidence, however, is able to provoke investigations despite the fact that by its very nature it does not directly arouse the reflective mind. Historical truths do not engage in the investigation of their own truth; they are protected by authority as long as the intellect does not dare to test them and "to create its own principles of possibility and probability, irrespective of these artificial historical constructions, which it sets aside." [11] Hence, belief in the historical Jesus as the Christ is not grounded in any practical need of the intellect but rather upon the testimony of others, and for this reason it is limited from the outset in its origin, validity, and extent. Nevertheless, this belief is supposed to determine the fate of all men for all eternity. Here, Hegel anticipates the question of Kierkegaard: how can everlasting salvation be based upon historical truth? Hegel, however, finds no profound paradox here, but only absurdity. For either the greater part of mankind is excluded from the blessing which "trickles down upon us, the chosen ones" from this historical belief, or else we must admit that Jesus does not have the "enormous importance" which we ascribe to Him as the sole condition under which men can grasp something of their purpose in the world and have value for God and the mind. Furthermore, since Christianity teaches much which is beyond our intellect and imagination, the intellect, whose insights are in principle accessible to every intelligent person, can only reject this teaching even though it may be recorded with the holiest of seals in the historical faith of the people. Thus, to this day Christ is still proclaimed the Savior and gratitude is demanded toward the Person who has suffered for us—"as if millions had not already sacrificed themselves for lesser purposes—smiling, without the blood and sweat of fear, and with joy . . . for their country or a loved one." [12] In the face of the many improbable and difficult-to-believe truths in historical Christianity, Hegel wonders how it could possibly have managed to overcome the natural religion of the Greeks and Romans and to have regarded itself as superior to the "blind" heathens, whose virtues Hegel looks upon as "splendid vices."

How could a religion be replaced when it had established itself for centuries as part of the state and was intimately bound up with its constitution? How is it possible that belief in the gods ceased? These cities and kingdoms attributed their origin to the gods. The people made sacrifices to them every day and asked for their blessing in every undertaking. Only under the banner of the

11. *Hegels theologische Jugendschriften,* ed. H. Nohl (Tübingen, 1907), p. 66.
12. *Ibid.,* p. 59.

gods had their armies been victorious; they thanked the gods for their victories. The joy of their songs and the seriousness of their prayers were dedicated to the gods. The altars, monuments, and statues of the gods were the pride of the people and the glory of art. The worship and feasts in honor of the gods were occasions for universal joy—How could the belief in gods such as these be severed from its manifold connections with the entire texture of human existence? [13]

To this question, Hegel gives the same answer as the historian Gibbon had given: revolution, such as this, produced by Christianity's penetration of the ancient world can only be explained by the decay of the ancient world, by the complete disappearance of political and intellectual freedom from public life.

The image of the state as a result of his own activity disappeared from the mind of the citizen. . . . All activity, all purposes were related now to individuals. There was no longer any action for the sake of the whole, the idea—either each worked for himself or was compelled to work for another. The freedom to obey self-imposed laws, to follow superiors chosen by oneself in peace and in war, and to carry out plans which included oneself, vanished. All political freedom disappeared. The right of the citizen provided only a right to the security of his property, which now made up his entire world. Death robbed man of the entire system of his purposes and must have become for man something horrible, for nothing survived, as the republic might survive the citizen.

In these circumstances there was no belief to hold onto, no absolute. One was required to obey a strange will and a strange legislation, without a fatherland, in a State without joy, whose presence weighed upon the citizen while public worship, celebrations and feasts could not restore the happiness which had gone out of his life. Circumstances were such that the slave, who very often surpassed his master in ability and education, could no longer see in the role of master the advantages of freedom and independence. Under conditions such as these, a religion was offered to man which was either appropriate for the needs of the age . . . , or else lent itself to the satisfaction of man's needs. [14]

The Christian teaching about the corruption of man's nature and his need for salvation could have taken root only during a period when everything was in flux, in a period of withdrawal from a common public existence into the private inner life of the individual and his soul's welfare. However, when the coming of the kingdom of God, the revolution anticipated by the early Christian communities, did not take place, "one was content to look forward to that revolution at the end of the world," while the Jews returned to their hope for a Messiah. The community

13. *Ibid.*, p. 220.
14. *Ibid.*, pp. 223f.

as a union of free citizens was replaced by the hierarchy of the church. The Absolute took refuge in a supernatural world and a supernatural God, to whom man was only connected by faith, hope, and desire. This "objectivity" or "positivity" of the divinity "went hand in hand with the corruption and slavery of man," just as, in general, the idea which man has of God always corresponds to the idea which he has of himself and reveals the common "spirit of the age."

> In this way, through its objective God, this spirit was revealed. Men began to know an astonishing amount about God; many secrets about his nature in a variety of forms were spread throughout the entire world. These secrets were not spread, as secrets usually are, by one person whispering into the ear of another; they were loudly proclaimed and children knew them by heart. The spirit of the age revealed itself in the objectivity of its God. It located Him, not in infinity, but in a world that was foreign to us, in whose domain we had no share and in which we could not establish ourselves through our own doing. At best we could either beg or bewitch ourselves into it. This spirit revealed itself when it posited man as a not-I and his divinity as another not-I. But this spirit was revealed most clearly in the mass of miracles which it produced. For the purposes of decision and conviction, these took the place of insight. But what was most monstrous was that people fought, murdered, slandered, burned, stole, lied, and cheated for this God. In such a period the Divinity must have ceased completely to be something subjective and to have become totally an object.[15]

Jesus had attempted to elevate the established positive form [*Positivität*] of the Judaic religion of law (the religion which Hegel described—and Nietzsche after him—as a slave morality based on resentment) by "the active relationship of love" to God as His father and to men as His brothers. But the community of Jesus bound itself to this particular man, who had been sent by God who had given them these commandments, and had humbly renounced all his own possessions. However, if human nature is radically different from the divine nature, if both confront one another without being able to communicate, and if they can only be reconciled miraculously through a particular individual, then the Christian preaching itself reverts back to a "crude positivity," which rules out a personal subjective assimilation of the divine. Everything then depends only upon believing and being baptized —"two positive acts" [16]—and "the Christians have returned to the same condition as the Jews." Everything was based upon the absolute power of Jesus and, for this reason alone, regarded as

15. *Ibid.*, p. 228.
16. *Ibid.*, p. 164.

God's will. Thus, the commandments of Jesus lost "the inner criterion of their necessity."

The chief question with which Hegel is concerned in his critique of "positivity" is not primarily the alienation of man as a finite creature from his natural world,[17] but rather from eternal truth as a whole, in theological terms, the relation of the *fides quae* to *fides qua creditur*. He was led by his reflection on the relation between objective truth and subjective opinion to the question concerning the "totality," the original whole within which man can have a relation to God in general, either in harmony or discord. If the truths asserted by positive belief are true simply because they are asserted by divine authority and thus "independent of our own opinion," then it is not clear how they can also be "truths for us" or "subjective."[18] Whoever grants to God absolute power over our entire being and ignores the fact that God is also for us[19] and, as spirit [*Geist*], can only be known by spirit, and whoever renounces the assimilation [*Anbildung*] of the divine cannot free himself from a merely positive belief. The capacity for such a belief presupposed the "loss of freedom and reason" and the independence of self-consciousness. God remains unrelated to and unreconciled with man and the world. But, in fact, belief in the divinity is only possible "because there is in the believer himself something divine and he discovers, perceives himself and his own nature, in the object of his belief,"[20] even though he is not necessarily conscious of the fact "that what he has discovered is his own nature."[21] "The belief in the divine

17. Under this narrowed viewpoint, the "*Positivität*" of G. Lukács, E. Bloch, and A. Kojève is explained with reference to Marx.

18. *Theologische Jugendschriften*, p. 223.

19. Cf. Feuerbach's appeal to Luther's *pro nobis* to his goal of the reduction of theology to anthropology (*Wesen des Christentums*, Chap. 14).

20. *Theologische Jugendschriften*, pp. 312f.

21. Later, in the introduction to *Lectures on the History of Philosophy*, the relation of *fides quae* to *fides qua creditur* is grasped more precisely in terms of the concept of perception: "A separation is posited in self-perception, and spirit [*Geist*] is the unity of the perceiver with what is perceived. The Divine Spirit who is perceived is the object which the subjective spirit perceives. But the spirit is not passive, or rather, its passivity can only be momentary; it is *one* substantial spiritual unity. The subjective spirit is active, but the objective spirit is itself this activity; the active subjective spirit who perceives the Divine Spirit and insofar as it perceives the Divine Spirit, *is* the Divine Spirit. This relation of spirit to itself alone defines it absolutely; the Divine Spirit lives and is present in His community. This perception is called "faith," though it is not historical religion. We Lutherans —and I am one and want to remain one—have this basic belief alone. The unity (of subjective and objective spirit) is not the Spinozistic substance; it is the knowing substance in self-consciousness, which makes itself infinite and universal. All the talk about the limits of human thought is shallow, for the sole aim of religion is to know God. The testimony of the spirit as to the content of religion

originates therefore in the divinity of one's own nature," [22] for only a "modification" of the divinity can recognize the divine—a proposition which can scarcely be distinguished from Feuerbach's reduction of religion to anthropology and which, in its influence, extends to the Nietzschean critique of Christianity.[23] For even the young Hegel considered it the chief task "reserved for our age" to claim, at least in theory, as the possession of man "the treasures which have been squandered on heaven." [24] "At least in theory" because it remains questionable which age will have, in fact, the force to maintain this right to the reassimilation of the divine, to make it its own and to take actual possession of the Absolute.

In Hegel's judgment, the life and fate of Jesus is an incomplete step on the way towards the reassimilation of the divinity of God from which man was alienated when the divinity of God became "positive." Jesus himself had wanted to restore the "totality" of the active relationship between God and man through the love which unites them. Love, by its very nature, rises above positive religious law and positive morality; hence it cannot be demanded as a duty.[25] Love, as a mutual relationship of one person to another, is a "feeling for the whole." Jesus, opposing all of humanity to the positivity of Judaism, had "sublated" [aufgehoben] "the immorality of the positive man." [26] All genuine virtues, according to Hegel, are only "modifications" of love. However, Jesus remained trapped in the destiny of the Jews. In order to hold himself apart from the spirit of his age, he had to carry the kingdom of God in his heart alone and in the hearts of his disciples who shared his world. "But, he had to avoid an active relationship to the 'real' world for everything lay under a sentence of death" [27]—a flight of the schöne Seele from the "real" world to heaven.

---

is itself the essence of religion. It is a testimony which both testifies and engenders. The spirit engenders itself first in witnessing; it exists only insofar as it produces, testifies, manifests, or reveals itself." (Works, XIII, pp. 88f.)

22. Theologische Jugendschriften, p. 313.

23. "I demand that all the beauty and sublimity which we have lent to things both real and imaginary be returned to man, for it is his property and his possession—his most beautiful apologia. Man as poet, thinker, god, love, power—with what princely generosity has he made a present of all this to things, in order to impoverish himself and to feel wretched! Until now, his greatest act of selflessness has been that he knew how to revere, worship, and yet suppress the fact that he himself is the creator of all that he reveres." (Nietzsche, Works, XV, p. 241.)

24. Theologische Jugendschriften, p. 225; cf. p. 71.

25. Ibid., pp. 267, 296.

26. Ibid., p. 276.

27. Ibid., pp. 325ff.

In the further development of the Christian community into a church, from the beginning the idea of the God-man was reduced to "a historically objective," that is, to a "positive" outlook. The world remained unreconciled with God, for it is impossible to unite oneself to a particular unique individual—to "This One," as Hegel was later to call Him—and to bring about the development of a "complete existence" through consciousness of Him as a divine human being. Since then, all forms of Christianity have moved within the antithesis of the divine and the worldly—radically ascetic sects; the Catholic church, which is so involved in everything worldly, but reservedly so; and Protestantism, which reduced everything to inwardness. "The Christian church has run full circle" [28] about the extremes of world-denial, world-involvement, and indifference. It goes against its grain to find peace in an impersonal and active beauty. Its fate is that church and state, the worship of God and life, piety and virtue, spiritual and worldly activity, can never be "fused into a unity." [29]

The young Hegel was still far removed from finding in Christianity the "absolute religion" and the "axle" of the totality of world-history. He had not yet based the concept of spirit and its freedom upon the appearance of Christian self-consciousness. His comparison of Jesus and Socrates leaves no doubt that he saw Socrates and not Jesus as the embodiment of the freedom of the spirit. Hegel begins his characterization with a comparison of the relation each had to his disciples or, as it were, apostles.[30] "Christ had twelve," a "fixed," definite, unchangeable number. These twelve had to break off all other relationships in order to follow their master exclusively. It was not enough for Christ to exchange ideas "with men of intelligence and admirable hearts, to kindle a few sparks in their souls, some new ideas, which, when the material they fall upon . . . contains no fuel of its own, are lost

28. Cf. Nietzsche: "All possibilities of Christian existence—the most earnest, the most casual and the most harmless, the least reflective and the most reflective —all have been tried. It is time to invent something new, or else we will fall into the same rut once more. Of course it is difficult to get out of the whirlpool after it has whirled us about for two thousand years. But even mockery, cynicism, antagonism toward Christianity is played out. One is reminded of a field of ice when the temperature rises: the ice is torn up, dirty, full of puddles of water, dull and dangerous. It seems to me that only a respectful and rather considerate distance is now called for, from which to venerate religion, even though it is already dying. Our business is to comfort and console, as one comforts the mortally ill; only against bad, thoughtless, bungling doctors (usually the learned ones) must protests be raised. . . . Christianity will very soon be ripe for a critical history, i.e., for dissection." (*Works*, X, p. 289.)

29. *Theologische Jugendschriften*, p. 342.

30. *Ibid.*, pp. 32f., 163.

all the same." Jesus says instead: "whoever here believes in me, he will enter the kingdom of God," and the Apostles understood this as a reference to His Person: "whoever believes *in me . . .*"

How different is Socrates, who had an indefinite number of friends and pupils! "The thirteenth or fourteenth was just as welcome to him as the others," if he were only like them in heart and mind. Nor did he preach—"How could it even have occurred to a Socrates in Greece to preach?" He wanted only to instruct men and to enlighten them about that which ought to be their principal concern. They were his pupils and his friends but in such a way that "each retained his independence. Socrates did not live in them, and was not the head from which they as limbs received the elixir of life." There were Socratic disciples to be sure, but not in the same way in which there were Christians. Socrates brought forth from the soul ideas which were already contained in it and needed only a midwife. "He left behind no command to spread his name abroad, no method for giving the soul a good scolding and pouring morality into it—the good (*agathon*) is born with us and cannot be preached into us."

He gave no one any cause to say: What—is this not the son of Sophroniscus? Where did he acquire such wisdom that he dares to instruct us? He did not offend anyone by boasting about his own importance or by mysterious, profound expressions which would impress only the ignorant and the naive.—He would have become a laughing-stock to the Greeks.[31]

The opening sentences of Hegel's dissertation, *Concerning the Path of the Planets (De Orbitis Planetarum,* 1801) indicate that Hegel saw more in Socrates than a teacher of men concerned solely with *human* things.

The praise that Cicero bestowed upon Socrates, that he had brought philosophy down from heaven and introduced it into the lives and homes of men, is either incorrect or should be interpreted to mean that philosophy cannot serve the life and lodging of man well unless it descends from heaven in order to aim its whole mission back towards heaven.

That is, philosophy would not be what it is, if it did not strive for the divine, like religion, whether the divine is understood as the physical cosmos or the transcendent world-spirit. For only in the Highest and the Whole can man be with himself or truly at home.

In the "Fragment of a System," which also originates during the period of the dissertation, Hegel summarized the aim of his

31. *Ibid.,* p. 34.

early theological writings in the form of a systematic outline. "Life," "love," and "spirit" are equivalent concepts in these writings. Through the leading conception of "the active relation of love," Hegel developed the mediating activity of spirit, which at the same time fuses and "sublates" [*aufhebt*] everything "positive," i.e., whatever is immediately given, fixed, and determined. The life of the spirit bestows life; this life consists above all in the fact that spirit is activity which sets everything in motion and which negates and dissolves what is apparently permanent or "positive." What Hegel wanted from the beginning was what, for him, is the most profound and most fundamental insight, the truth which supports everything else: the transformation of the lifeless contradictions of the "abstract" or "one-sided" understanding into the active relation of the speculative principle—"one-sided" because these contradictions come from that other aspect of the abstracting understanding which also belongs to it. The speculative principle not only contains but also "sublates" [*aufhebt*] the contradictions of being and nothing, life and death, the limited and unlimited, subject and object, willing and thinking, belief and knowledge, freedom and necessity. If only the "whole" is "the truth" [32] and "the truth" cannot exist without the mediation of our mind or spirit which perceives the truth and is essentially the freedom of being-with-itself through being-with-the-other, then every mere positivity which confronts us is "outrageous," whether it concerns religious dogma, miracles, and laws, or, as with Kant, merely moral laws and the conflict between duty and inclination. True "life" or "being" cannot be an absolute division and discord.[33] True being is unity and there are just as many kinds of unity as there are kinds of being. The linguistic expression for the latter is the "is" of the copula, the connective.[34] When Hegel speaks of the whole and attributes only to the whole the entire truth, he is not referring to the sum of all parts, to any synthesis effected by the understanding or to a mere "encompassing" [*Umgreifendes*], but to the outcome of a mediation from an original "center." The whole is the "absolute," [35] the one absolute world-spirit, which contains all its modifications or moments together and in motion. In this sense, the "Fragment of a System" refers to "the limitless totality of life" and also to the "spirit of the whole" which man,

32. Hegel, *Phenomenology of Mind*, ed. J. Hoffmeister (Leipzig, 1937), p. 21.
33. *Works*, I, pp. 168ff.
34. *Theologische Jugendschriften*, pp. 379ff.
35. *Ibid.*, p. 288.

to be sure, as a limited, finite creature places outside of himself. This is done so that he may free himself from those limits of which he is conscious, to raise himself from the finite life to the infinite, an ascent which is only possible when both lives, finite and infinite, are one. Hegel calls this ascent to the infinite activity of the spirit "religion" and the "worship of God" [36] whereby he definitely distinguishes his own view from what is called "pantheism." For, according to Hegel, it could never occur to any intelligent man to regard each and every contingent thing as divine.

Spirit is the law which animates everything just as the science of logic is the spirit which animates all sciences. This active spirit of the whole is just as much active *relation* and mutual connection as it is *difference*, separation, and opposition.

If I say that life is the unity of opposition and relation, then this unity can be isolated once again and it can be objected that it stands in opposition to disunity. Instead, I must say that life is the unity of unity and disunity.[37]

Or, as Hegel phrased it shortly thereafter in his work, *The Difference Between the Systems of Fichte and Schelling*, "the identity of identity and non-identity," in which opposition and unity belong together. It is only possible for the totality, or the absolute of the active spirit, to set itself forth in one thing and another because it differentiates and alienates *itself* in order to merge with itself through this division.

Because philosophy divides, it cannot posit the entities it divides without positing them in the Absolute. For otherwise, they would be pure antitheses which would have only the character that if one exists, the other cannot. This relation to the Absolute is not "sublation" of both (for then they would not be divided). They must remain divided and not lose this character insofar as they are posited in the Absolute or the Absolute in them. And since both must surely be posited in the Absolute—by what right would one come before the other? Not only the same right, but the same necessity applies to both, for if only one were to enter into the Absolute and not the other, then their essences would be posited as unequal and the task of philosophy, which is to sublate divisions would be rendered impossible.[38]

Whoever posits the ego or the world as absolute has not yet reflected on the nature of the Absolute. In the "Fragment of a System," Hegel had not gotten this far in his reflection on the

36. *Ibid.*, p. 347.
37. *Ibid.*, p. 348.
38. *Works*, I, pp. 246f.

Absolute. Philosophy, he tells us there,[39] must stop at religion, for only religion, because it perceives the Whole, is in a position to raise finite limited existence to the level of the infinite, while philosophy, on the contrary, as reflection upon the opposition between thinking and not thinking and between thinking and thought, never surpasses these distinctions and therefore can only postulate "the completion" of the finite, which is a fundamental need of human nature. Only in a vivid image was Hegel able to express how the finite, limited individual life can enter into the universal whole of life:

The custom of John the Baptist (no such activity on the part of Jesus is known) to baptize with water those who were of the same spirit as he, is symbolically significant. There is no feeling which is as much like the desire for the infinite, the longing to flow over into the infinite as the desire to bury oneself in the fulness of water. He who plunges in has an unknown confronting him which encircles him immediately and which he can feel in every part of his body. He is taken from the world and the world from him. He is only the feeling of the water which touches him where he is and he is only where he feels the water. There is in the fulness of the water no gap, no limitation, no multiplicity, or determination. This feeling is the least diffuse of all, the simplest. The baptized rises again into the air and separates himself from the body of water. Although he is already separated from the water, it still trickles from him on all sides. As the water leaves him, the world takes on definite outlines again, and he returns strengthened to the multiplicity of consciousness.[40]

How far removed is this image from Nietzsche's despairing desire to find an "ocean" in which the solitary soul could "drown"! [41] Hegel had already shown in the fragment on the positive form of the Christian religion [42] that if the problem concerning the relation of the Christian religion to man should become the object of a radical reflection from a conceptual standpoint, then it must turn into a metaphysical consideration of the relation of the finite to the infinite. This relation constitutes "the most difficult issue, one might say, the only subject matter of philosophy." [43] Hegel, however, will not carry out this project until his lectures on the philosophy of religion, though he prepares the way in the essay, *Belief and Knowledge*.

39. *Theologische Jugendschriften*, p. 348.
40. *Ibid.*, p. 319.
41. *Zarathustra, der Wahrsager.*
42. *Theologische Jugendschriften*, p. 146.
43. *Ein Hegelsches Fragment zur Philosophie des Geistes*, ed. F. Nicolin. In *Hegel-Studien*, I (Bonn, 1961), pp. 9–48; cf. pp. 28f.

[II] BELIEF AND KNOWLEDGE (1802)

IN THIS ESSAY, Hegel sets himself against a rationalistic characterization of religion based on the conflict between
belief and knowledge. If we can know nothing about God, if we
can only believe in Him, or if He is only a postulate of practical
reason or of conviction based on religious feeling—if, in short,
reason is unable to know God as the "truth in and for itself"—
then there is neither genuine belief nor true knowledge, but only
the lifeless conflict of religion and philosophical truth. Against
this "enlightened" standpoint Hegel argues that the progressive
development of his age has advanced so far beyond this conflict
that the distinction between reason and belief now falls within
philosophy itself, that is, in the difference between a merely rational mode of thinking and a *speculative* rational mode of thinking. Whereas the rational mode needs religion for its completion,
the speculative mode is itself already religion. On the other hand,
the "enlightened" understanding has spoken with such authority
in religious matters, for example, in its critique of the belief in
miracles, and in general, in what today would be called "de-
mythologizing," that no one can still consider making philosophy
a handmaiden of belief, as it was in the Middle Ages. Even a
philosophical dispute about the positive belief in miracles is rightly
considered outmoded; and if Kant was not successful in his attempt to revive the positive form of religious belief with meaning
drawn from his own philosophy, the reason is that religion no
longer seemed worthy even of that honor.

Five years later, in a section of *The Phenomenology of Mind*
which treats of the "struggle of the Enlightenment with superstition," Hegel reached the conclusion that each had infected the
other, that both had moved within the same element. The reason
which had already been reduced to a mere rational understanding,
which grasped religion as something positive, only revealed its
own emptiness when it placed what is higher than the understanding in a "beyond," in a belief outside and above itself, which
not only lacks but is also opposed to reason. Both the knowledge
of the Enlightenment and religious belief, which for the Enlightenment is a dreary superstition, are "sublated" by Hegel into what
he calls the absolute knowledge of the Absolute. In this absolute
knowledge, philosophical reason and Christian belief, which "perceive" the same absolute subject matter under different forms,[44]

44. In a similar manner, the Catholic philosopher, F. von Baader, tried to show
that the separation of faith from knowledge is responsible for the decay of our

are to be reconciled. If Kant had been correct in maintaining that reason cannot know the transcendental, the infinite, and the eternal because all knowledge is limited to objects of sensory experience, then the highest idea—God or the Absolute—would have no reality since God is no *res*, no thing, not a being among other beings at all. But the entire point of the ontological proof for God's existence was to show that precisely the highest idea, and only this idea, is the highest reality. It was this idea which Kant destroyed and Hegel, in opposition to Kant, restored in a different form.[45] For reason cannot renounce "its being in the Absolute," [46] if it is to be philosophy and not just a rationalism of the understanding, which fills out the empty space of its ignorance with subjective longing, anticipation, belief, and postulate. In this way, the understanding posits its own finitude as absolute because it fixes itself in opposition to the infinite. This understanding is not able to enter the "internally clear and desireless" region of the reason; basically, it is acquainted with human beings only, and, from an equally narrow perspective, it regards the natural world as no more than a multiplicity of concrete things.[47]

Since the fixed standpoint which the sovereignty of time and culture has established for philosophy is that of the reason as it is affected by the senses, such philosophy cannot aim at knowing God but only at what is called the human being. This human being and humanity are its absolute standpoint, that is, its established, incontrovertible limit; from this standpoint, reason is not a reflection of eternal beauty, nor the intellectual focus of the universe, but an absolute sensuous perception which still, however, has the capacity of belief, whereby it can clothe itself now and again in a super-sensible form that is alien to it.[48]

Kant only touched upon "the idea of an absolute medium of an intuitive understanding" in *The Critique of Judgement*. Fichte,

---

society, and that the antagonism between faith and knowledge is only a struggle between one faith and another. (*Works*, I, pp. 321ff., 357ff.)

45. See D. Henrich, *Der ontologische Gottesbeweis* (Tübingen, 1960).

46. "Speculation recognizes as the reality of knowledge only the being [*das Sein*] of knowledge in its totality. For speculation, everything definite has reality and truth only in its known relationship to the Absolute. For this reason, the Absolute can be recognized in that which forms the basis of the claims of common sense. Because, moreover, for speculative philosophy, knowledge is only real insofar as it is in the Absolute, that which is known, that which is enunciated to philosophical reflection and therefore takes on a definite form, is at the same time negated. The relative identities of ordinary common sense which seem to claim absolute validity in their limited form, become mere contingencies for philosophical reflection." (*Works*, I, p. 180.)

47. *Works*, I, p. 138; XV, p. 520.

48. *Ibid.*, I, p. 15.

in his *Vocation of Man,* tried to bridge formally the irreconcilable contradiction between man's determination by nature and his self-determination by means of an empty philosophical belief.

This enormous pride, this dark insanity of the Ego which is horrified by thought, detests thought, and grows melancholy about the fact that it is one with the universe, that eternal nature is active in it. Its resolution not to submit to the eternal laws of nature and their sacred and strict necessity, but to detest them, to recoil from them in melancholy, is based upon the pettiest of perspectives on nature and its relation to individuality, one that is devoid of all reason. The same applies to the despair of this Ego because it is not free, free from the eternal laws of nature and their strict necessity and its belief that it is made indescribably miserable through that obedience. This is a perspective to which the absolute identity of subject and object is totally foreign; its principle is absolute non-identity.[49]

It is noteworthy that in these early writings Hegel does not yet refer to the "absolute medium," the framework of his thought, so-called because it brings forth from itself disunity as well as mediation exclusively as God, but also as "eternal nature," "the universe," and a few pages later, "the wisdom existing in the development of the world." [50] But at the same time, he points to the Christian doctrine of the Incarnation and the likeness between God and man, in order to argue against Fichte that the world is sanctified from the Christian standpoint in an entirely different way than it is in Fichte's bleak moral order of the world. The essay concludes with the elevation [*Aufhebung*] of the dogma of Christ dying for our salvation to a "philosophical existence" in the concept of "a speculative Good Friday." [51] The eternal suffering, "God himself is dead," is at the same time the highest triumph because the divine God only becomes free from his alienation and finitude in a particular man through the death of the crucified God and then is resurrected in the universal holy spirit of the Christian community, the kingdom of God. The eternal suffering upon which the "religion of the modern age" is based, the feeling that God himself is dead, must be understood philosophically, that is, conceptually, as a moment in the highest idea of the absolute spirit as absolute freedom. God must die so that the difference and the separation, which God posited when he became finite in Christ, is once again restored to totality.

Whatever is positively historical and empirical in the eternal

49. *Ibid.,* p. 138.
50. Cf. *Theologische Jugendschriften,* p. 80, for the equating of "spirit of the divinity" with "spirit of the rational world."
51. Cf. *Phenomenology,* p. 523; *Phil. of Religion,* Part 3/1, pp. 158, 166, 170, 172.

history of God is inessential. The God of which Hegel speaks is, following Pascal, not the God of Abraham, Isaac, and Jacob, but a "God of the philosophers." It is the highest idea and as such the highest reality, a spirit which alienates itself and returns to itself from its determinate otherness. Hegel's essay, *The Scientific Treatment of Natural Law,* deals with the Absolute, with no reference to God's death and resurrection.[52] The tragedy performed eternally by the Absolute is that it generates itself into objectivity and hence into a determinate finitude, thus giving itself over to suffering and death, to raise itself from its own ashes to glorification. In the same way, in the essay on *Difference,*[53] Hegel claims that disunity is *one* factor in "life" which develops eternally out of antithesis and that totality is only possible through restoration from the highest of separation. The Whole, as such, is the Absolute, which is a continual process of going out of itself and returning to itself, in which disunity mediates progressively with itself. Historically, this mediation appears in Christ as mediator, but in and for itself, it is the anonymous "logical essence" of God. Whoever, like Hegel, grasps the Christian religion as philosophically absolute can just as readily call the absolute spirit "a relation of God to Himself," for it is "the eternal being-in-and-for-itself," which opens itself up, differentiates itself from itself, takes its differentiation back into itself, and "sublates" it. Hegel carried on ceaseless investigations of this logical essence of God, or spirit existing in and for itself, and its formal structural movement in all the concrete phenomenal manifestations of the intellectual life, such as language, work, and not least of all, in the philosophical interpretation of the dogma of God's Trinity, as Father, Son, and Holy Spirit.

[III] THE RELATIONSHIP OF PHILOSOPHY AND RELIGION IN THE LECTURES ON THE PHILOSOPHY OF RELIGION (1821–1831)

HEGEL'S LECTURES, of which only the smallest part has survived in his own handwriting, the largest part consisting of a compilation of notes taken by various students, integrate all the themes of his early theological writings and the first essays. But now the critique of Christianity is withdrawn in favor of its justification in conceptual thought. The beautiful features of the natural Greek folk-religion dissolve in the light of the absolute

52. *Works,* I, p. 376.
53. *Ibid.,* p. 170.

religion of the spirit which is Christianity. The contrast between Socrates and Christ is revoked insofar as it is now an "irreligious" consideration to look upon the Christ as a common man with uncommon claims and to ignore the man-God character which makes him distinctive. The life and death of both men are only comparable for the unbeliever.[54] The great turning point in the development of truth for the spirit to grasp, is first reached with Christ; the truth in and for itself is revealed because only Jesus as the Son of God knows the Father. However, the absolute religion needs a philosophical justification in thought [Begriff] because Christianity as mere belief concerning "the relation of the limited to the Absolute" [55] is now no longer justifiable, but merely persists and is asserted with tenacity because its forms have been retained.[56]

However, the philosophical justification of the Christian religion cannot be apologetic, for although apology makes use of the understanding it does so only in a supplementary and apparent fashion because it cannot make a move without appealing to authority for support.

But just as it is unavoidable from this standpoint that reasoning must extend into the infinite, in the same way the highest divine authority too is of such nature that it requires a foundation and rests upon authority. For we were not there and did not see God when He revealed Himself. It was only others who related it to us and guaranteed it. And precisely the evidence of these others, who experienced the historical and knew it first through eye-witnesses, should, according to apologetics, produce conviction about matters which are spatially and temporally separated from us. But this mediation is not certain, for it depends upon how the medium which stands between us and these matters is provided by the perception of others. The capacity to perceive requires a prosaic understanding and the formation of this understanding, conditions which were not present with the Ancients. They lacked the capacity to grasp history in its finiteness and to extract what is of inner significance in history, because for them the opposition between the prosaic and the poetical had not yet been posited in its sharpest form. And if we posit the divine in the historical, then we fall into the uncertain and the changeable which is peculiar to everything historical. The prosaic and sceptic understanding is opposed to the miracles which the Apostles reported, for it finds an incongruity between the miraculous and the divine.[57]

Everything depends on drawing forth the inner "significance," the living spirit from these lifeless letters, from the stories of the

54. *Phil. of Religion*, Part 3/1, pp. 154, 169f.
55. *Works*, I, p. 181.
56. *Phil. of Religion*, Part 3/1, p. 229.
57. *Ibid.*, Part 1, p. 290.

Bible and the teachings of the Church. One must dismiss all positive theology which is related to its object dogmatically, apologetically, or even historically and critically. The scholarly "goings-on" with historical criticism have nothing to do with the matter, for they concern only thoughts and conceptions which others have had, defended, and fought for, with events which do not take place in our own minds. Moreover, "this paramount preoccupation with the historical aspects of objects which are eternal truths of the spirit itself should be discouraged." [58] It is but a variation on the renunciation of one's own power of understanding Christian doctrine to appeal uncritically to the "word of God," as if that word were something immediate and completely given, something established and positive, which did not require a mind [*Geist*] to grasp it so that it may come alive.

Exegesis takes over the written word, interprets it, and alleges that it aims only at a valid understanding of the word in order to remain true to its meaning. However, if interpretation is not just the clarification of a word but the explanation of its meaning, then it is easy to see that exegesis must bring its own ideas to bear upon what is basic to the word. The simple interpretation of a word consists only in putting in the place of an unknown word a known one. Explanatory exegeses, on the other hand, introduce wider notions, although their apparent intention is to abide by the meaning of the word. It is in this way that commentaries usually make us more familiar with the view-points of their age than with the works commented upon. Whatever meaning the words contain ought to be accounted for. However, such an account requires that their meaning be brought into consciousness, into ideas [*Vorstellungen*]. In this way, the other ideas of the consciousness of the age assert their rights in the interpretation of what the meaning should be. Is it not the case that even in the interpretation of a fully developed philosophical system, for example, of Plato or Aristotle, that the explanations turn out differently according to the mode of interpretation adopted by those who have undertaken the investigation? Thus, the project of taking the Bible as a foundation, either out of respect or in fact, with complete seriousness, brings with it the sort of interpretive explanation whose ideas will correspond to its intentions. The ideas themselves contain determinations, principles, and assumptions which are then made valid in the business of interpreting. Thus, exegetically, the most opposed views have been proven by theologians by reference to scripture and the result is that the so-called Holy Gospel has an everchanging face. All heresies, together with the church, have appealed to the Scriptures.[59]

Precisely because an explanation independent of one's own mind is impossible, Hegel defends the formation of Christian principles undertaken by the fathers of the church, against the

58. *Ibid.*, Part 3/2; cf. Part 1, pp. 27f., 47f.
59. *Ibid.*, Part 1, p. 38.

Protestant bias which would have us believe that these great theologians corrupted the original form of Christianity.

It is well known that Luther conceived the purpose of his reformation to be a return of the church to the simplicity of its original form in the first century. But in this form there is already a doctrinal system which is extensive and involved, a fully developed body of teachings about the nature of God and the relation of man to Him. For this reason during the Reformation a definite system was not produced at all, but only a tangled construction into which the most complicated things are woven. This "knitted stocking" has been completely unraveled in more recent times since the desire has arisen to lead Christianity back to the plain threads of the word of God as it is found in the New Testament. Thus, the aim of extending the system, i.e., Christian doctrine determined through the idea and according to the idea, has been given up in favor of a return to the character of its original appearance (with the exception of what is no longer applicable). Now, only what is reported about its original appearance is regarded as fundamental to Christianity.[60]

However, since any understanding of Christianity and the Bible requires a mind to make it live, everything depends upon *which* mind is brought to the task. Biblical exegesis in the first century was quite different from what it is today, when, for example, it is considered as settled that we can know nothing about God himself but "only about our relationship to Him," or as we would say today, our "existential" relation. Every theology proceeds on the basis of presupposed "forms of thought" which affect the nature of God, man, and their relation. The investigation of these forms belongs to philosophy alone, because only philosophy can think about thought itself.

Theology, when it turns against philosophy, is either unaware of the fact that it uses such forms, that it too thinks and that everything depends upon proceeding according to thought, or else it deceives. It wants to reserve for itself arbitrary, accidental thought but knows that knowledge of the true nature of the mind [*Geist*] is detrimental to arbitrary thinking. Here, arbitrary, accidental thought is the element of positivity. Only the concept itself is truly and thoroughly free from what is positive, for thought as such, which is this ultimate freedom, is found in philosophy and religion.[61]

Hegel claims for his thought absolute relevance and absolute necessity. The perception of the Absolute, through which the Absolute itself first becomes established in human nature and confronts itself, is, for Hegel's self-consciousness, nothing less

60. *Works*, XV, p. 96.
61. *Phil. of Religion*, Part 3/1, p. 25.

than union with God's spirit and the world-spirit.[62] Both the spirit of God and the world-spirit are interchangeable in Hegel's language and thought, because the absolute spirit becomes finite through its activity in the world. The notion that the kingdom of God is not of this world has only polemical importance and, considered in isolation, is an abstract, one-sided determination from the earliest period of Christianity. This idea would lose its limited importance if the Christian truth were given a "secure existence," [63] i.e., if the principle of Christianity were made into a principle of the world.[64] Although the self-unfolding of the eternally present spirit falls within historical time, this explication of the principle of Christianity is not intended to be "intellectual history," but is to be understood metaphysically. The Christian religion is absolute, not because God was revealed through a particular individual two thousand years ago in a "dead historical distance in a corner of Palestine," [65] but because this revealed religion is itself revealing, that is, because the eternal spirit in and for itself makes itself manifest so that since that time there has been nothing more concealed or hidden from the human mind. "There is no longer anything hidden about God." [66] The spirit has now overcome all limitations and has become for itself what it is in itself.

This knowledge which the spirit has of itself, about what it is in itself, is the in-and-for-itself of the spirit, that is, the complete, absolute religion which reveals what spirit is and what God is. It is the revealing, not just the revealed religion. For now the spirit is clear about itself whereas previously it was only able to grasp itself through one of its conceptual determinations. Then the spirit as spirit remained concealed and religion was still hidden and not in possession of its truth. . . . When the time finally came, the spirit revealed itself to itself, for this path on which the spirit achieves its purpose leads through time and must pass over existence.[67]

62. Hegel replied in a letter to Hinrichs: "Concerning the other matter, that is, the impression that has been created that the Absolute has first come to knowledge of itself in my philosophy, there is much that might be said. But the shortest reply is this: If we consider philosophy as such, then there is no particular problem concerning *my* philosophy, because every philosophy grasps the Absolute and not what is alien to it. To conceive the Absolute, in any case, is, in itself, its self-comprehension. This is what theology was formerly conceived to be. . . . But in these matters, misunderstandings cannot possibly be avoided. . . ." (*Letters by and to Hegel*, II, p. 357.)
63. *Phil. of Religion*, Part 3/1, pp. 150ff.
64. *Works*, XV, p. 94.
65. *Ibid.*, XIII, p. 90.
66. *Phil. of Religion*, Part 1, p. 75.
67. *Ibid.*, p. 74.

If the time has come to pass, says Hegel, in a word-play upon the original Christian annunciation, "that a conceptual justification is needed," then Christian faith no longer lives in the immediate religious consciousness. "What truth, one might ask, can still be found in the content of the Christian faith?" "The salt has lost its savor," and when "religious truth is treated historically," as in modern Protestant exegesis, "then religion is finished." [68] Regarded historically and from the standpoint of the world, Christianity, for Hegel, had already reached its end as a stage in the history of the world. This dissolution, like its origin, however, involves only the external historical aspect of contingent events to which philosophy cannot conform, though even philosophy is, in its appearance, contemporary with its age.[69] Religion must take refuge in philosophy, precisely because it is now disappearing, both historically and world-historically, and is no longer acceptable in its religious form, although philosophy, to be sure, is for the few and not, like religion, for the many.[70]

Hegel's indifference to the "external" and "accidental" applies to everything merely "historical" from which the possibility can never be excluded that it might have happened otherwise. In contrast, there is the inner necessity of the true "history of God" or of the absolute spirit which is an "eternal" process and not a unique event.[71] Because, however, what pertains to the spirit comes to us, first of all, in an external manner, that is, empirically and historically, through authority and tradition, absolute religion is at first positive religion. Even the historical Jesus is such a historical externality, a matter of indifference to the "absolute content" in and for itself.[72] But how do we reconcile this with the fact that what is peculiar to the Christian religion is that the historical person of Jesus Christ as the Son of God belongs to the nature of God and therefore cannot remain indifferent to the absolute content? To this question about the distinction or identity of the historical Jesus with the revealed Christ, Hegel answers that even the historical form should not be understood in its positive historical particularity when it ought to exist for the perceiving spirit. It must itself be grasped as something spiritual. No matter by what particular individual the truth is revealed, something external and

68. *Ibid.*, Part 3/1, pp. 240f.

69. *Ibid.*, Part 1, p. 53.

70. *Ibid.*, p. 69. The same distinction is used by Origen against the philosopher Celsus as an argument *for* Christianity.

71. *Ibid.*, Part 3/1, pp. 95f., 198. Concerning "chance and necessity," see Part 2/2, pp. 134ff., 150ff.; Part 3/2, pp. 88ff., 95ff., 124ff.

72. *Works*, XIII, pp. 87f.

historical remains because the person is not the absolute content of Christian doctrine as such. We should not attach ourselves to a definite teacher but perceive the truth of his teaching and this is only possible when we perceive the truth "in the spirit and in the truth."

For the same reason, the actual testimony to the truth of the Christian religion cannot be "positive." The sentient human being demands tangible "evidence" and finds it, for example, in miracles. This, however, is an attestation outside the spirit by means of which no testimony to the spiritual essence of absolute religion can be produced, precisely because the testimony of the spirit cannot be of an empirical sort. "That I believe, for that end the testimony of my spirit is needed," and the spiritual can only be established in and through itself.[73] In its highest form, however, the testimony of the spirit is philosophy, the essential thought which unfolds the truth of things and knows the truth in its concept. Religion can only be justified by philosophy, whereas devotion is a mere approximation of thinking. Whoever opposes the immediate certainty of belief, of heart and feeling to this thought about the truth, does not understand himself, for the heart and feeling of a human being are not those of an animal, but the reflective heart and feeling of a being who in his essence is spirit and self-knowledge.[74] Belief, to be sure, is an essential moment in the Christian religion which is absent from other religions, but the immediate *certainty* of belief does not yet guarantee the *truth* of what is believed.[75]

But what then is this self-certifying "spirit" which has been our subject throughout, and how are we to understand the relation of the finite human spirit to God as the Absolute? The first answer which Hegel gives is the following: the spirit is essentially an active going-out-of-itself, a revealing or manifesting of itself.

If we make a preliminary inquiry of our consciousness of the nature of mind or spirit, we find that spirit is what manifests itself, it is being for the spirit. Spirit exists for spirit and not in a superficial accidental way; it *is* only spirit in so far as it exists *for* the spirit. This makes up the concept of spirit itself.[76]

In the act of self-manifestation, there is already implicit the relation to another similar mind or spirit; and the relation of the absolute spirit to the finite and the finite spirit to the absolute, according to Hegel, makes up the essential content of Christianity,

73. *Phil. of Religion*, Part 3/1, pp. 191ff.
74. *Ibid.*, p. 23.
75. *Ibid.*, Part 3/2, pp. 29f.; cf. Part 3/1, p. 141; cf. *Encyclopedia*, §63.
76. *Phil. of Religion*, Part 1, pp. 50f.

whose central doctrines are the Incarnation of God and the elevation of man to God. In order to grasp and to unfold this teaching philosophically, there is no need to appeal for support to empirical events which have come down to us through tradition and instruction. The only possible way in which the truth of the Christian religion can be established—to whatever extent it still makes sense to speak of finding the ground of the eternal at all and not just of the conditioned, limited, and phenomenal [77]—is, without support from any external authority, to see why and how God or the Absolute as spirit eternally reveals or manifests itself and comes to consciousness of itself in the finite mind of man.

Since Hegel interprets the dogma of God's revelation in man philosophically, in terms of fundamental and universal principles, the personal and unique character of the Incarnation of God—this most positive miracle of all Christian miracles—is lost. A problem then arises as to what extent infinite God and finite man, the human and the divine, belong together. Is a relation between man and God possible perhaps because every relation, and therefore the relation of the divine to man, is already, *as* a relation, not onesided, but a reciprocal and mutual relation which will have, therefore, two sides and two senses? But how can the relation between God and man really be reciprocal when the one spirit is infinite and the other finite? Hegel does not dispute the fact that finite and infinite, subject and object, internal and external are different, for "who does not know that?" But it is something else again to see that such determinations are different and at the same time inseparable.

Granted that we say of two things that they are as different as heaven and earth. This is correct; both are simply different, but they are inseparable. One cannot point to the earth without pointing to heaven and vice-versa. It is difficult to make this point against those who argue against the philosophy of religion in that way for they show too great an ignorance and a complete lack of familiarity with the forms and categories with which they make their attack and pass judgment upon philosophy. They say very straightforwardly that immediacy is something quite different from mediation and utter trivialities as something original ... without having reflected upon these matters, how these determinations are present. Reality is not present to them but strange and unknown. For this reason the talk which they aimed at philosophy is the rigmarole of the schools caught up in empty insignificant categories whereas with philosophy we are not in "school" but in the actual world.[78]

77. *Ibid.*, Part 3/1, p. 199.
78. *Ibid.*, Part 1, p. 60.

Hence, even God cannot be grasped as mind or spirit if one abstracts from his own mind for which the divine is what it is and in which the divine reveals itself.

On the part of God, nothing can stand in the way of His being perceived through man. The failure of man to perceive God can be "sublated" [*aufgehoben*] if we admit God has a relation to us, that God exists for us since our spirit has a relation to Him, or as it has been said, that He has imparted and revealed Himself. God is supposed to reveal Himself in nature but he cannot reveal Himself to nature, that is, to stones, plants, and animals because He is spirit. Hence, if nothing stands in the way of God's perception, then only the human show of humility must prevent it, pretending, as it does, that a finite knowledge can be established and fixed absolutely only in contrast to the divine.[79]

It is not human reason in its so-called limitation which God perceives at all, but "the spirit of God in man," or in speculative terms: "It is the self-consciousness of God which knows itself in the knowledge of man." [80] That is, "Man knows God only insofar as God knows Himself in man. This knowledge is God's self-consciousness but also God's knowledge of man. God's knowledge of man is also man's knowledge of God. The spirit of man which is to know God is only the spirit of God Himself." [81] The beginning and the end of the absolute Christian religion as well as of the absolute philosophy of the absolute spirit is that God as spirit essentially manifests or reveals Himself because he differentiates Himself or delivers and imparts Himself in such a way that man participates in Him. The Absolute, however, does not divide itself in two opposed parts, into a divine object on the one hand and into a subject who believes in an alien object on the other.

The unity and totality of the spirit which exists in and for itself returns undivided to itself out of this self-differentiation and separation. Just as man knows himself in God as a "universal self," [82] that is, in his universal essence, so, on the other side, the

79. *Ibid.*, Part 3/2, pp. 48f.

80. Cf. *Ibid.*, Part 1, p. 257: "Theologians of former times, particularly Catholic theologians, grasped this profound truth in all its inwardness; contemporary Protestant theologians have only criticism and history. Baader relates that a Dominican monk of the thirteenth century, Meister Eckhart, delivered sermons in which he said such things as these: 'The eye with which God sees is the same as the eye with which I see; His eye and my eye are one. I will be judged in God's righteousness and he in mine. If God did not exist, neither would I; if I did not exist, neither would God.' But it is not necessary to know this, for there are things which are easily misunderstood and can only be grasped in the concept."

81. *Ibid.*, Part 3/2, p. 117; cf. Part 3/1, pp. 6, 14.

82. *Ibid.*, Part 1, pp. 141f.

universal spirit of God comes to self-consciousness through man. In this dual "being-with-itself in being-for-the-other" consists the "freedom" of the spirit which exists in and for itself.

This freedom for the assimilation of the other, whose objective alienation is negated, increases as subjectivity develops for itself, asserts itself effectively, and frees itself from everything which prevents a return to itself. In the light of the French Revolution, in which man for the first time "stood on his head" and called into question everything which was out of harmony with his own will and spirit, Hegel calls the French philosophy of the Enlightenment "the treasure of the Spirit itself." For whatever the atheistic and materialistic consequences of the emancipation might be, even freedom as abstract caprice and destruction of the *status quo* belongs to the essence of the human spirit. The French philosophy is the

... absolute concept which turns against the entire realm of existing ideas and accepted notions. It destroys everything established and gives itself the consciousness of pure freedom. The certainty which lies at the basis of this idealistic activity is what exists, what has value in itself, is the universal essence of self-consciousness; and neither the concepts ... of good and evil nor those of power and wealth, nor the accepted ideas about belief in God and his relation to the world ... or the duty of self-consciousness towards Him— none of these are truths existing in themselves which could be independent of self-consciousness. All these forms, the real in-itself of the actual world, the in-itself of the transcendental world, are therefore sublated in the spirit which has become conscious of itself.[83]

Hegel, in a bold use of the statement "In this sign you shall conquer," applies it to the modern notion of the freedom of conscience, and provides the revolution with its justification in world-history, not against the meaning of freedom in the Christian doctrine, but for it!

... because they (the revolutionaries) only had in view what had been done under the sign of the cross—because they saw how the sign of the cross had been devalued. Lies and deception had conquered in this sign and under this seal institutions became indifferent to all vile actions. As a result this sign came to represent the epitome and the root of all evil. Hence, in a different form they completed the Lutheran reformation.[84]

The German Reformation and the French Revolution broke with the "positivity" of religious and political conditions and this

83. *Works*, XV, p. 457. Cf. in the *Phenomenology* the chapter concerning the realm of self-alienated culture.
84. *Works*, XV, pp. 473f.

alone justifies them. Hegel saw in Christianity the historically remote yet ever present origin of these revolutions, both of which had self-determination as their purpose. Thus, when Hegel speaks of the "modern" world in contrast to the "ancient," he has in mind the "quarrel of the ancients and the moderns," but "the moderns" begin with Christianity.

The greatness of the standpoint of the modern world is that the subject has plunged more deeply into himself, that though finite, he knows himself as infinite and, with this conflict, he is driven to resolve it. The question, then, is how to resolve it. This is the conflict: I am a subject, free, a person in my own right, but for this reason I also free the Other, which confronts me and thus remains an Other. The ancients never experienced this conflict, this antithesis which only spirit can endure. It is a mark of supreme energy to come to a realization of this conflict. This alone is spirit—to grasp oneself ceaselessly as conflict.[85]

For the first time in the history of the world, Christianity bestowed value upon "the peak" of subjectivity—being a self and being self-conscious, because it brought every man as man into direct relation with God as the Absolute. Since God appeared in human form, the presupposition of all post-Christian philosophy has been that absolute divine truth is there for man.

The meaning of Christian life is that the peak of subjectivity has become familiar with the notion that there is a claim upon the individual himself, which also makes him valuable, to strive towards this Unity, to make himself worthy of becoming a place of residence for the spirit of God, for His grace, as it is called.[86]

By refining substance into subjectivity, Christianity produced a revolutionary "reversal" in world-history. Man is no longer looked upon as a creature included in the cosmos, a creature who is mortal in contrast to the immortal gods and subject, together with the gods, not to the highest law of freedom, but to unchanging necessity. Instead, the divine is placed at the peak of self-consciousness and God Himself takes human form. As a result of God's Incarnation, a Christian "anthropo-theology" arises out of the cosmo-theology of the Greeks.

The Greeks were anthropomorphic; their gods were humanly formed. Their defect, however, is that they were not anthropomorphic enough, or rather that Greek religion is on the one hand too anthropomorphic and on the other hand not anthropomorphic enough. It is too anthropomorphic because immediate qualities, forms, and activities are absorbed into the divine. It is not

85. *Phil. of Religion*, Part 3/1, p. 46.
86. *Works*, XV, p. 87.

anthropomorphic enough because man is only divine as a form in the other world and not *as* man, not as a creature of this world and a subjective being.[87]

Thus, the Incarnation and the relation of Father, Son, and Holy Spirit are central to Hegel's philosophical interpretation of the Christian religion. In his lectures on the history of philosophy, Hegel deals with Christianity in connection with neo-Platonic philosophy, which was also a philosophy of spirit, though it had not yet attained the peak of subjectivity. The essence of the Absolute is first revealed in Christianity: "It is a man, but not yet man or self-consciousness in general." However, because positive belief knows the absolute essence of the divine spirit in *this* particular Person only, in the immediacy of existence, this domain does not yet belong to philosophy but to religion.

This individual Man who lived in a certain time and in a certain place, is the absolute spirit but not the concept of self-consciousness; self-consciousness is not yet known, not grasped.[88]

In contrast to neo-Platonism, Christianity has the advantage of perceiving the absolute divine spirit as man in his immediate presence. Compared to the philosophical concept, however, its defect is that it is not yet aware of the unity of the divine and the human in its universal essence, but only in an empirical person, in this one Man.

God appears in the empirical present. He has no other form than that of the empirical mode of the mind [*Geist*], that is, the form of the *particular human being*—this is the particular empirical form of the spirt. This is what is extraordinary, and we have seen its necessity, for now divine nature and human nature are posited as not in themselves different: God appears in human form. The truth is that there exists only one reason, only one spirit. We have already seen that finite spirit as such does not truly exist.[89]

The isolated particularity of the Person is the "simple obduracy" which refuses to go over to another, to surrender itself and be "sublated." [90] Accordingly, the relation of Father and Son also is not to be represented as a relation between persons; it is to be understood in terms of the eternal and universal essence of spirit, that is, through the categories of logic: universality, particularity, and individuality.

The first is the idea in its simple universality for itself, which has not yet advanced to otherness and has not yet disclosed itself for division—the Father.

87. *Ibid.*, p. 88.
88. *Ibid.*, p. 7.
89. *Phil. of Religion*, Part 3/1, p. 137.
90. *Ibid.*, p. 80.

The second is the particular, the idea in its appearance—the Son. Insofar as the first is concrete, then to be sure the being-of-the-other is already contained within it. The idea is eternal life, eternal process. The second, however, is the idea in its externality, so that the external appearance is converted into the first and becomes known as the divine idea, the identity of God and man. The third then is the consciousness of God as spirit. This spirit, insofar as it exists and realizes itself, is the community (of the Holy Spirit).[91]

Spirit is not spirit when it is made the object of a direct, simple, and calm reflection, for it is essentially movement and activity manifesting itself through division, differentiation, and mediation. In all its stages, it realizes the absolute totality which it already is in itself, for itself.

The spirit which does not manifest and reveal itself is dead. Manifestation means to become for an other. As a becoming for an other it meets with opposition, difference in general, and this is what makes the spirit finite. Something which exists for an Other is, in this abstract characterization, finite. It must confront the Other and has its purpose, its limits, in this Other. Thus, the spirit which manifests itself, determines itself, enters into existence, and makes itself finite is the second (person). The third, however, manifests itself conceptually, takes back its first manifestation into itself, sublates it, becomes aware of itself, and is for itself what it is in itself.[92]

Consequently, spirit is three-in-one; without this determination, spirit would be an "empty word." And if the true spirit is the consciousness of absolute truth, hence of that which God is in and for Himself, then the eternal activity of the mind must be grasped as the logical "rhythm" of concept, judgment, and conclusion in which the three moments in the movement of *Logos* are joined together. "In the eternal sphere God is the union of himself with himself, this joining together of himself with himself." [93] God has revealed the truth through His Son and the outpouring of the Holy Spirit. Truth, however, concerns not only the Absolute as such, but also all its appearances. There is nothing in the realm of spirit which is not an example of the sublation of opposites and of the production of a unity of subject and object, because the structural movement of the spirit, which is the logical foundation that underlies everything, is present in each of its appearances, "and occurs in every living activity." [94] For this reason, Hegel can also explain the Christian Trinity through other modes of appearance of the universal spirit: through progress

91. *Ibid.*, p. 198; cf. p. 72.
92. *Ibid.*, Part 1, p. 65.
93. *Ibid.*, Part 3/1, p. 170; cf. Part 1, p. 66.
94. *Ibid.*, Part 1, p. 221.

and decline in the process of organic life,[95] in the linguistic expression of the human mind, in work, in love, and in being loved.[96]

Finally, we wonder, where does love fit into Hegel's version of the Christian religion? It was love which played so significant a role in the early writings when the problem was to set forth the "totality" of living relations or the Absolute. Is love, like spirit, capable of putting into concepts the absolute universality and totality of being? According to Hegel, one can really love only individuals, particular men, not all men and not everything. The desire to love "humanity" is an "empty pouring forth of a mere image, the opposite of love." However, if one analyzes and understands love, then it reveals a logical structure identical to that of spirit.

If one says "God is love," then that is a very important and true statement. But it would be senseless to understand this merely as a simple definition without analyzing the nature of love. Love is a distinction of two persons who are nevertheless not separate for one another. Love is the consciousness, the feeling of this identity, to be outside myself and to exist in the other. I do not have my self-consciousness in myself but in the Other. However, it is *this* other in whom alone I am at peace and am satisfied with myself—and I exist only because I am at peace with myself. If I do not have the latter, then I am a contradiction which splits apart. The other, which in the same way is outside itself, has self-consciousness only in me. Both (myself and the other) are only this consciousness of being distinct from each other and of being identical—an intuition, a feeling, a knowledge of unity. This is love and it is useless to talk about love without knowing that it is this differentiation and the sublation of this differentiation.[97]

Expressed "in terms of feelings" one can call the Holy Spirit "eternal love" and the relation of God to Himself through His Son "a play of love with itself" because in this three-in-one relation of Father, Son, and Holy Spirit, "there is never any serious otherness, separation, or division." [98]

[IV] THE END OF "ONTO-THEO-LOGIC" AND THE QUESTION
      CONCERNING THE TOTALITY OF THE WORLD

HEGEL'S "TRANSLATION" of the Christian religion into speculative philosophy aroused controversies during his own lifetime, among orthodox theologians as well as free-thinking phi-

95. *Ibid.*, p. 70.
96. *Ibid.*, Part 3/1, p. 72; cf. p. 79.
97. *Ibid.*, p. 75.
98. *Ibid.*, p. 93.

losophers. The former criticized him because so philosophical a religion would destroy not only the religious mode of representation but also the dogmatic content of Christian doctrine as well.[99] The latter objected that Hegel's philosophy of religion restored orthodoxy in a philosophical form and ignored the historical critique of religion. Both criticisms are a result of the fundamental ambiguity of Hegel's critique of positive religion which is simultaneously a conceptual justification of religion. Hegel defended himself against both objections. To the charge that he ignored critical-historical exegesis, he replied that it is not essential to know whether this or that passage in a text should be read one way or another and whether the church fathers, widely acquainted as they were with neo-Platonism, made use of Alexandrian philosophy in their interpretation of the Trinity in order to understand what they believed. For the really essential question is whether such teaching is true in and for itself, no matter where it originates and *even if* it is based on texts which are uncertain for textual criticism. But precisely this decisive question is ignored by historical-critical theology, even though the doctrine of the Trinity, together with the creation and fall of man, God's Incarnation, and the Resurrection of Christ are fundamental to the Christian religion.

If a large part of the educated public, even many theologians, were made to say, hand on heart, whether they consider these doctrines indispensably necessary for eternal salvation or whether their rejection leads to eternal damnation, then there is no doubt what their answer would be. Terms such as eternal damnation and eternal salvation are not even supposed to be uttered in polite society. Such expressions count as *arreta*. Although no one would deny them, still it would be embarrassing to have to explain what they mean. And if anyone who has read the dogmatics, devotional books, and similar materials of our age in which the basic teachings of Christianity are supposed to be set down or even provided with a foundation, were asked to judge whether those doctrines are proclaimed unambiguously and without "loopholes," then we need not even wonder how he would answer this question. Since theology no longer places such importance upon these doctrines or else couches them in such nebulous terms, one difficulty in the way of the philosophical understanding of dogma is thereby removed. Now that these teachings of the church have lost so much of their former interest, philosophy can deal with them unencumbered.[100]

That is to say, if the content of religion is true in and for itself, philosophy can make it comprehensible again. Furthermore, religion does not require philosophy for its destruction,

99. *Ibid.*, Part I, pp. 295f.
100. *Ibid.*, p. 47.

because the matter has already been taken care of by historical-critical theology and there is nothing more which could be destroyed. In contrast, it should be recognized that Hegel's philosophy of religion contained more church dogma than the dominant Protestant theology of his age. Philosophy, as Hegel understood it, was the true theology because it did not despair of knowing "the logical essence of God."

Nevertheless, a definite destruction did come about through Hegel's "sublation" of Christianity into philosophy, a destruction of both the Christian religion and that philosophy which it engenders. D. F. Strauss, Feuerbach, B. Bauer, and M. Stirner brought to its conclusion that critique of religion which in Hegel's sublation was only the reverse side of his justification. With Marx, the "critique of heaven" was transformed into a critique of the "earth" and the critique of theology into the critique of political economy, for when the "holy form of human self-alienation" disappears, one must unmask its unholy form, which is not self-alienation in the form of sins of the spirit, but material exploitation.

Marx, however, worked out his analysis of the capitalistic processes of production of "labor" and "goods" with the help of Hegel's categories of the spirit. Also, he understood the future kingdom of freedom as Hegel had understood it, as a "freedom of the highest community," [101] and freedom itself as "being-with-one-self in otherness," in the sense of a complete reassimilation of an alienated world. Marx's critique of Hegel is not concerned with the formal structure of movement (alienation, objectification, and the return from self-differentiation) which he took over from Hegel, but with its logical universality. Hegel applied the abstract categories of logic to everything in the same way and passed over the historically conditioned modes of alienation and objectification. Ultimately, in the absolute knowledge of the Absolute, he allows the objective side of every human activity to dissolve into absolute self-consciousness and interprets this as the essence of human existence. For Hegel himself, this criticism would have been pointless because the formal categories of logic are the "all-activating spirit of all the sciences" and determine the significance of the universal essence of things.[102] Unintentionally, Marx corroborates Hegel's view, in that he makes the essence of economic relationships transparent by means of just these Hegelian categories. The difference between them consists, however, in the fact

101. *Works,* I, p. 231.
102. Cf. *Ibid.,* XIII, p. 72.

that Hegel was realistic enough to want only to mediate and "sublate" "contradictions," whereas Marx, although he speaks of "sublation" as does Hegel, wants in fact to do away with them completely and he calls this utopian intention "scientific socialism." But even though Marx departs radically from the aim of phenomenology and "onto-theology" and considers "being in the Absolute" to be a groundless fiction, he proceeds nonetheless on the basis of absolute presuppositions. Thus, he assumes that the finite human being is the only "real" Absolute, that his "universal self" is a social *Gattungswesen* whose only essential activity is "labor," and above all that nature is there "for man"—as, with Hegel, spirit is there for spirit. Since Marx regarded Feuerbach's critique of religion and metaphysics as decisive, he made the actual historical existence of laboring humanity into the All and the Absolute. A century earlier, Alexander Pope had said in his *Essay on Man* that "the proper study of mankind is man" and this was taken to mean that we are not to study what is beyond man and hence what does not concern him. From this standpoint, Hegel's "absolute idea" becomes a mere ideology and religion a "topsy-turvy world" which will last only until man is no longer alienated from his human world. The beginning and the end, then, is no longer God or the Absolute in which man has his being, but the radical secularization of man which corresponds to a similarly radical humanization of the world.

These themes have their origin in the Enlightenment, and in Hegel's lifetime they had already found a significant expression, which has lasted up to now in *The New Christianity* of Saint-Simon and in the *Positive Philosophy* of his pupil, August Comte, for whom man is the highest creature. Hegel ascribed the indifference towards a knowledge of God as the Absolute and Infinite to the general intellectual direction of his time. The extent of the knowledge of God decreased in the same proportion as the knowledge of finite things began to stretch out into infinity. Whereas in the Middle Ages all science was the science of God and philosophy was theology, our age is characterized by "knowing everything and anything—only nothing about God." "Our age has done away with the need for such knowledge and its problems; we are finished with it." [103] Even on Sunday, modern man no longer has time for anything so lacking in purpose as religion, whose own purpose is the highest purpose of serving no useful purpose at all; like metaphysics, it is purposeless and useless.

103. *Phil. of Religion*, Part I, p. 5.

As on the highest peak of a mountain, when we are far removed from any definite view of what is on the ground, when we look into the empty sky and with calm and distance survey all the limitations of the landscape and the world—without working at it, theoretically—so in religion and philosophy, through the eye of the spirit, man is carried beyond the limited purposes of his immediate existence. His sole concern is no longer to attend to his changing condition and to realize his own interests; now he wants only to "proclaim the glory of God."

In this way, Hegel achieved the purpose which he had set for himself from the beginning, that is, to realize "the kingdom of God," or the eternally present spirit which is therefore without desire, and to draw near to God or the Absolute. Who can fail to recognize, in this language, which is so far removed from everyday concerns, the basic theme of all religious and philosophical "elevation" [Erhebung], namely, the ethos of the Greek *theoria* and at the same time the diametrically opposite mood of Christian contemplation which frees itself from the earthly for the divine? Nor can we avoid this question: why does this grand attempt to give to the Christian religion once again a philosophical existence come to an end with Hegel? Cannot the same be said about this attempt that Hegel said about Kant's far less ambitious work on religion, i.e., that it "had no luck" in its attempt to animate the positive form of historical belief with philosophical meaning, for religion no longer appeared worthy even of this honor? Is it an accident or only the consequence of a defective understanding that Hegel's radical followers could see in his philosophy of religion and his philosophy of spirit in general only "the negation of theology from the standpoint of theology" (Feuerbach), in Hegel himself a concealed "atheist and Anti-Christ" (B. Bauer), in the Absolute "absurdity" and "an imaginary subject" (Marx), and in Hegel's entire philosophy the last grand attempt

... to restore the lost, vanished Christianity by means of philosophy in such a way that ... the *negation* of Christianity *is identified with Christianity itself*. The highly praised speculative identity ... of the infinite and the finite, the divine and the human, is nothing other than the accursed contradiction of the modern age—the identity, at its highest point, at the summit of metaphysics, of belief and unbelief, theology and philosophy, religion and atheism, Christianity and paganism. Only in this way did Hegel remove this contradiction from sight, obscured it, so that the negation of God, atheism, is made into an objective determination of God.—God is defined as *process* and atheism as a moment in this process. But just as a belief which comes out of unbelief is no true belief because it is always burdened with its opposite, so the God who comes out of his negation is no true God; He is, rather, a God who contradicts Himself, an atheistic God.[104]

In comparison to the narrow, critical acuity of Hegel's left-wing radical pupils, the academic "revival" of Hegelianism at the beginning of our century was antiquated and out of date from the start. The time is long past when one might still see in Hegel, as did G. Lasson, the distinguished editor of Hegel's philosophy of religion who was both a Hegelian and a Protestant minister, the "profoundest mystic of the modern age" and "the most dedicated believer." The time is also past, however, when, like Feuerbach, one could reduce philosophical theology to "anthropology," or else, like Marx, to a theory of the relations of production in society, that is, to what in Hegel's political philosophy is called "the system of needs," which has merely a secondary significance in his system as a whole. The natural man and the social world of man are not the totality of being which Hegel constantly has in view. What is crucial to the Hegelian philosophy is not that as philosophy it still had as its object the absolute totality of being conceived upon the Greek model as "eternal presence," an always-existing totality which is only disclosed to pure thought devoid of all practical interests, to *theoria,* nor is it that Hegel conceived the nature of human existence within this totality. On the contrary, what is crucial to Hegel's thought is that, in the context of the Christian tradition, he undersood the Absolute as an *other-worldly* and *transcendent spirit* which makes itself finite in the natural world and in the self-consciousness of man. The limits of Hegel's philosophy of spirit are revealed therefore in its limited concept of nature and world.

The physical world, which was the subject of Hegel's dissertation and which Kant had distinguished as *mundus sensibilis* from a *mundus intelligibilis* had, for Hegel's "eye of reason," no genuine reality. The truth of the world is its "ideality," that is, its origin in the absolute idea, the eternally creating and preserving divine spirit which releases the world as the "other" and the "external" into a relative independence. In relation to the other-worldly spirit, the world is "externality itself." God cannot exist without the world, but this only means that God would remain an empty abstraction if He were not an active mind, creating, revealing, and differentiating Himself from Himself. In order to be God, He cannot "do without the finite"; He makes Himself finite in the

104. Feuerbach, *Grundsätze der Philosophie der Zukunft* (Zurich and Winterthur, 1843), §21.

world of nature and in the finite human mind. Only by means of the world and man *is* He creator.[105] Although man, alone among all creatures, is in his essence, thought and spirit, and stands in an essential relation to God as infinite spirit, nature has a relation to man only and "not also for itself a relation to God." For Hegel, nature is, from the start, determined by the spirit which knows itself as an externality which does not know itself.[106] As a creation of God or spirit, nature is, of course, rational too *in* itself and therefore a possible object of rational knowledge, but it has no spiritual and rational being *for* itself. The "contingent" belongs to nature [107] and not to the inner necessity of all spiritual being. Nature lacks the self-determination and self-consciousness of spirit,[108] and "everything which happens in heaven and on earth" strives solely towards the end when the spirit "will be for itself." [109]

In his fundamental assumption that true being can only be being which knows itself, Hegel stands not only within the tradition of Cartesian philosophy and the idealistic ontology of being as consciousness [*Bewusst-Sein*] which followed it, but also within the Christian tradition whereby only the man who knows God and himself is God's likeness, and in which God is neither the world nor nature, but world and nature are his work (*natura ars Dei*). Because Hegel accounts for the story of creation philosophically, the world and nature become the external and finite "otherness" [*Anders-Sein*] of the absolute idea and the infinite spirit. As a Christian thinker, Hegel sees the world no longer as an eternal Greek cosmos which has its own *logos*, but as essentially lifeless because, unlike God and man, it does not know itself. With what justification, however, can we regard all of nature and its activity as deprived of spirit just because it does not know itself as man does? Is it not the case that many "essential" things, if not most of them, function and happen in us without knowledge and self-consciousness? [110] And religions other than Christianity do not "elevate" man to a knowing and willing spirit, but rather submerge him consciously in the unity and totality of a positive "nothing," which does not attain to consciousness, knowledge, or dialectic.

105. *Phil. of Religion*, Part 3/2, pp. 27f.
106. Cf. Pascal, *Pensées*, §§793, 347.
107. *Encyclopedia*, p. 248. See D. Henrich, *Hegels Theorie über den Zufall*. In *Kant-Studien*, Part 2 (1958–59).
108. *Phil. of Religion*, Part 3/1, pp. 94f.
109. *Works*, XIII, p. 64.
110. See Nietzsche's allusion to Leibniz's "incomparable insight," whereby he corrected not only Descartes, but all those who philosophized before him, that

The fact that Hegel produced a philosophy of nature as a part of his system, in addition to a logic and a philosophy of the self-knowing spirit, and discovered in organic life the same structure of movement which, with consciousness, determines spiritual life, does not detract from the proud depth of his disdain for nature. It was this disdain which led him to describe the stars as only a sort of "light-eruption, no more astonishing than a crowd of men or a mass of flies." And Marx, who shared with Hegel this contempt for nature, quoted with delight Hegel's extraordinary remark that all the wonders of starlight are nothing in comparison with the most criminal thought of a human being, because only man as *spirit* knows himself!

Hegel had indeed "translated" the positive form of the story of creation into speculative philosophy, but he could not escape its consequences. In the account of creation, man as the sole likeness of God has an *absolutely* unique position in nature. Thus, because of his uniqueness, he stands outside the evolutionary order of living creatures and cannot be regarded as a biological accident. In connection with Kant's critique of the teleological proof for God's existence,[111] Hegel raises this question: what is the relationship of organic nature to inorganic nature, which appears to be a necessary pre-condition for life?

The plants, the animals, human beings come afterwards as an addition. The earth could exist without vegetation, the plant kingdom without animals, the animal kingdom without man. Thus, all these appear to be independent. Experience also confirms that this is so. There are mountains without any vegetation, animals, and human beings. The moon has no atmosphere. The meteorological processes required for vegetation are not present on the moon, and it exists therefore, without any vegetative nature and so forth. The inorganic appears to be independent; man arrives as an external addition. Thus, one has the impression that nature in itself is a productive force which produces blindly and that from this force vegetation results and then from this, animal life.[112]

If this were the case, the existence of man would be something adventitious, accidental, contingent. Man's absence from the universe would not diminish it in any way and the existence of purposive living creatures whose continued existence or cessa-

being conscious is only an accident of perception [*Vorstellung*] and *not* its necessary and essential attribute, and therefore that what we call "consciousness" is only one aspect of our mental and spiritual world (perhaps even a pathological one) and by far *not this world itself*. (*Fröhliche Wissenschaft*, §357.)

111. *Phil. of Religion*, Part 3/2, pp. 164ff.
112. *Ibid.*, pp. 166f.

tion depends upon the natural conditions of life would be an accident. In opposition to this view, Hegel asks whether it is a true "determination of the concept" that life and man are conditional and dependent—and he denies that they are. The true determination on the basis of the concept, then, can no longer be taken from experience, for there is revealed both in nature and in the history of man, as much progress as failure and unfulfilled purpose. Nevertheless, man is sure that he is related to the other external nature as its ultimate goal and that the significance of this nature lies in its being his material, just as the inorganic is material for the organic. Man is no accident in the totality of the natural world, and the truth about organic and inorganic nature and their relation is a "third thing" which is spirit or, in ordinary discourse, "God." If, in contrast, the principle of harmony in the totality of the world is called *nous, logos,* or *world-soul,* as it is in Greek philosophy, where Plato, for example, conceives of God as a huge living creature and the world as a visible God, then only vitality has been posited and not the higher principle that the world-soul as spirit is different from its mere vitality. A grasp of absolute spirit is not yet reached with the recognition that the universe is a system of vital energies, that is, a cosmos; this first appears with Christianity. In a fragment of Hegel's we are told that

The Greeks were given the *human* as their portion, that is, the *free* spirit which has not yet grasped its *infinity.* This spirit spread throughout the Greek world. . . . It is not the absolute spirit, the *holy* spirit. Rather, it is man as *free within* nature so that he carries his power of consciousness within nature and remains encompassed by nature . . . he cannot, therefore, arrive at the *concept* of spirit as such.[113]

Thus, Hegel assumes that the emergence of Christianity into the Greek and Roman world was an "advance in the consciousness of freedom" and that, in general, truth has the "tendency" to "develop" with time. But why is it an "advance" for man to no longer know himself as free *"within nature"* and to preserve his power of consciousness within nature? And why is it an "advance" for man to believe that he has "infinite" freedom because he appeals to the outpouring of a "holy" supernatural spirit and interprets the miraculous history of the New Testament philosophically in order to justify the loss of a positive form of faith? If we can neither understand how an other-worldly and supernatural God, which is spirit, is supposed to have created man, nor yet as-

113. *Ein Hegelsches Fragment zur Philosophie des Geistes,* pp. 47f.

sume that man brought himself into existence through his own will, then man can only exist and be as he is because nature produced him. Physical generation, whose product is man, does not require any "testimony of the spirit." [114] The "book" of nature, a biblical metaphor still used to refer to nature at the beginning of the development of modern natural science,[115] is not a holy scripture upon which an absolute religion can be based. And a philosophy which "translates" historical, biblical belief into speculative thought is not in itself Christian, though it is a philosophy based upon Christianity which, in giving a philosophical justification to faith, betrays how unsure of itself faith has become. At the point where Hegel asks whether there is, in fact, anything in the content of Christian doctrine which can still be believed, he severs his relations from it, for to speak of "dissolving it" would mean ending with a "dissonance." Today, a century after Nietzsche wanted to bring about a "crisis and supreme decision about the problem of atheism," it would strike a false note were we to conclude with the assurance that Christian belief and philosophical questioning can be harmonized. "He who said that 'God is spirit' —took the greatest step and jump forward to unbelief that has yet been taken on earth; on earth it is not easy to make such words good again." [116]

114. *Works,* XIII, p. 89.
115. See E. R. Curtius, *Europäische Literatur und lateinisches Mittelalter* (Bern, 1948), pp. 321ff.
116. Nietzsche, *Zarathustra,* "Das Eselsfest."

11 / Can There Be a Christian Gentleman?

THE SOCIAL PHENOMENON of the Christian gentleman as we observe it in England and New England lives by two principles or principal ways of life. These principles are, however, at first not noticeable as two different and even opposite principles, because it is the very achievement of the Christian gentleman to blend one with the other in such a way that the result seems to be a harmonious perfection. To show the essential difference between a "gentleman" and a Christian, we may start with a historical reflection on the ideal of the former.

I

THE GENTLEMAN-IDEAL has no Christian origin. Many great civilizations before Christ and outside the Christian world have set up and developed such an ideal as a pattern of perfect behavior. First of all the Chinese. In the *Analects* of Confucius,[1] many passages describe the gentleman or Chün-Tzu. Chün means ruler, Chün-Tzu son of a ruler. As a member of the upper class, he is contrasted with the lower class of "small" people. He is a superior man by birth, character, and behavior. He is bound by a particular code of manners and morals, the latter not independent of the first but reflected in them. His deportment is one of perfect propriety and ease. He is well tempered and well balanced, a man of perfect self-control and self-respect. Thanks to his moral training, he is without fear and fret, indifferent to success and adversity. "A true gentleman is calm and at ease; the small man

1. See in particular IV, p. 16; VII, p. 36; XIII, pp. 25, 26 in the translation of A. Waley.

is fretful and ill at ease. . . . The gentleman is dignified but not haughty, common people are haughty but never dignified. . . . The true gentleman is easy to serve but difficult to please, common people are difficult to serve but easy to please." The gentleman avoids all such extremes as lavishness and frugality; he follows the middle way between too much and too little. This maxim is not particular to Confucius, but common to all rational ethics; it is most explicitly developed in the classical Greek ethics.

The Greek term for the gentleman is *kalos-kagathos*.[2] The Greeks felt keenly the difference between the well-bred and the *banausos*, between the noble and vulgar. The gentleman is well-bred, good-looking, and in perfect proportion, while the manners of the *banausos* are vulgar, like those of artisans, porters, and slaves. In Plato's ideal state, the education of the gentleman begins when children begin to play. Etiquette about sitting, or rather lying down and rising up, about haircuts, about shoes and garments, and about bodily posture belongs to the education of a gentleman.

To us who have been brought up within a religious tradition which has intensified man's moral sensibility but disengaged it from manners and class distinctions, most of the Chinese and Greek concern about "manners" seems to be trivial, for we do not think of morals in terms of manners. But in all genuine cultures, manners imply morals and vice versa. Morals are at first *mores*, i.e., habits. It is the privilege but also the predicament of Christian ethics that its extreme standards of love, humility, and self-surrender cannot be standardized and adequately embodied in habits and manners.

The most complete description of the Greek ideal of a gentleman we have from Aristotle.[3] The gentlemen is *megalopsychēs*, i.e., magnanimous, generous, and high-minded. His excellence and virtue appear in very concrete details, e.g., in the right use of wealth. He will expend freely but well, upon the temples, sacrifices for the gods, on his city's navy, on the chorus of the theater, and preferably on works of permanent value, while the *banausos* spends big sums on trifles to show off. The high-minded man respects himself, for he regards himself as worthy of high things. "The man who thinks himself worthy of less than he is really worthy of is unduly humble." The proud claims what is in accordance with his merits, while the others go to excess or fall short—

2. See T. R. Glover, *Greek Byways* (New York, 1932), pp. 157ff. on "The Manners of a Gentleman."

3. *Nic. Ethics*, 1122a–1123a; 1123b–1125a.

a perfectly natural and reasonable ethic, but not at all Christian!

Further, high-mindedness can only exist on a large scale and in a big frame. Little people, says Aristotle, may be neat and modest but cannot be beautiful and high-minded. The gentleman has a sound pride in giving as well as in accepting honors. He will, however, prefer to give, for in giving he remains independent while in receiving he becomes obliged to others. He will ask for scarcely anything, but will give help readily. He is unassuming toward those of the middle class, but dignified towards people of good fortune and high position. He will not regard trivial compliments from trivial people. He does not make cheap compliments or speak ill of others, not even of his enemies "unless it is purposely to insult them." He is essentially truthful, open in his love and hate. The Greek gentleman is, like the Chinese, slow in his movements, sedate in his manners; he will not hurry and say "I am busy." He never lacks proportion. He has the gift for knowing the right things to do and to say, the right way to do and to say them, and the right company in which to do and to say them. His brothers are not his neighbors but other gentlemen. He is a man of taste and a law to himself, self-contained and self-sufficient like the eternal circular motion of the heavenly spheres. The life of a gentleman, says Aristotle, will never revolve around another person unless he be an equal or a friend. To Aristotle, this true proportionate pride is "the crown of the virtues the price of which is honor." But, says Aristotle, it is hard to be truly proud, for it is impossible without being *kalos-kagathos*. Proud men, he concludes, are often thought to be disdainful, but the proud man despises justly while the many do so at random. That is his kind of "righteousness." Measured by the standards of St. Paul and Augustine, all these virtues are but "splendid vices," refined expressions of human pride, though of a pride which is disciplined and well-balanced.

About two thousand years lie between the Chinese and Greek conceptions and our modern, predominantly English ideal of a gentleman, and yet our Western ideal shows all the essential features of the *Chün-Tzu* and *kalos-kagathos*. The reason for this identity is that the gentleman-ideal is a common product of higher civilization and as such is independent of the Christian religion or any transcendent ethics. The English word "gentleman" [4] is derived from the Latin word *gens*, i.e., race and family. *Gentilis* is one who belongs to a noble family, to the ruling or upper class, the gentry. Up to the nineteenth century, the gentleman was dis-

4. See the article "Gentleman" in the *Encyclopaedia Britannica*.

tinguished by his social status and the possession of a coat of arms. As such, he is distinguished from the yeoman, tradesman, and husbandman who are not well-born and well-bred and are thereby incapable of being "gentle." The gentleman as we know him from Lord Shaftesbury, Chesterfield, and innumerable minor figures is, like the Chinese and Greek gentleman, a man of self-control and self-respect, well-tempered, conscientious, considerate, and gracious. Now, gentleness, modesty, and conscientiousness are usually held to be Christian virtues also, though perhaps not the most exacting ones. But even apart from the outstanding virtues of Christian ethics, there is a very deep though subtle difference between the conscientiousness, considerateness, and modesty of a gentleman and that of a Christian, as J. H. Newman has so beautifully pointed out.[5]

The gentleman is not a creation of Christianity but of civilization, even if civilization simulates the virtues of Christianity. To the gentleman, the source of conscience is not the will of God but the dictate of his own cultured mind. He is conscientious out of self-respect, but self-respect is not a Christian virtue. And when he does wrong, he does not feel contrition of which God is the object, but remorse and a sense of degradation. He is modest and his modesty may seem like humility, but Christian humility is the most difficult of all virtues for a self-respecting person. The gentleman's modesty is a temporary relinquishment of the privileges of his own station; it is an act of condescension toward those on a lower level, yet as a gentleman he never loses his sense of superiority which even increases by the natural pride of being capable of condescension. To claim this kind of modesty as humility would be hypocrisy. There is a world of difference between the gentleman's prudent moderation, modesty, and condescension on the one side, and the "twelve degrees" of humility on the other side. But even a saint can never be sure that natural pride does not enter into his spiritual and bodily self-abasement. If the gentleman is consistent, he will have to admit that his standards are not those of a follower of Christ but the standards of a man of the world, i.e., honor and decency, self-respect, and distinction.

It is in particular self-respect, "the very household-god of good society," as Newman calls it, which directs his conduct. Dean Inge once remarked: "If you said to an Anglican bishop you are no Christian, he would hardly feel surprise. It would be a point of debate; but if you say to him you are no gentleman, he would

5. *On the Scope and Nature of University Education* (Everyman's Library), Chap. VII.

probably never speak to you again." Much can be said in favor of cultured self-respect, but much can also be said against it. For the reverse of it is an intense dislike of exposure. The self-respecting gentleman is an enemy of extravagances of all kinds. He shrinks from scenes and he does not make confessions. He always controls his temper and suppresses his emotions. He carefully avoids whatever may cause a jar in the minds of those with whom he is cast. He avoids irritating topics, clashing of opinions, collision of feelings, and all those things which are regarded as out of place. He never hurts another's feelings because he himself does not want to be hurt in turn.

Jesus certainly *did* expose himself, cause disagreement, and hurt the feeling of others, in particular those of his fellow Jews, for he was passionate and his message radical and, to a decent Roman, rather shocking. As Nietzsche has put it in his "Anti-Christ": There is only one gentleman in the whole New Testament, viz., the cultured and skeptical Roman governor Pilate. Nietzsche, in his attempt at restoring the natural and classical virtues of a proud master-morale over against what he called a Christian slave-morale, wrote an impressive passage describing the ideal of a well-bred gentleman. He calls him a *Wohlgeratener* (one who is well-bred), and he says of him:

He is carved from one integral block which is hard, sweet and fragrant as well. He enjoys that only which is good *for him;* his pleasure, his desire ceases when the limits of that which is good for him are overstepped. . . . He is a selective principle; he rejects much. He is always in his own company, whether his intercourse be with books, with men, or with nature; he honors the things he chooses. . . . He reacts slowly to all kinds of stimuli with that tardiness which long caution and deliberate pride have bred in him. . . . He believes neither in ill luck nor guilt; he can digest himself and others; he knows how to forget, he is strong enough to make everything turn to his advantage.[6]

It is obvious that this human wholesomeness is not Christian saintliness but a modern version of the Aristotelian high-mindedness.

II

THE CHRISTIAN GENTLEMAN is a contradiction in terms, because a gentleman is a man of the world while a Christian is a follower of Christ. The most striking proof of the incom-

6. *Ecce Homo,* 1, 2; cf. *The Will to Power,* nos. 1003, 175.

patibility of the one with the other is the life of a Christian saint who was indeed a gentleman—namely, before he became a Christian! St. Francis was by birth, upbringing, and manners a young gentleman. But after his conversion and decision to follow Christ, he became a vagabond, quite careless about his former social status and good manners, training himself instead in the most austere ascetic discipline. Indeed, he practiced the Christian virtues of humility and charity, hope and faith. These Christian virtues are far from being a rational middle way between extremes. The Christian ethic is full of paradoxical tensions between such extremes as life and death (of saving one's life by losing it), of sin and grace, despair and faith, sorrow and joy, power and weakness, the cross and the crown. The Christian virtues are not natural and reasonable virtues of a golden mean but radical virtues of grace.[7] For humility means more than modesty, charity more than benevolence, hope more than looking forward, and faith more than rational belief. Charity to the deserving is not charity, but plain justice; it is the undeserving who require charity. Hope means hoping when, against all empirical evidence, things are hopeless; it is not the natural effluence of a cheerful temperament, but a religious duty and its substance is faith in things invisible. And having faith means believing the incredible and being certain about things we cannot prove and demonstrate. A gentleman may be very just and generous, but the paradoxical justice and apparent injustice of the parables of the prodigal son and of the laborers in the vineyard is beyond his scheme of reference.

On the other hand, it is also impossible to imagine the Apostles and the "internal proletariat" of the early Church as gentlemen. These men who conquered the Roman world of the conquerors would never have evoked the least interest, either hostility or enthusiasm, if they had been as wise and philosophical as the gentleman who cares so much about propriety and is therefore unwilling to expose himself and to challenge his fellow men. It is impossible to be a *Christian* gentleman because it is impossible *as a gentleman* to follow Christ. The birth, life, and death of Jesus Christ are anything but gentleman-like, and the birth, life, and death of a true gentleman are anything but Christ-like.

If, nevertheless, it seems as though the Christian gentleman were combining the virtues of the one and the other, the reason for this deceptive appearance is that both the way of the gentleman and the way of the Christian have deteriorated and are now leveled down to the common standard of an average decency.

7. See G. K. Chesterton, *Heretics,* Chap. XII.

Modern Christianity has degenerated because it wants not only to live in this world but also to be of it and to benefit from all its inventions. And the gentleman-culture has degenerated because the modern world has become a mass society which has little place for the superior refinement and distinction of the gentleman. This process occurred during the nineteenth century and is strikingly illustrated in the change of the definitions of the gentleman in the *Encyclopaedia Britannica*.

In the edition of 1815, a gentleman is still a man of the upper class who bears a coat of arms. In the edition of 1845, the social status of a gentleman is extended to all above the rank of yeoman. In the edition of 1856, the title is generally accorded to all persons above the rank of common tradesmen. The gentleman has become a gentle*man*. He is no longer distinguished by blood and circumstances. This change indicates that the middle classes have come into their own. And with the growth of modern mass society, the gentleman became almost synonymous with man though there are still some curious remnants of the earlier and stricter meaning, for example, in the idiosyncrasies of certain gentlemanly sports like golf and fishing. But on the whole, the leveling process is going on and eventually, if everyone who has some education can claim to be a gentleman, nobody will stand out any longer as a superior man. All of us are now gentlemen because none of us is "well-born" and everyone is making a living by earning money. Likewise, all of us are now Christians because we agree with Jews and gentiles on the general principle of tolerance without specific religious convictions. The freedom from business and money-making which formerly was a prerequisite for the education of a gentleman (as it still is for the training of a Catholic priest) became something almost negative in our modern world of labor, business, and industry, where leisure has become mere laziness. As Darwin once wrote in a letter: "Now I am so completely a gentleman that I have sometimes a little difficulty to pass the day." Thus, the gentleman is dying out with all that is gracious in him; his code of behavior disappears even in the diplomatic profession, on account of political, social, and economic changes.[8] That is regrettable but unavoidable since the gentleman's morals and manners depend on a certain upbringing, leisure, and wealth.

If the Christian way of life were also essentially dependent on political, social, and economic conditions, then the Christian-

8. See H. Laski, *The Danger of Being a Gentleman;* cf. F. M. Powicke, *History, Freedom and Religion* (London, 1940), pp. 40f.

ity of the twentieth century could only be a semi-religious version of secular philanthropy and gentleness, socialism, and pacifism. But how can Christianity be dependent on worldly conditions if its very meaning is to transcend the loyalties, standards, and conditions of the *saeculum?* Nothing can prevent serious Christians from bearing witness in the modern industrial world as they did in the ancient pagan world. As a "Christian civilization" and world-historical religion, Christianity may decay and even disappear, but it does not therefore disappear as a faith in the kingdom of God as an imitation of Christ. It was the merit of St. Francis within the Roman church and of Luther in revolt against it to have reformed Christianity according to its genuine standards. Now the time has come to distinguish once more between essential Christianity and the humanistic stream derived from Hellas,[9] for the time has arrived where decisive distinctions have to be made lest Christianity lose all its vigor and taste, as it did for men like Nietzsche and D. H. Lawrence,[10] who did nothing but yearn for a transcendent faith in something more than the all-too-human. Their blasphemies are therefore nearer to the Christian faith than to the decency of the gentleman whose supreme standard and concern is self-respect and self-perfection.

If Christianity were not reduced to an adjective of "religion" but were maintained as an unconditional and specific faith, the question whether a perfect man of the world can be, at the same time, a Christian, would immediately prove its absurdity. For how could one ever combine self-respect with self-surrender? If anything is beyond doubt in the Old and the New Testament, it is the emphasis on a distinction: in the Old Testament, between the chosen people and the gentiles; in the New Testament, between the kingdom of God and the standards of the world; and in the whole Bible, between the will of God and the will of man. To proclaim the Gospel in a world of sin and death cannot be done by way of adjustment but requires a critical distance and disengagement. The Church cannot address the world religiously and efficiently if she has no distinct vantage point from which to address the world instead of pretending to be extensive with it by offering a Christian version of modern secular culture. The world has not essentially changed since the times of early Christianity, nor has the possibility of proclaiming the Christian message to a hostile world by a faithful minority. To be a gentleman in our time may be much more difficult than it was in the times

9. Cf. *Theology Today* (Oct., 1944), p. 295.
10. See D. H. Lawrence, *Posthumous Papers* (New York, 1936), pp. 731ff.

of Aristotle and Shaftesbury. To be a Christian in our time is no more and no less difficult than it was in the first centuries.

The crucial test of being a Christian will always be the attitude toward suffering. When St. Paul was imprisoned, he wrote to the Philippians that the things which happened to him would serve "the progress of the Gospel." Those who were imprisoned by the "praetorian guards" of our time felt exactly the same way, if they were really Christians. They did not make an attempt to escape, nor did they think about future improvements of state prisons. They took what had happened to them as an opportunity of becoming firm in the faith and of spreading the Gospel. A gentleman too, in such circumstances, will behave differently from a vulgar man. He will nobly bear the hardships, even torture and death, but he will not take up his cross for the sake of the Crucified. Both the gentleman and the Christian are distinct from the natural man who cannot but despair and rebel or adjust himself if deprived of his civil liberties. The external result may thus seem to be almost the same in the case of a Christian and of a gentleman, but the way both achieve their inner freedom is as different as their motivation and aim. The gentleman will patiently suffer for the sake of preserving his self-respect; the Christian will enthusiastically suffer for the sake of Christ who suffered for him. A similar difference could be easily shown in the attitude toward the suffering of others. There is not a single human passion and action which does not have a different key and tone, motive and meaning, if experienced by either a man of the world who has disciplined himself in order to stand it, or a follower of Christ who has, by grace, overcome it and is, therefore, able to stand it. However similar the external appearance may seem, a discerning understanding cannot fail to see the essential difference, so admirably expressed by Augustine in his discussion of Stoic ethics.

To be sure, the Christian message as recorded in the Gospels does not live by any essential polemics against the world or the state or the man of the world who wisely engages in or retires from it. The message of Jesus is quite affirmative on account of its eschatological setting. All his parables presuppose a freedom from the world's concern with success and human respectability, a freedom which is so radical and perfect that only saints have ever approximated to it. A critical distinction between Christianity and the world was unnecessary so long as the primitive Church lived in small groups apart from Roman society. But a critical distinction became necessary when Christianity spread out and consolidated within the pagan world, and it becomes even more necessary in our modern world where everything up to a certain degree is still Christian and to an equally uncertain degree is non-Christian, if not anti-Christian. In our ambiguous "Christian world," the Christianity of the gentleman is like the Christianity of a Christian democracy and civilization—an adjective which fails to determine the noun. This ambiguity derives from the worldly success of the Christian church and, at the same time, her failure to make the world Christian. Thus, we live in a Christian world which still reflects the religious faith in the kingdom of God, but only in its secular transformations. All modern history of the West is still inspired by the quest for the kingdom of God— but it sets its hope in a "better world" on material production, progress, and welfare. It was St. Paul's verdict on pagan society that "it had no hope," and it is the verdict on our modern, progressive society that it has hope—in the wrong thing and without substance. The Christian gentleman of the Christian world is only one instance out of many which indicates a general confusion of principles.[11] We may meet a "Christian gentleman" in the flesh, as a social matter of fact, but he does not exist in spirit and principle.

11. With the exception of Clement of Alexandria, I know of no early Christian writer who ventured to adapt the Christian way of life to that of the ancient gentleman. At a time when the pagan philosopher Celsus dismissed the Christian church as an association of bakers, fullers, and slaves, Clement stands out as a refined scholar fond of the ancient gentleman. Since at his time, families of the pagan upper class began to come over to the Church, he thought it a timely task to baptize certain details of gentlemanlike deportment, dress, entertainment, and expenditure, so that they might be acceptable also to Christians. Clement's *The Pedagogue* is a book of instruction in conduct, morals, and manners, in what one might call the Christian gentleman. He discusses, e.g., whether a Christian should use the customary signet ring of gold. He decides that he may use it, but the device on it should not be a pagan idol, but rather a Christian symbol like a dove or a fish. (See T. R. Glover, *op. cit.,* pp. 175ff.)

Selected Bibliography of Works

by Karl Löwith

Gesammelte Abhandlungen Zur Kritik der geschichtlichen Existenz. Stuttgart: Kohlhammer, 1960.

Heidegger: Denker in dürftiger Zeit. Frankfurt a/M.: S. Fischer, 1953. Second expanded edition, 1960.

Das Individuum in der Rolle des Mitmenschen. Tübingen: Mohr, 1928.

Jakob Burckhardt: Der Mensch inmitten der Geschichte. Luzern: Vita Nova, 1936.

Meaning in History. Chicago: University of Chicago Press, 1949. German Edition: *Weltgeschichte und Heilsgeschehen.* Stuttgart: Kohlhammer, 1953. Dritte Auflage, 1957.

Nietzsches Philosophie der ewigen Wiederkehr des Gleichen. Stuttgart: Kohlhammer, 1956.

Von Hegel zu Nietzsche. Stuttgart: Kohlhammer, 1941. Vierte Auflage, 1958. English Translation: *From Hegel to Nietzsche: The Revolution in Nineteenth-Century Thought.* Translated by David E. Green. New York: Holt, Rinehart and Winston, 1964.

Wissen, Glaube und Skepsis. Göttingen: Vanderhoeck u. Ruprecht, 1956. Zweite Auflage, 1958.

Index